Klonopin Lunch

A MEMOIR

Jessica Dorfman Jones

Crown Publishers
New York

Library of Congress Cataloging-in-Publication Data
Dorfman Jones, Jessica.
Klonopin lunch: a memoir/Jessica Dorfman Jones. —1st ed.
    p.   cm.
   1. Dorfman Jones, Jessica. 2. Dorfman Jones, Jessica—Marriage.
3. Dorfman Jones, Jessica—Relations with men. 4. Young women—
United States—Biography. 5. New York (N.Y.) —Biography.
6. Drug abuse—United States—Case studies. 7. Promiscuity—
United States—Case studies. 8. Life change events—United States—
Case studies. 9. Self-destructive behavior—United States—Case
studies. 10. Self-actualization (Psychology)—Case studies. I. Title.
CT275.D8643A3 2012
974.7'043—dc23 [B]   2012004503

ISBN 978-0-307-88697-2
eISBN 978-0-307-88699-6

Printed in the United States of America

Jacket design by Christopher Brand
Jacket photograph: (mouth) Image Source

10 9 8 7 6 5 4 3 2 1

First Edition

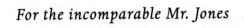

For the incomparable Mr. Jones

If you bring forth what is within you, what you bring forth will save you. If you do not bring forth what is within you, what you do not bring forth will destroy you.

—THE GNOSTIC GOSPELS

Contents

Author's Note

The story that follows is entirely true, much to the author's amazement, amusement, and occasional chagrin. In an effort to safeguard the privacy of the individuals whose lives touched mine and are in any way represented herein, I have changed their names and identifying details. This policy applies to those who were very good and those who were very naughty; no favoritism was applied. In some instances, it was necessary to rearrange and/or compress events and time periods to further the narrative, preserve the aforementioned's anonymity, or because my own mind-altering activities as related in this book left me no choice. Finally, the dialogue in this book was re-created to the best of my abilities, and if not verbatim, it matches what was said to the best of my recollection. If the words are not exact, the spirit in which they were said and the content as I remember them are represented as accurately as possible.

Klonopin Lunch

— 1 —

ARE YOU READY TO ROCK?

And so it was that, by the time I was on the doorstep of thirty, I was in a job I'd grown to hate and had been married for four steady, if plodding, years to my college boyfriend Andrew. Sweet, predictable Andrew. While he had once been a wildly hilarious partier up for any crazy scheme at a moment's notice, now he loved nothing more than a night spent at home reading quietly and turning in early. I tried my best to be equally content with his vision of a cozy and homely pas de deux, but inevitably, at least once a year, I would wind up running into the night to kick up my heels. Andrew thought these outbursts of mine were amusing and they barely registered with him as he flicked through the latest Grisham novel before turning in for the night.

The job I'd grown to detest was a high-level position at a dot-com that, like so many others of its ilk, had managed to burn through close to one hundred million dollars in just over two years without actually producing anything. The New York Silicon Alley era had been fun while it lasted, but it was drawing to an obvious close and I was burned-out, unmotivated to figure out what my next move would be, and feeling dull as dirt. Gone were the days of three-hour steak lunches at Les Halles, the weeklong sales meetings in Vegas, and exorbitant expense accounts. Knowing that our days were numbered, everyone had basically just stopped working; instead of the hustle and bustle we had all experienced in the early days, going to work now consisted of sitting at your desk and waiting for the phone to ring. That ring had become the inevitable death knell from human resources announcing that the gravy train had dried up.

I occasionally considered going back to work as a lawyer, but I had hated law school, it took several tries to pass the bar, I had worked for sadists, and the day I left that world was one of the happiest of my life. I detested the legal profession and it seemed the feeling was mutual. So there I sat, sliding into thirty, with an unused law degree, soon to be unemployed, and in a mildly geriatric marriage that had become as predictable as my morning oatmeal.

I shared an office at beenz.com with an old friend, the very person who had roped me into this job in the first place. Brynne was the head of Web development and I was the director of business development, and we shared an office mostly because nobody else liked playing Jerky Boys tapes at top volume as much as we did. Brynne was also struggling with what her next steps in life would be and like me marveled daily that she'd made it to thirty and hadn't yet figured out who or what she wanted to be when she grew up. We were both young but feeling old

in our newfound adulthood and filled to the brim with
the tedium being heaped upon us daily at the office.

On a lazy Thursday in January filled with Web surfing and vending machine abuse, we were both killing
time by reading Salon.com to each other from our lap-
tops, nestled deep inside the beanbags our company had
thoughtfully scattered around the office. Why were these
oversized bean-filled hacky sacks the only available seat-
ing other than our desk chairs? Because our company
was called beenz.com.

"I can't take this anymore. We have to do something so
we don't go insane. What should we do?" Brynne asked
from the depths of her vinyl cocoon.

I had no idea what to do. The rigors of killing time had
robbed me of my ability to make plans. Was my inertia
the warning sign of an oncoming clinical depression? At
that point even a descent into madness would have been
an interesting change of pace.

"Go for a drink?"

That had become my answer to just about everything.
Brynne was unimpressed. "No, I don't mean that. I mean,
we don't have anything to *do*. Let's take up a hobby. Some
activity that we would never do under normal circumstances. Let's just go nuts!"

Going nuts seemed like a fine idea, but I had long ago
lost any sense of what that really meant. During my college years, that might have meant spending almost every
summer night staying out until dawn, going to drag
clubs, and doing ecstasy. Now, except for the very occasional party, "going nuts" meant buying the deluxe edition of Scrabble for a rousing weekend at home.

"Sure, let's do it. But how?" I rolled out of my bean-bag and onto the floor, which still smelled slightly of stale beer from last week's intraoffice beer-pong tournament. Staring up at the acoustic tile, I said, "Well, I always thought it might be fun to learn how to play mah-jongg."

Brynne gagged on a mouthful of Skittles. "What are you? Ninety?! Next stop orthopedic shoes! Vomit."

"Jesus, okay, fine. Remain calm! Just pretend I didn't say anything. What do *you* think we should do?"

Brynne remained silent as she carefully arranged the Beanie Babies on her desk into lewd positions. "I think that we need to get our groove on."

I dug deep and really tried to conjure up an image of what getting my groove on would look like. Try as I might, all I had to work with was a blank wall of fuzzy white static glowing like a broken TV set in my mind's eye. Shit. I had no clue. My life was so fucking lame.

Brynne lowered the boom. She had already cooked up the perfect plan. Brynnie explained that there was a guitar store across the street from her place in Chelsea and that the guys who sold guitars there also gave lessons. She had popped in a few days earlier, sussed the scene out, and was happy to report that lessons were affordable and readily available. The store had enough guys working there to make it possible to basically call up anytime for next-day service. Before I could fully process what she was talking about, Brynne snatched up her phone and called right then and there from our office. She booked lessons for both of us from the same guy. Hers would be the following Wednesday and mine would be the day after that. I didn't want to rain on her parade, but the speed with which Brynne was changing our routine was making me uneasy. It wasn't much, but the little foxhole of ennui that I had dug for myself was, well, mine. I didn't like it, but I knew its parameters and how to operate in it. I had grown to rely on my discomfort zone to steer me through my days, and losing it seemed just as scary as staying put.

From that moment on, all Brynne could talk about was our guitar lessons. I was still trying to wrap my head around the idea of doing something new; was I really ready and willing to change up my familiar if stultifying routine? While Brynne prattled on, I concentrated on embracing the unknown. Slowly, my anxiety loosened its grip and excitement about our project, as well as possibly rediscovering some of my old audacity, crept in. I had to admit that Brynne was on to something. We hadn't even learned how to play a C chord yet but the spell of boredom and lassitude that had held us in its grip for the previous year was breaking down. We were suddenly as sure as we had ever been about anything that we were going to take the East Village rock scene by storm with our searing riffs and bad attitudes. We discussed the pros and cons of dyeing our hair.

Wednesday night rolled around and Brynne headed off to her lesson, while I hurried home to have one of my Martha Stewart OCD meltdowns of after-work bread baking. I baked bread for two reasons: the manual labor helped to keep me calm and focused, and it allowed me to indulge my need to always go the extra mile, be perfect, and do everything right all the time. I couldn't get close to being comfortable unless the apartment was immaculate, I was a great cook but still as thin as possible, and my job was prestigious. In the grand scope of things, baking bread was one of my healthier obsessions.

I was halfway through the second kneading and my dear, sweet, patient husband was watching *Celebrity Deathmatch* on MTV in the other room. A few words about my husband, Andrew. He was an absolute saint. Since our freshman year of college he had been my biggest cheerleader and best friend. No one was funnier, smarter, or more understanding of all the weird neurotic bullshit that I could manufacture than him. Back in college we'd been partners in lunacy (like entering a dance contest in Columbus, Ohio, at a drag bar and winning) but that part of Andrew and our relationship had died down to almost nothing. I missed that part of him. Now, despite the angel on my shoulder telling me to be nice and behave myself, the devil on my other shoulder would tempt me to do something bananas just to get a rise out of him. I'd fantasize about making him go dancing with me and then ripping my top off while standing on the bar. Or, if public nudity wasn't appealing to me at that moment, I'd picture myself just starting a plain old bar fight that he'd have to leap into. Anything to mix things up. I never actually did any of this stuff but even if during one of my nights out I had one drink too many and acted like an idiot, Andrew was always so very good and so very kind and so very understanding. Which could be so very boring.

Just as I was checking to see if my dough was doing well with its second rise, the phone rang. It had to be Brynne! I wiped my hands off on my apron and grabbed the phone off the counter. Without even confirming it was her, I started questioning whoever it was on the other end of the call. "How was it? Was it awesome? Did you have the most fun ever? Can you rock? More to the point, do you think I'll be able to?"

There was a pause on the line. Which was weird. I was expecting a torrent of crazed excitement to flow through the receiver and knock me back against the wall of the kitchen. But no. There was a big, hanging, flabby pause. Oh God, maybe it wasn't her. Maybe I had just verbally accosted a telemarketer from Bangalor. But then Brynne cleared her throat and I knew it was her. And then she said the one thing I didn't expect her to say in a zillion years.

"I think you should cancel your lesson tomorrow."

"What the *fuck* are you talking about?"

"No, seriously, dude, I don't think it's a good idea for you to take lessons from this guy."

I was immediately worried for Brynne. All of my worst, and most frequently obsessed over, paranoid fantasies rose up to choke me. What could have happened? Had the teacher done something untoward? Was he weirdly pervy? Did he try to steal from her? Had he insulted her? Was he unkempt, or even worse, unwashed? Did he try to teach her Air Supply? What could possibly have gone wrong?

I replied slowly, trying not to sound hysterical. "Why? Are you okay? Did he do something to you? What happened?"

"Oh please, no, nothing like that. I liked him and he can definitely teach. It's just that, well, I don't think he's *right* for you. I think we should just call someone else from the store to teach us."

Her obfuscation was driving me off the deep end. "Brynnie, cut the shit. What's the deal?"

She finally blurted it out. "Dude. He's totally cute. He's an obvious sex machine and potential lothario. Complete with winking, tight pants, shooting finger guns, big blue eyes, the whole nine yards. You're going to think he's totally insanely delicious. He'll probably think you're cute too, or at least flirt shamelessly. I just don't think it's a good idea."

Let me interject here to say that there had been an episode a few years earlier when I had enjoyed an unconsummated but still notably hot and heavy flirtation with a friend of a friend who had recently moved to the city. Nothing irreparable had happened, but my attraction to the guy had been unmistakable. Even so, I'd been pleased that all zippers had remained zipped and everyone had remained unschtupped. So I was amazed at Brynne's reaction. I had lived through temptation before; why on earth would she think it would be a problem now?

"Okay, Brynne, I appreciate your concern, but I don't think there's any danger here. He's just some guy who's going to remind me what the circle of fifths is and teach me how to bang out three chords and the truth. No problemo here."

"It's the banging I'm worried about." She snickered on the other end of the line.

I was getting irritated. This was clearly all about her fantasy life and not about me in the slightest. "Dude. Stop it. I'm not banging anyone. Is it possible that *you're* attracted to him? Maybe? Feeling unsatisfied at home? Stirring up a little trouble, my love?"

"No. Not one bit. All is well in my world. I'm telling you, dude, be prepared for major trouble."

There was no question in my mind that Brynnie was hot for the guitar guy. No woman on the face of the earth calls her friend to warn her of an imminent boning if she is not secretly hoping to be on the receiving end of that boning herself. That is a fact. It didn't help Brynne's case that she was dating a lawyer at the time who, at the age of thirty-two, was still wearing braces. I secretly believed that he had *Star Wars* sheets lurking in the back of his linen closet. So now, despite Brynne's best efforts, I was completely desperate to meet Guitar Boy because I had to know what would make her have this bizarre sexual meltdown.

The next day passed with the usual insanity of firings and recriminations at work. I got in a little before noon and Brynnie was already there, working on her résumé and chatting with a bunch of her programming minions. When I walked into our office she gave me the hairy eyeball and dismissed her coterie of flunkies so we could pull our beanbags together and gossip. Brynne refreshed her Cassandra-like warnings, but they continued to fall on deaf ears. Realizing there was nothing she could do to reverse the wheels she had set in motion, Brynne switched gears and turned on the Jerky Boys for a while so we could listen to the ranting of the Egyptian Magician and forget about our bizarre standoff. We made feeble attempts at doing our jobs and by four thirty I was on my way downtown to prepare for my guitar lesson.

"Preparing" meant getting home in time to change into jeans and a T-shirt, picking up some beer, calling Andrew at the office to say hi before one of his rare nights out with the other attorneys on his team, and relaxing for just a few minutes before the big event. None of that happened. I was running late as usual. My upstairs neighbor, an old friend from law school, had waylaid me in the grocery store. Halfway through chatting, I realized I had ten minutes to get home and get myself squared away before the teacher showed up. I grabbed a six-pack of Stella and bolted. The second I got into the apartment, the doorman buzzed to say that Gideon was on his way up. Gideon? Oddly, I hadn't even thought of the teacher having a name until that moment. Brynne and I had referred to him exclusively as Guitar Boy. In a panicked rush, I threw my coat on the bed; tossed the beer in the fridge; and still wearing the semicorporate heels, skirt, and blouse combo I had worn to work, reached for the doorknob just as the doorbell gave its halfhearted little cough of a ring.

I opened the door.

For some reason, probably because of all the buildup and drama that Brynne had concocted for what I had assumed was her own entertainment, I became instantly flustered when I swung the door open. I felt disoriented and anxious. I couldn't look the guy in the face. I was totally derailed, which never, *ever* happens to me. I'm an extrovert. I'm the one who usually can't stop talking. But there I was, mute and shuffling in my own doorway. I dropped my eyes to the floor. An internal monologue of totally unhinged dementia began:

Oh my God, what's wrong with me? I have poise and aplomb to spare! I had etiquette lessons, for Christ's sake! Pull it together and greet this guy so he doesn't think he's arrived at some adult day-care facility! Do it, Jones. Now!

As I forced myself to drag my gaze upward from Guitar Boy's feet before I could look him in the face, I took in a pair of scuffed motorcycle boots and a worn-out pair of light brown corduroys that had bald patches in a few places and frayed hems. They could not have been tighter. There was no way. This guy had to lube up to get into his pants, because I could see clear as day that he wasn't wearing any underwear. At. All. He had one of those tall skinny boy bodies (he must have been about six foot two)—not quite heroin-strung-out looking, but it definitely begged the question of whether or not food was part of his lifestyle choice. Tight body. Tight pants. Giant belt buckle. Of course. It was brass and looked old and kind of seventies-ish, but God help me if it registered, because I was already on to the perfectly draped and soft Led Zeppelin concert T and faded denim jacket. I would have laughed out loud at this extra from *Dazed and Confused* if it hadn't all been just so raw and *hot*. By the time I got to his face I knew I was dead. Crooked smile; perfect teeth, but a little yellowed from the Marlboros I could see poking out of the jacket pocket. Pale skin and the bluest blue eyes I had ever seen, ice blue. Thick black lashes. A long, aquiline nose with a sculpted tip and a very slight bump at the bridge that immediately identified him as being a member of my tribe. And black hair in a perfect, parted-down-the-middle seventies flip. He was *ridiculous*. It was like a Jewish Vinnie Barbarino had landed on my doorstep. But it didn't matter, because what was even more ridiculous was that Brynne had been right. Righter than rain. Of course she was right. She knew me like the back of her hand. *Fuck.*

This guy was sex. Not sexy. Actual sex. For the first time in my life I really understood what pheromones were all about. I fully appreciated what it meant to smell sex emanating from another person—not the remains of a sexual encounter but the indisputable chemicals that flowed out of his pores and made my stomach lurch and my palms clammy. It was the first time in almost ten years that I'd felt that inexorable urge to lunge at another person and lick him. Anywhere on his body, I didn't care where. An eyebrow would have sufficed. I knew I was blushing because I could actually feel the roots of my hair burst into flames. As if that wasn't shameful enough, Guitar Boy just grinned wider and wider as my mortification practically became another physical entity sharing this psychotic out-of-body experience with us. I think I salivated. Out of nowhere, faintly, oh so faintly, I could hear the whispery sound of clothes being torn off and underpants hitting the floor in the future. Holy shit, was I hallucinating? I still hadn't said anything and we'd been on my doorstep for an interminable and silent ten seconds or so. Finally, Gideon brought us back to earth with a wink and a gravelly, "Can I come in?"

Yes, baby. You can come in.

And in that split second I knew two things: I was going to sleep with this guy and my marriage was over. I wasn't capable of acknowledging the first truth for about three months, and the second and much more horrible truth took about eighteen more months to hit home. But in hindsight, which we all know is the best and cruelest perspective you can have, I knew it all in that moment. The door to my world of being the hostess with the mostest slammed shut, and my days as a coke-snorting, skinny-jean-wearing, band-fronting, wild-sex-having babe began.

I was ready to rock.

2

FREE BUFFET

Before I race forward with the dirty and pruriently delicious details about what happened next with Guitar Boy
and the tectonic life shift that was rumbling beneath my
feet from the moment I set eyes on him, I have to admit
that it wasn't the first time I had fallen in love, or the kind
of lust that stands in for love, on the spot. The truth was
I had a habit of losing my mind over boys to the point of
total insanity that started in grade school and continued
unabated through college. Guitar Boy was part of a narrative arc of wanton desire that had begun a very long
time ago.

There had been boys in grade school whose Wallabies
and perfect bowl haircuts made me swoon as if Scott
Baio himself was sitting next to me in math class. There
were boys in high school whom I worshipped from afar
and a few I managed to play with whose awkward teenage fumblings eventually quelled whatever passion they
had originally stirred up in me.

But then came college. College supplied a steady
stream of delicious and strange boys whose attention I

wanted and whose attention I got. First there was Mitchell, he of the perfect eighties hair and ability to drink a fifth of rye in under five minutes. Then came Ben, the soccer player whose beauty had all the girls in his dorm swooning from day one of freshman orientation. He eventually checked himself into a mental institution. Then came Wade, king of the wake-and-bake, who was too stoned to notice I had broken up with him. Ian followed on his heels with his ever-present cloud of patchouli and disturbingly exciting habit of shoving his hand down the back of my pants in public. Each one of these guys had me at hello and left me gasping for breath by the time we were finished with each other.

And then there was Andrew. Andrew was by no means an instant crush. It took me about a month of knowing him to realize that while all those other boys were dangerously exciting and sexually fascinating, the most interesting, nicest, and sweetest guy was the friend I had been confiding in about all the nutcases I was fooling around with.

Andrew was anything but mainstream. While everyone else at our college wore fisherman's sweaters, bluchers, and corduroys like they were the last word in fashion, Andrew arrived on campus sporting a buzzed haircut save for one long forelock that swung over his left eye. He had a tiny gold loop in his left ear, which I later found out he had pierced in the bathroom of the airplane on his way to Ohio, and favored wearing brocade fifties tuxedo jackets over Cramps concert T-shirts. All his jeans were black and skinny and his shoes were pointy. He was so cool. One night Andrew asked me to see a play on campus with him, knowing I was likely to say yes as a friend of mine was in it. While we waited for the doors to open I saw him turn toward me. I knew that this was the moment we would finally kiss so I turned toward Andrew and kissed him back, hard. His shoulders sagged and then stiffened again as he grabbed me to him, kissing me back even harder. It wasn't until many years later that I learned that Andrew had been turning toward me to ask me to remind him of the name of my friend who was in the show. So in reality, I had kissed him first. And while I've never regretted it, Andrew's hesitation and my impulsive gesture spoke volumes about our personalities and the course of our lives together.

I loved Andrew for his proto-hipster chic and outrageous intelligence. He read Wittgenstein for fun and was an endless source of weird and wild facts. He loved my bred-in-the-bone New York attitude and cozied up to my bookish weirdness like a cat curling up next to a radiator, warmed in the glow of my neuroses. And when I changed gears and partied like mad, drinking like a sailor and dancing on tables, he loved that too.

We had been consistently together for five years by the time I turned twenty-five, and things had become sedate, wholesome, and what I supposed was considered normal. I was restless. And when I was restless I got cranky and bitchy. I went through a period of raging at Andrew for what I perceived as domestic errors or social gaffes. I didn't want to make out with him anymore, much less have sex. I dealt with my agitation not by finding an activity or job that would add to my life and fulfill me, but by stirring up ridiculous chaos with Andrew and kicking up enough drama to keep me interested in whatever was going on between us. I knew somewhere in the deepest and darkest reptilian part of my brain that this situation was madness and couldn't go on forever. It was uncomfortable and destructive. I had to find a solution. I didn't want to keep the crown of Queen Bitch firmly shoved down around my ears just to keep from being bored or in a rut.

In a move that privately shocked even me, I decided that the solution to our problems was to get married. We needed movement forward as a couple, and what could be more forward movement than marriage? Andrew hadn't made any decisive moves in that direction, so I romantically informed him that it was time to shit or get off the pot. That is, regrettably, the phrase I used. Andrew, displaying infinite patience and love, didn't throw up and leave when I made that announcement. So we took the leap and got married. After my stint as Queen Bitch, I wonder to this day what possessed Andrew to make that leap. And while I loved him dearly, I remained essentially the same person I was the day I fell in love with the boy in the Wallabies in 1978. Despite having the best intentions I was, still, recklessly susceptible to the call of sudden and wild attraction. But I had managed to behave myself well enough, despite certain men catching my eye, during Andrew's and my time together.

And so, despite all my previous best efforts and successes in the self-control department, there I was, standing on the doorstep of my marital home holding the door for a sex God in tight pants and inhaling whatever pheromone brew it was that made me salivate just looking at him. I backed up in a daze and started manically dancing around the room fluffing pillows, offering him a seat, asking what he'd like to drink, and generally behaving like June Cleaver had she downed a fistful of bennies just in time for Ward to get home.

Gideon was still playing the mysterious and silent card that he had so winningly displayed on my doorstep as he slid around the apartment, casing the joint. Jesus, what was he doing? Was he planning to rob me later? I did a quick visual sweep of the apartment to see if I had left any valuables lying around. Finally, Gideon focused in on the dining room and rearranged the chairs so two of them were in the middle of the room facing each other. Clearly, this was where we were going to sit. Facing each other. Dear God, I didn't think I was going to be able to survive blushing for a full hour. The only way this was going to end was with me crumpling to the floor in the throes of an aneurism. I randomly wondered if it was too late to cancel the lesson. It would be like trying to put toothpaste back in the tube, but I was willing to try. I had clearly gone insane. Thankfully, just as I was about to implode into a pinprick of mentally unwell dark matter, Gideon broke the silence.

"Um. I'll have a beer, okay?"

"Of course! A beer! Sure! A beer! I've got Stella. Is that cool? Great. A beer!"

Up until this moment, the worst that Gideon could have suspected me of being was nervous and horny. Now it was clear that I was retarded.

From start to finish, the lesson was pure torture. I was far too turned on to absorb a single thing he said. Any shred of a chance I might have had to seem cool was blown. I had officially gone from former Queen Bitch to reigning Queen Dork.

As Gideon leaned toward me to position my fingers on the strings, I could tell that he had eaten a falafel before he arrived. Normally that particular scent, tahini-infused garlic breath, would have me backing up, gagging, and generally making a fuss. Had Andrew been the falafel eater, I would have demanded that he brush his teeth thoroughly before he could get within five feet of me. I might have even lobbied for a second brushing. In this case, I leaned in. And inhaled. I had the vague awareness that this was the behavior of a bona fide pervert.

Throughout the hour of my humiliation, Gideon was adorable. He was funny, a careful teacher, and as professional as anyone could be when his student has drooled all over her shirtfront. At the end of the lesson, he packed up his gear and asked if I'd like to keep the time slot for next week. I emphatically said I would and handed over his cash. Gideon grinned and thanked me, and everything seemed like it was going to be okay. Normalcy had returned. I relaxed enough to show him to the door without tripping over the rug or doing anything else too hopelessly pathetic to recover from. But just as we got to the front door, he stopped and turned around to look at me. And then he did the unthinkable. Standing on the same doorstep where lightning had struck me not seventy-five minutes earlier he said, "I'm glad you had *such* a good time." Then he winked. Knowingly. My jaw was hanging down as I let the door slam behind him.

Fuck! With that wink, I knew I was in serious trouble.

Rather than call Brynne, who would no doubt want every juicy detail but would then totally shame me by crowing about how right she was and that I was a simp to have gone ahead with the lesson, I called my friend Edward. Brynne was one of my closest gal pals, but as any girl knows, it's your best gay pal who is truly the One. He's the one you can tell the worst and craziest crap to. He's the one who won't judge you or compare your lives when you're calling him from inside your closet, crying, with a serving spoon of Chubby Hubby wedged between your trembling lips. He won't judge you, simply because he's a guy and you're a girl and no matter how gay and empathetic he may be, that divide provides enough perspective to make that gay friend a loyal but impartial spectator at the comedy of errors that is your life.

Edward is the best. When you're with him, life is fanciful and magical. You're a character in a novel and you shine in the reflected glow of his brilliance, which he magnanimously always claims emanates from you and you alone. You're invariably funnier, more glamorous, and definitely more exciting when you're with Edward. Ergo, he is never without a dinner engagement. Also, it doesn't hurt that he looks like a young Rupert Everett. Edward's loyalty knows no bounds. We have revealed our most vulnerable underbellies to each other. And thanks to having known each other since our teens, and experiencing most of our truly formative moments together, we come across more as telepathic twins than as mere friends.

I dialed Edward's number with trembling fingers, still jangled from the adrenaline rush brought on by the guitar lesson of the damned. After about half a ring, he snatched the receiver of his ancient rotary phone from the cradle and made a noise that sounded like, "Mmm-hmmmm."

"Edward, is that you? That's how you answer the phone now?"

"I'm getting ready to go out. What's up? How was your guitar lesson? Are you Joan Jett yet?"

I was silent, twisting the phone cord around my finger. Apparently the three seconds it took to do this was enough to set off his radar.

"Oh God. What's wrong?"

"Well . . . the lesson was okay. I was a little nervous so I didn't really play that great the first time, but it was kind of fun. The teacher was . . . nice."

Amazingly, I suddenly couldn't bring myself to tell Edward what had happened and how I felt, despite the original purpose of the call. I was paralyzed. Was I ashamed of how I felt? Was it my loyalty to Andrew, who was also good friends with Edward, that was keeping me mum? Again, my silence spoke volumes.

"You think he's hot." Not a question from Edward. A statement.

I wailed into the phone. "Yes! Yes I do! What am I going to do? Edward, I'm serious. I actually drooled a little when he was close to me. He's so hot. And he knows that I think he's hot. And he winked at me when he left, and I have another lesson next week. What should I do? I feel so, so, so totally insane! Like, 'psycho killer *qu'est-ce que c'est*' crazy."

This time the pause was on the other end of the line. In his most patient voice that broadcasted exactly how stupid he thought I was being, Edward delivered the following withering statement. "You're not going to do *anything*. So what if you think he's hot? I think practically every boy I meet is hot, or has the potential to be hot, but does that mean I hump everyone on the F train? No, it does not. A little self-control is what makes the world go 'round, darling. I think the question is less 'What do you do?' and more 'Why are you so torqued up about this?' So you think someone is cute. Get over it." That was delivered all in one breath. Edward inhaled deeply, gave it a beat for dramatic effect, and dumped another bucket of ice water over my head. "And what does Andrew think about all this?"

"Jesus Christ, Guitar Boy left five seconds ago. I haven't said anything to Andrew."

Edward interrupted me quickly with, "And you never will."

"Okay, whatever. I'm just trying to say that this was different. This wasn't just a standard cute-boy meltdown. Being near him made me feel nuts, like I would do anything to keep the mojo going. Oh come on! You know what I mean!"

"Yes, I do. But I went to your wedding at the botanical gardens and I stood next to you and Andrew while you got married. You have got to pull your panties back on and get with the program. Get over it, my love. And before you accuse me of being mean, I'm not trying to be. I just don't want you to suffer the consequences of what I know would be a whole new kind of jackassery."

This was Edward's version of a warning. Florid, yet

piercing. I heard it but surprised myself by bristling a little. I proceeded to shake it off and dismiss it summarily.

"Fine, whatever. It's no big deal. Enjoy your night out."

"Come on, now, don't be bitchy with me. If you're so hot and bothered go have sex with your husband tonight. Use it or lose it, baby. And seriously, the big question is why this has you so freaked out. Seriously."

"I don't know! Whatever. It's no big deal. Have fun wherever you're off to."

"It's dinner with the Claudes. First drinks at Splash, then dinner at Bruxelles. You remember the Claudes, right? They're usually amusing. Okay, enough of this. Cheer up, chicken, I'll talk to you tomorrow."

And with that he was gone. I couldn't believe judgment was forthcoming from this unlikely source. I was furious. Who was Edward to moralize? For God's sake, he flirted shamelessly with anything in trousers in front of his own boyfriend just to make sure he knew that Edward was, and would always be, a hot commodity. Hypocritical jerk. I'd show him. I could flirt as wantonly as he could and make Andrew sit up and notice big-time.

Holy shit. Was that it? Was I desperate to make Andrew crave me like he did when we first started dating? Did I just want Andrew to rouse himself from the rest-home snooze he had slipped into a few years after we got married when he knew he had me for life? Did I simply want him to display the passion I had once been so knocked out by? Was I missing the guy who not-so-secretly left gladiolas at my door, the guy who drew cartoons for me of us as two little fanged monsters in love just to make me laugh? I loved that guy. I had a flash of clarity. My attraction to Gideon was freaking me out because I felt like I needed it. The looks we exchanged and the pheromone cocktail he splashed in my face had hot-wired me back into an alert, turned-on state I had forgotten all about. I hadn't gotten that feeling from Andrew in far too long, nor was there any hope that I would again anytime soon.

Andrew was my dearest friend and the person who loved me unconditionally, always letting me have my way. He reveled in my outspokenness and drive, frequently taking a backseat just to enjoy the show. His adoration was palpable but lacked any kind of edge. His total acceptance of me left me frustrated and cranky and seriously unfulfilled. I wanted someone who could provide resistance, a little bit of fight. Instead of a sparring partner, I had a warm and welcoming down pillow. And because he was so sweet, of course I felt like a dick. I knew I was a horrible ingrate but couldn't help myself. I hadn't actually done anything serious about my dissatisfaction yet, but I was like a spoiled child who, midtantrum, comes to the realization that her behavior is abhorrent but feels powerless to stop the tornado she's created. My growing sense of frustration led to bouts of guilt that usually kept me from facing my mounting irritation with Andrew head-on. I took refuge in the "sweep it under the rug" approach. But the jolt from Gideon's glossy hair and crooked smile had me comparing the two guys whether I meant to or not, and I couldn't help but feel pulled in what I knew was the wrong direction.

Eventually I heard the key turn in the front door lock

and Andrew came home. All lanky six foot one of him, dark hair cut super short and a pair of gold-rimmed glasses lending the slightest bit of gravitas to his boyish, elfin face. Long gone were the brocade jackets and skin-tight jeans. Today, like he did every day, Andrew sported the uniform of his job as a tax attorney: gray flannel suit, white oxford shirt, repp tie, and wing tips. He was the stark opposite of Gideon's scruffy juiciness. Andrew looked like a freshly made bed. He was crisp, clean, and a safe place to land.

Andrew walked into the kitchen and put his arm around me, asking how my day was. I mumbled something about it being fine and shooed him into the bedroom to change out of his gray flannel armor and into his usual jeans and Izod. It was only after we were snuggled on the couch watching *The West Wing*, again, and silently chewing our dinner that he remembered I had had my first guitar lesson that day and asked how it went. I said that it was fun even though it was kind of difficult, but that I was definitely going to try another lesson. I told him that the teacher was a total cheese ball and then launched into an excoriating description of Gideon, mocking every detail of his getup as well as the fact that he referred to other musicians as "cats" without irony. I had Andrew rolling around on the couch with laughter, and as he giggled his head off I felt a wave of relief crash over me. I had declawed Gideon and felt like I was on firm ground again.

That night Andrew and I had sex for the first time in about a month. Edward's admonition to channel all my lusty Sturm und Drang into my marriage rang in my ears, so I heeded his advice and plunged in. Like the rest of our life together, the sex wasn't in any way offensive or horrible. If it had been, that might have actually spiced things up a little. Instead, it was the same choreography of positions and tricks that we knew so well we could do it in our sleep. Sometimes, I felt like we were. But I tried to feel inspired and get into it. And it was nice. Totally familiar and nice. But I had to acknowledge that my fantasizing about Gideon throughout that love session had helped things along, and certainly wasn't quite right. If I had declawed Guitar Boy so effectively, there was no reason he should be climbing into my head at precisely the moment when he least belonged there. The worst part was that I felt like I had gotten one over on Andrew even though I hadn't meant to. Now I had a dirty little secret to keep from my husband. One that I could savor and pull out for viewing whenever I needed a little shiver of naughtiness that could make me feel recklessly alive. A little secret that would also make me feel slightly nauseated just as it was also getting me off.

The next day dawned and brought with it another day at The Dot-com of Doom. As usual, I arrived late and left early and in between kibitzed with Brynne to while away the day. We kept low profiles in a joint effort to remain inconspicuous as executives bickered in the hallways, jockeying for positions that would only last another few weeks at best.

As the day dragged toward its merciful end, Brynnie finally got around to asking me about the lesson. I could tell that my not bringing it up had been killing her all day but I didn't want to risk revealing my feelings by sounding giddy or overexcited. She'd know the score instantly and I didn't know if I was ready to divulge just how confused and unsettled I was. And after the censorious warning Edward had delivered, I wasn't interested in hearing further judgment or unwanted opinions that might dissuade me from seeing where my lightning-bolt attraction would go. It had been so long since I felt truly breathless about anything; I couldn't bear to kill off this little dark desire of mine. So when Brynne asked, I managed a few nonchalant grunts and tried to distract her by segueing into a discussion of what songs we'd cover if we ever got good enough to start our band. No fool, Brynne paused her flow of questions and appraised me with a single raised eyebrow and a stony silence. After enough time had passed for her to feel that her silent message of "Don't think you're bullshitting me" had been effectively delivered, Brynnie allowed the conversation to flow on to fantasizing about learning how to play Kiss, Queen, and maybe even a little Cheap Trick. By four o'clock we were too exhausted from feigning industriousness to stay any longer and left without knowing if our company's new tradition of firing people late in the day on Friday had continued. We figured that if they really wanted to can us, they'd call us.

Saturday morning came and I woke up to realize that I didn't have anything planned for the weekend. Andrew and I had received an invitation to dinner that night with our friend Laura and her trust-fund boyfriend, but the thought of going through with it was unbearable. I couldn't handle another night of pretentious wine ordering and loud discussions about what Trust Fund did at JP Morgan. I was mulling over other possibilities and brushing my teeth when the phone rang. Assuming it was Edward or one of my girlfriends, I answered the phone with a mouth full of toothpaste and slurred, "Shello?" into the receiver.

A gravelly voice that seemed vaguely familiar asked if it could speak to Jessica. I spat into the bathroom sink and asked who was speaking. In the nanosecond between my asking the question and receiving the answer I knew who it was. My stomach lurched and I sat down on the toilet lid to steady myself.

"Yeah, um, hi, it's Gideon. Your guitar teacher? Is this Jessica?"

I was stunned. Rooted to the spot and gripping the edge of the sink with white knuckles, I took a deep breath, alarmed by how quickly this person's intrusion into my morning routine had thrown me. Was he really this magnetic or was I creating drama out of thin air? My head spun as I struggled to come up with the appropriate response to his question.

"Yes, this is Jessica." Brilliant rejoinder.

"So, you know who this is, right?" I could sense a smile in Gideon's voice.

"Yes, Gideon, I think I can remember someone I met two days ago." My heart beat so hard my throat hurt as I waited for him to chuckle. Nothing. Crickets chirped in the distance. Did he not get the joke? Oh God, I was probably being re-filed in his mental Rolodex from "Queen Dork" to "Queen Bitch." Maybe he was just a little slow?

"Right. Sure. Well, I'm calling all my students to let them know that I'm playing a gig this weekend and it would be cool if you wanted to come and see my band play. So, you know, you'd be chilling out watching me and the guys play guitar, see what you're ramping up to. It'll be a good hang." I had nothing to do this weekend and now this guy calls to invite me out to watch him play. This was a total social deus ex machina. It was weirdly convenient and very tempting.

"You invited all your students, huh? Is that something you normally do?" I tried to sound innocent as I fished around to get a better handle on exactly what this invitation entailed.

"No. I just thought it would be cool this time. It's a good band and we're really gelling so I thought I'd get some people in the audience. It's at Freddy's in Park Slope. Do you know it?"

"Nope. I'm never in Brooklyn. I'm Manhattan all the way. Born and bred on the Upper East."

"Oh, Upper East Side girl never goes to Brooklyn! Maybe you'll make an exception for me." Holy. Shit. He was definitely flirting. He'd swallowed the bait I'd thrown out and taken his time to play with me.

"Well, we'll see. I'll see if my husband and a few of my friends are up for it. When is the gig?"

"Tonight at nine."

"That's short notice. Is this how you always make plans?" I thought I'd go back to teasing him. If he was up for a little verbal slap and tickle, so was I. Gideon laughed and said that he wasn't so good at making plans; he was more of an "in the moment" kind of guy.

"Doesn't that tend to get you into trouble?" I couldn't resist.

"What do you think?"

"I think it probably does." Dear God, where was this going? We had flown past flirting and were veering off into a danger zone where everything that fell out of our mouths implied some kind of intent. Intent to do what remained to be seen, but it couldn't be good. Too confused and annoyed with myself for having the over-wrought yearnings of a teenager to continue on this track any further, I wrapped things up.

"Well, I've got to go, but if I can make it I'll come."

"Cool, thanks. Hey, what were you doing when I called? You sounded funny."

"I was brushing my teeth. Sorry if that was weird, you just caught me off guard."

"No, I was just wondering. You were in the bathroom this whole time. That's kind of intimate, don't you think?"

Oh help me, please. This guy was relentless. The strain of all this come-hither banter was going to drive me to drink well before an acceptable hour. I looked up and An-drew was making weird hand gestures in the doorway to the bathroom in a silent plea to have a moment to him-self in there. I had to end this insanity, stat.

"I don't know. Maybe. Maybe not. It really didn't occur to me!" I gave a light giggle and said good-bye before Gideon could say anything else. I hung up, limp from the exertions of keeping my head on my shoulders and my heart in my chest. The whole conversation had taken no more than a few minutes, but I was so rattled I felt like I needed to be booked into the nearest sanatorium.

By seven o'clock that night, I had managed to assemble a group of friends to go to Freddy's with me. My pal Larry, another college friend, was already sitting on my couch drinking beers with Andrew and gossiping about a mutual friend who might be pregnant. Larry was a great guy whose fatal flaw was his absolute inability to keep a secret. So while we benefitted from his endless divulging of other peoples' secrets, Andrew and I always tried to be careful only to share details we wouldn't mind having printed in the *New York Times*. Andrew was pretty good at keeping mum. I was usually less successful. Brynne was there too with her boyfriend Danny, who was already annoying her by asking if she'd be open to having a threesome with any hotties we might find in the wilds of Brooklyn, and we were waiting for our friend Jake to show up. Jake was habitually late because he loved making an entrance, even if it was only in my living room. Which was fine because we still had about forty-five minutes before we had to find a cab that would take us over the Brooklyn Bridge.

While the guys shot the shit in the living room, Brynne and I sat in my bedroom staring into the depths of my closet. I had nothing to wear. When did all of my clothes become so beige? I always thought that I was kind of preppie but with a certain je ne sais quoi that tipped the scales over to hip. I realized in a flash that I was sadly mistaken. At this critical moment, when looking effortlessly cool was so vital, all I had to work with was the wardrobe of a fifty-year-old school administrator. Gideon, in his infinite dude-dom, would take one look at me in my off-the-clock gear and write me off as a tight-ass who was the mayor of Dullsville. Why hadn't any of my friends told me that I looked so drab? I turned on Brynne in a vicious panic.

"I can't believe that you never told me that I look like shit all the time. I look like a dead librarian and it's all your fault."

"Are you retarded? You're conservative, but you always look nice. Just wear some jeans and that nice short-sleeve sweater with the cardigan that goes over it and some loafers. Perfect!"

I stared at her in disbelief. She had just told me to wear a twinset and Weejuns to a bar to hear a band play. We had clearly fallen into a wormhole and emerged in 1962. "Brynnie, I don't know if you noticed, but I'm not Jackie Bouvier. Wearing a twinset to a bar is absurd. I need something gorgeous and extremely, ridiculously sexy to wear." Just as I said this, Andrew popped his head into the bedroom and clearly heard my anguish over my lack of slut-wear. Nothing registered on his face at all. No curiosity about my sudden need to be a hot piece. I had clammed up the moment he appeared and in the resulting silence, Andrew said chirpily, "Hey, honey, what time are we leaving?"

"I don't know, whenever everyone's here I guess."

"Cool." And with that he was gone. Brynne and I just stared at each other. Then she resumed where she left off. "You don't own anything sexy. Just go with jeans, a T-shirt, and Converse. Wear some makeup and smile a lot; you'll be fine. But I want to go on the record saying that you are way too invested in going to this gig. Nothing good will come from flirting with Gideon. I totally get the sex-appeal thing going on here, I told you it was going to happen, but you're too jacked up. It'll be weird. What does Andrew think of all this anyway?"

"That's what Edward asked. Andrew thinks nothing because there is nothing to think. We're just going to hear our guitar teacher's band. You're the one who wanted to take lessons so badly and start a band of our own. So this is the first gig we're going to see with someone we actually know playing, and now you're freaking out. Seriously, there is no big fucking deal here." And with that I dove into my closet to find a decent pair of jeans that didn't make my ass look too fat, and so that Brynnie couldn't get a good look at my lying face.

Finally dressed in something that resembled what a normal person would wear going out on the town and with Jake having finally made his grand entrance, I left the apartment with my friends and we hailed cabs on the corner of Sixth Avenue and Twelfth Street. Brynne, Andrew, and I got into one cab and Jake, Danny, and Larry took another. It was freezing but we didn't bother trying to convince the cabbie to break code and take all of us since there were enough cabs speeding up the avenue to accommodate us. It was still early so the downtown revelers hadn't really hit their stride yet, drunkenly stealing taxis from each other and generally making public transportation as hellish as it can be on cold winter nights in New York. We all gratefully snuggled down into the seats of our stale, BO-scented rides as we cut over to Fourteenth Street and got on the FDR to go over the bridge and into the hinterlands of Brooklyn.

When we pulled up to a nondescript brick building with a neon Guinness sign in the window I had second thoughts. If it was lame in there, it might kill this passionate spark I had for someone who got me more cuckoo-demented than I had been in years. I couldn't afford to lose that. Or what if my arrival was of absolutely no interest to Gideon? Would the embarrassment of showing up with a posse in the face of his indifference be so cringe-worthy that I'd have to cancel my next lesson and nip all of this fun in the bud? With my heart in my throat I got out of the taxi, and after all six of us assembled on the sidewalk, we walked into the heat and noise of the bar.

Gideon and his band, curiously called Love Craft, hadn't hit the stage yet and were milling around setting up their gear and trying to look as important as possible in a performance space that was clearly an afterthought at best. I later learned that the band's name referred to the lead singer's favorite sci-fi writer, which definitely put the band's overall allure in jeopardy. But I was blissfully unaware of this dork factor the first time I saw them play. Andrew, Larry, and the rest of the gang elbowed their way to the bar and grabbed Budweisers for all of us and managed to find an unpopulated corner where we could set up camp and comment on the scene. My anxiety about what I was going to wear that night was, to put it lightly, misplaced. Jeans, T-shirts, and checked flannel were the fashion statement at Freddy's, except for the band, which sported a look that veered between Gideon's Zeppelin tribute and a bargain-basement Mick Jagger thing for the lead singer and the rest of the band.

Clutching my beer and trying to look like I was the last word in nonchalance, I slouched in the corner with my crew, scanning the crowd for Guitar Boy. I telepathically willed him to come over to say hi but knew that once he did I would most likely do something lame, like stutter or spill my beer on my shirt. I felt like I was in seventh grade but was perversely enjoying it this time around. Oh God, just what I needed. Now I was into masochism. Great. While I busily lost myself in self-flagellation and navel-gazing, Brynne had been talking to a new addition to our group. I snapped out of my reverie when I saw that it was Gideon. He had spotted us and came over to thank us for coming. Despite his penchant for pants of alarming snugness, Guitar Boy's manners were impeccable.

It was only after I heard a few statements like "Yeah, man, that's cool" and "Did all you cats come from Manhattan?" that I deigned to turn to my left and acknowledge our host. As I did, he turned to his right and our eyes met across a divide of less than two inches. Startled, I stepped backward onto Andrew's foot and promptly fell into the wall behind him. I had all the sex appeal of Don Knotts. Laughing hysterically, Andrew scraped me up and draped his arm around me as I stammered something about needing to lay off the hooch. Gideon's gaze barely wavered as he let a slow smile play across his lips. Unable to look at him without doing something else that would land me in the slapstick hall of fame, I ducked my head and stared at the floor, hoping it would open up, swallow me, and spit me back out on Sixth Avenue so I could go home and pretend none of this humiliation had ever happened. No such luck. By the time I had composed myself and could join the conversation again, Gideon was in a spirited discussion with Jake about humbuckers and Andrew was asking me what I wanted to do about eating something after the gig. I wondered how it was that I could have just had yet another sizzling jolt of unparalleled sexual electricity nearly send me to an early grave, yet no one around me seemed to notice. Andrew was definitely oblivious as he nattered on about whether we should have burgers or Thai food later. I was pretending to care enough to mull it over when the lights dimmed and Gideon excused himself to join the rest of the band onstage.

If the guy I had been dreaming about licking for the past few days weren't in the band, I don't think I would have made it to the end of the set. It wasn't that Love Craft were bad musicians; it was just that they were so ridiculously silly. There was no question that each one of the band members had memorized every move from their "How to Be a Rock Star" playbooks, delivering performances soaked in so much self-conscious rocki-tude that I found myself curling my toes just to brace myself against my own embarrassment. The drummer twirled his sticks over his head, then threw them out to the crowd as mementos. No one caught them. The lead singer pranced around and twirled the mic stand with the aid of a long chiffon scarf. The bass player wore huge shades and never looked up while Gideon and the other guitar player delivered windmills and knee slides, occasionally holding their guitars like machine guns to point at the crowd. For some reason, in the midst of all the silliness, Gideon's windmills didn't disturb me at all. I actually thought they were kind of sexy in an ersatz Townsend kind of way. But I nearly needed someone to order me a crash cart when the lead singer climbed onto the bass drum, only to either fall or leap awkwardly from his perch. I turned to check out Brynne's reaction and found her staring at the stage with her mouth hanging open.

As for the songs, they were too reminiscent of the entire Led Zeppelin and Stones catalogs to be truly awful, but there wasn't anything remotely memorable or notable about them. Except, perhaps, the lyrics. I was profoundly confused when I managed to decipher the lead singer's bluesy shrieks and growls enough to hear him sing, "All it takes is a free buffet." And then he repeated it for what felt like twenty minutes. Free buffet? What the hell was going on here? Was this a band of British-blues-loving gastronomes who were short on cash? Were they renegade Zagat reviewers who had committed their research findings to song? Who on earth would sing about a free buffet? Thankfully, "Free Buffet" was the band's final offering, and after it blazed to its conclusion in a haze of fuzz pedals and reverb, we were released from the cacophonous confusion that was Love Craft's set.

Needless to say, we had to stay to tell Gideon how much we liked the gig. Doing anything to the contrary would have been the height of rudeness and my friends and I were nothing if not well mannered. So we hung around nursing our beers, waiting for the band to finish packing up their gear and reveling in the attention of the formerly gyrating women who now crowded the stage. It was clear that I was not the only admirer of Gideon's charms. He was knee-deep in girls wearing tight jeans and halter tops, and while I craned my neck around the two fratty dudes standing in front of me who were high-fiving each other over what I assumed was some recently committed date rape, it was impossible to make eye contact with the object of my obsession. Finally, I broke away from my pack to approach the stage. I walked over to Gideon and tapped him on the shoulder. I sparkled my best debutante-circuit smile at him and chirped, "Hey! That was really fun, thanks for inviting us!"

Gideon stopped winding his guitar cable over his forearm and shook his hair out of his eyes, grinning at me. "I'm really glad you liked it. It's some cool music, right?" I allowed myself the briefest of hesitations and then let loose with a string of accolades.

"Oh yeah! You guys were great. You have so much energy and the music is really great. Very, um, rocking. Anyway, it's fun to see what Brynne and I might be able to do someday! Definitely something to look forward to. It was awesome. Really, you guys were fabulous. You have to tell me the next time you're playing."

As I delivered this pile of absolute horseshit, I managed for the first time to keep my eyes locked with Gideon's in a steady gaze that radiated confidence. An inexplicable feeling of total calm came over me as I smiled prettily, joked around a little about how smelly the bar was getting, and in a moment of rash daring, put my hand on his upper arm to give it a squeeze as I delivered my final thanks and farewell. Gideon's eyes flickered to where my hand rested and darted back to my face. I thought I saw his super-groovy veneer crack for just a fleeting moment as his sly grin flattened out into a straight line. Ha! Now I was back on top. I had regained my composure and despite my earlier droolings and weak knees, I was delivering the message that I could handle whatever sexy charm Guitar Boy had to dish out.

I congratulated myself for being the biggest alpha girl in town, and after gracing Guitar Boy with another sweet smile, I turned to go. As I turned, my hand fell from his arm, and just before it swung to my side he caught it. He squeezed it quickly but held on as I leaned away, pulling me ever so slightly toward him. No smile danced around his pretty face now. Gideon pulled me a little closer to him once more and said in a quiet voice, "Really glad you came. I'm looking forward to next week." And in an instant, he let go of my hand, propelling me away so he could turn to the next woman hovering around him. I searched the crowd for my waiting friends and the starving Andrew and made a few hand gestures to say that they didn't have to wait to congratulate the band, I had done it for them. Relieved, they rushed out of Freddy's and into the bracing cold air outside.

We eventually got a livery cab to stop for us and take us back to the Village to Jane Street and burgers at the Corner Bistro. As we devoured our late dinner we laughed about the band, dissecting the performance and trying to figure out whether they really thought they were cool or if they had actually delivered some kind of performance piece that was a commentary on the absurdity of rock attitude. I piped up, asking the panel if they could make heads or tails of "Free Buffet." Larry rolled out of the booth laughing. He wiped his eyes and informed me that the band had, in fact, been singing "leap of faith" for that last twenty minutes. As I giggled, acknowledging that the song was now slightly less bizarre, Brynne jabbed her knuckles into my thigh under the table in what I knew was a silent plea to go to the bathroom together to discuss what had gone down with Gideon and me in those last few minutes in the bar. She had witnessed everything but had the good grace to keep her lip zipped until the time was right. I jabbed her back, hoping she would understand that I meant I would talk to her privately later. Right now, I had bigger fish to fry. As I sat in the booth in a state of mild discomfort, I had to acknowledge my sneaking suspicion that when Guitar Boy had pulled me to him I had, ever so slightly, wet my pants.

3

DE-FLOURING

There's only so long you can stave off the inevitable. True, I spent hours obsessing over Gideon and the thumpingly lusty effect he had on me, but I also spent an equal amount of time mired in self-loathing and flat-out anxiety over the situation. I knew that I wanted to rip his threadbare corduroys off with my teeth, but I held back. It was one thing to think about it, but leaping on a strange man was too deranged to actually do. And Andrew certainly wouldn't be down with it, to say the least. So I spent most of my time both during and after our lessons gyroscoping between panty-melting passion and mental cold showers, trying to analyze my desire into the ground and hoping to render it boring and pointless in the process. No dice. With every passing day and each excruciatingly chaste guitar lesson, I knew that my combined desires to lick Gideon from stem to stern and to shake up my life were undeniable. Worse than that, they felt compulsory.

By the time my fifth lesson rolled around, we had created a careful routine that mostly consisted of Gideon's trying to teach me a simplified version of a Beatles song and my yammering at him about my day and trying to pry information out of him about his life. I was desperate to know anything about him that would diminish his absurdly priapic status and make him vaguely human. This approach never worked. Gideon was no dope and clearly got off on our flirtation too much to let it die. He fielded my questions like a champ, only revealing the most tantalizing tidbits about himself that he knew would titillate someone who was obviously dying to burrow up his pants leg like a horny gopher.

He let me know that he grew up on Long Island but as a teenager would come into the city every weekend by sneaking onto the LIRR to hang out in Washington Square Park and the Village. He had been in bands since he was an early teen and worshipped Jimmy Page. He would allude to girlfriends, but so noncommittally that it was clear he liked playing around and was up for a good time. He would start to describe a woman he might or might not be seeing but then stop himself and say, "Oh, you know how it is." I didn't. I had no idea at all. But knowing that he was a hot piece who could, and would, make himself available for the taking was almost too much to bear.

By lesson number five, despite endless fantasies about all the suave methods I could employ to let Gideon know I was into him (although what I intended to do once my feelings were clear remained a mystery to me), I hadn't made any significant moves. The only thing I actually did manage to pull off was to put my bare foot up on his chair between his legs to position my guitar more comfortably in my lap. I looked up at him through my lashes in what I hoped was more Ava Gardner than Miss Piggy and asked, "Is that okay?" Gideon kept his head down, looking at my sweaty fingers on the fret board, and mumbled something along the lines of, "Oh yeah, sure. As long as you're comfortable." So much for the seduction of the century. That fateful lesson ended with me a little bit closer to being able to play the E-Z Chords version of "Blackbird" and a moment of awkward silence as I handed Gideon his cash.

As he pocketed the damp bills and headed for the door, Gideon turned back for a moment and asked if I was interested in having a drink. My heart stopped. I replied casually. "What, now?"

"Yeah, sure. I've got some time to kill before I have to meet up with some cats over at the rehearsal studio. Do you want to get a beer?"

I was thunderstruck. Had Gideon just asked me out on a date? Oh my God. My fantasy was coming true. Awesome! Then again, my fantasy was coming true. Which made me feel a little like throwing up, or, should I really go for drama, passing out right in front of him. What to do? It took about a nanosecond for me to make my decision.

"Oh, sure. There's a good restaurant downstairs with a nice bar. Want to try it?"

"Okay, cool. Sounds really good. Don't you want to take a jacket or something?"

I had already grabbed my keys and was headed for the

door wearing only jeans, a T-shirt, a cardigan, and loafers with no socks. "No, it's really right next door. No need to deal with a coat."

We waited for and got into the elevator in total silence, staring at our feet and then shyly grinning at each other as we descended to the ground floor.

We walked the five chilly steps it took to get from the front door of my building to the front door of Café Loup, the bistro next door, instantly glad they had their heat turned up high. The restaurant was filled with a mix of older people who had lived in the neighborhood for decades and young people out on dates, but the bar was empty so we made a beeline for it and chose seats right in the middle. I awkwardly climbed onto one of the high stools and waited for Gideon to stash his guitar in an inconspicuous place and climb aboard next to me. Still shy and a little dumbstruck, I didn't say anything, just smiled at him mutely and waited for him to get this show on the road. I figured that if he had the nerve to ask me to have a drink with him outside the sanctity of my marital home, the ball was definitely in his court.

He broke the silence with, "What would you like to drink?"

"Um, I'll have a Ketel One dirty martini with extra olives, thanks."

"Of course you will." He winked at me and ordered himself a beer. It was something domestic and I made a mental note that it might have been a statement made in response to my very specific and expensive choice. Rather than make a crack about this unspoken initial standoff, I uncharacteristically held my tongue. No need to antagonize him right off the bat, particularly when he was sitting so close to me I could feel the heat coming off his thigh. I took a sip of my drink, which had just arrived, to distract myself from the screaming impulse roiling in my head and belly to rest my hand on that thigh and stroke the length of it. Finally, Gideon turned to me and looked at my face for a long moment.

"So you grew up here in the city, right?"

"Yes, I did. Except for college, I've always lived here."

"That's cool. Where did you go to college?"

"Kenyon College. Do you know it?" He shook his head.

I told him about Kenyon, a liberal arts school in the middle of a cornfield in Ohio, how much I loved it, and how nice it was to be out of the city in such a rural atmosphere. I explained that I had been an English major with a minor in history. When I'd concluded this monologue, I asked the obvious question.

"And where did you go?"

"I didn't. That wasn't my thing, man. I got out of high school the minute I could and came to the city and started playing in bands and working. I've traveled a lot and played in Japan and China. Very cool. Very cool."

I wasn't sure if I had heard him right. I got the no-college thing. But was it possible to interpret what he had said as that he hadn't finished *high school*? Exactly how far off the straight and narrow was this guy, anyway? Somewhere in the back of my skull I heard blaring sirens and the sound of panic buttons being feverishly pressed. A hard little warning knot began forming in my stomach, threatening to dry up all my juicy feelings for Guitar Boy.

A crack in the floor between our bar stools suddenly appeared and threatened to throw us violently apart, reeling backward and away from each other. Just as I saw that crack split the parquet, Gideon's hand brushed against mine and brought all my attention to the square inch of my skin that his had touched. I couldn't breathe. Was that an accident? Did he mean to touch me? As I sipped my martini and tried to look nonchalant, the deranged Nancy Drew in my brain ran wild trying to solve the Mystery of the Sexy Hand. I snuck a look at Gideon out of the corner of my eye and saw that he was studying my face and smiling very gently but with dubious intent, sweet yet predatory. The fact that this turned me on was further proof that I was going slightly mad. I turned on my bar stool to face him, and before I could say a word, he took my hand in his.

The crack in the floor disappeared.

"Is this okay?"

It took me a moment to realize he'd spoken. The various rational warning signals that were going off in my head were drowned out by the sounds of blood rushing through my veins and a weird pounding in my throat. I felt my fingertips turn to ice. But from the waist down I was in flames.

"Oh, sure. Umm. Uh-huh. Okay."

Gideon held my hand in his, palm up. He smoothed my fingers out so he had a flat surface to work on and started tracing little circles on my palm and fingertips.

Again he asked, "Is this okay?"

I was beyond speech and only managed to grunt my assent to him. In the space of thirty seconds I had gone from wannabe Ava Gardner to an escapee from an adult day-care facility.

I stared at his hand as it played with mine and noticed how long his fingers were, with blunt tips and perfectly manicured nails. The hair on the back of his hand and wrist was light and very soft. Perfect. A brief digression about men's hands: they are incredibly important and can be a deal breaker. A cute guy with bitten nails, ragged cuticles, short fingers, weird knuckle hair, or any other physical oddity you can think of is in big trouble with the ladies. Guys never seem to understand this, but every woman knows it to be true. Bad hands can mean no second date. Gideon's hands were beautiful. Who cared what diploma he may or may not have had so long as those fingers could migrate from my palm to more exciting areas of interest?

Gideon kept tracing circles in my palm and gently transitioned into a little massage that crept up to my wrist and back down again. We hadn't spoken a word throughout his performance and I finally broke the silence by clearing my throat. I said as calmly and quietly as I could, "So, what's this all about?"

"You know." He grinned at me and stopped rubbing my hand but didn't let it go. "I really like teaching you. You know that?"

I regained a modicum of my usual composure and laughed lightly, saying, "Yes, I'm getting the picture." I tugged my left hand back a little but he held on. Interesting.

"I think you're enjoying the lessons too, right?"

I dropped the giggle and looked Gideon squarely in the eye and said very gently, "Of course. You know that. It's a lot of fun."

"That's cool. Because I think you can be really good. You should practice more, but I think you could really rock if you set your mind to it."

Maybe it was the cocktail that had gone straight to my head, but I was immediately incensed. That tends to happen. One stiff drink and I can go from zero to sixty in a flash. What the hell was he talking about? One second he's schtupping my hand, the next he's giving me a report card on my progress with "Blackbird"? This was ridiculous. Every time he got near me I wanted to bury my hands in his hair, or his pants, but I was not in the mood to play games or be played. Fuck it. Time to go home.

I hopped off the bar stool and said something about how it was getting late and I had to go home to make dinner. Gideon said it was no problem and paid the bill. He took his time to collect his things and didn't say a word about my abrupt shift from willing hand slut to brisk hausfrau. He held the door open for me as we exited Café Loup and lingered for a second outside the restaurant, both of us figuring out how to say good-bye after this odd and titillating little encounter. Gideon broke the silence.

"Hey, why don't you walk me to the end of the block? I can get on the train there."

"Gideon, it's freezing. I'm not wearing a coat."

"Well, that's your fault, isn't it? I told you to wear a jacket." He sounded like the perfect Long Island yenta. I laughed and admitted defeat on this particular point. I agreed to walk halfway. Neither of us really wanted to say good-bye so we trudged toward Seventh Avenue, chattering away about whether or not I should buy an electric guitar. As we walked, he kept bumping into me. At first it was imperceptible but it got more and more exaggerated as we walked until he was pushing me off the sidewalk into parked cars and frozen dog pee.

"Stop it! That's so annoying!" I was giggling like a kid, delighted that the weirdness between us had dissipated and we could just have a silly moment before he moved on to his rehearsal and whatever that entailed.

"Oh, so you don't like it when I bang into you?" We were back to flirting. Subtle he was not.

"Well, I don't want to be pushed around!"

Gideon stopped and threw his head back, laughing at me, clouds of vapor rolling out of his mouth into the cold air. "I seriously doubt that!"

For what seemed like the four thousandth time that night I was shocked. "What on earth do you mean? I have no interest at all in being shoved by you. Get off it!"

"Really? I thought you might like it."

"Okay, show me what you've got."

I expected him to give me another Gretzky-esque body check into a tree or a car, but Gideon was smooth and didn't miss a beat. With his guitar over one shoulder and one hand in his pocket to keep warm, he grabbed my upper arm with his free hand and wheeled me around so my back was to the buildings and we were facing each other. And then he shoved me backward over and over, forcing me into a narrow alley between a prewar apartment building and a church that had been made over into condos. Wedged into this nook, out of the wind, he set his guitar down and pressed his now-free hands against the fronts of my shoulders, pinning me to the side of the building. Without asking permission this time, Gideon swooped in and kissed me.

This kiss was something completely new and different. When Andrew kissed me, I was occasionally a little grossed out. Too much saliva or a flaccid lack of inspiration. Other times, I had no reaction at all. Our kissing had grown routine and was more a shorthand sign of partnership and affection than passion. I had forgotten what it felt like to be kissed thoroughly and expertly by someone you've been wanting longer than you'd like to admit.

So there I was, slammed against the building with Gideon clutching my shoulders and slightly stooping so his lips could reach mine. Before I knew it, Gideon's tongue was in my mouth, stroking the top of my palate, and his soft, soft lips were on mine in an airtight seal that literally took my breath away. I pulled away to gasp for air and as I did he let go of my shoulders, sliding one arm around my waist while the other snaked up behind me to grab the back of my neck, pulling my face even closer to his. Everything about that kiss was liquid. Our bellies were pressed against each other so firmly I didn't feel the sting of the cold air anymore. All I could feel was that heat that had been coming off his thigh in the restaurant, but now it was from all of him and it was all over me. That heat melted me down to nothing. My body was in flames and my joints felt loose and runny, like when you have a fever that makes you go out of your mind. The block of ice that was apparently normally set up in the space between my sternum and pelvis thawed into pure desire that I could feel pooling in my La Perlas.

Gideon kept kissing me, deeper and deeper; his mouth was so soft but relentless. I kissed him back, trying to swallow him whole. He ran the tip of his tongue along my front teeth and let it linger right under my top lip, then flicked it up to run it along the length of my lip before he forced my mouth wider so he could go back in and kiss me properly again. My hands had been dangling limply by my sides and now I let them creep up so I could hook my thumbs in his belt loops. As we continued to dissolve even further into each other, my hands moved up again so I could bury them in his hair, grabbing him and clutching him closer to me. He slipped his thigh between mine and gently ground it into the tight seam in the crotch of my jeans. I made that noise that you do when you're so very kissed and so very turned on. It's that involuntary noise that's somewhere between a moan and a grunt from the back of your throat that lets your partner know they've done a very good job. My arms went up around his neck, and I bent one knee, moving my foot up to brace me against the wall. I was trying to stand up straight and give back as good as I was getting but Gideon wouldn't have it. He grabbed my ass with both hands, pushed me back against the wall with his chest, and kissed me again, lightly sucking my lower lip before he let me go.

We stood there, dazed, staring at each other. He unabashedly shifted his erection to a less conspicuous spot and started grinning. I couldn't move. My legs were jelly and I knew my knees would buckle if I took a step. Gideon searched my stunned face for some indication of what I'd do next and when I remained slack-jawed and panting, he leaned in, kissed my lips gently, and asked if I was all right. I nodded. It took me another few seconds to find my voice.

I cleared my throat. "I wasn't expecting that."

Gideon stayed close to me and breathed into my ear. "Did you like it?"

I looked at my loafers and tried to figure out how to answer him without screaming "Yes! Yes! But I am horrified! This is unacceptable behavior!" The cold was creeping back into my bones and I shivered. I looked up at Gideon and said, "Of course. What do you think?" And I managed to smile what I hoped was a worldly and wry smile.

"I think you did. I know I did." And with that, my heart broke a little. For both of us.

"Well, I do have to go home and it's not a good idea to do this so close to my building. I'll see you next week?"

Gideon gathered his belongings and backed out of the alley. "Yeah, next week. Sounds good."

I nodded and wrapped my arms around myself for warmth. As I jogged to my door, I heard Gideon call after me.

"Hey, Jessica! Thank you!"

I didn't turn back or respond. But as I got into the elevator I ran my tongue along my lips to get one last taste of him before I brushed my teeth in anticipation of Andrew's arrival home.

• • •

From the moment that kiss began, my life changed. Or, to be more accurate, my thought process changed. Which in turn changed every aspect of my life. I went from being a normal person who could concentrate on reading a book, talk to friends, visit her parents, and basically do whatever it is that the average person does, to being a total mess. I had become a sex maniac on the same order as the average fifteen-year-old boy. Every day, all day, all I could think about was having sex with Gideon. Keeping the movie reel of kinky licking, tweaking, and sucking going in my head became a twenty-four-hour-a-day job. That incredibly erotic kiss ran on a constant loop in my head. And then I'd extrapolate into a fantasy collage of what he could do to me. If he kissed like that, there was no question that he was going to be something pretty special in the sack. He undoubtedly had some crazy *Kama Sutra*/tantric-sex-god training that equipped him with a library of positions and techniques cataloged in his head that would drive any woman insane.

Of course I felt pangs of guilt and like a creepy ingrate every time one of these lustful thoughts sprang to mind. I knew that Andrew deserved better than a wife who sat at her desk all day salivating at the thought of another man. But try as hard as I might, I couldn't rid myself of the obsessive underpants-melting insanity that had come over me. The even more shameful part was that when I was honest with myself I had to admit I didn't want to. I loved the frisson of excitement that thinking about sex and bodies and flesh and all the fabulous nerve-wracking stuff that went along with it brought me. I hadn't felt it in so long, and never this intensely. I wanted to wallow in the sheer physical pleasure of it. Unfortunately, the downside was that all that fun made me feel like I might throw up every time Andrew's face obscured the movie reel in my head, or if I thought of our wedding day and the smile on his face as I swanned down the aisle on my father's arm. But on the scales of crazy, fun outweighed nausea and getting groovy with Gideon kept winning out.

By the time my next lesson rolled around, the electricity between us simply didn't leave room for any attempts at pretense. Gideon walked into the apartment without saying a word, unpacked his guitar, tuned mine, and set them both carefully on the dining table. He gestured for me to sit in one of the two chairs that he had put in the usual position. I did; he handed me my guitar. After he had instructed me to play four scales and open C, A, and G chords, Gideon set my guitar gently on the dining table once again. He stood up and pulled me to my feet with him. He then turned to me and kept gently pushing me backward until I was standing directly in front of the sofa. And then with a little shove to my sternum, I was sitting down. Still, not a word had been said. He grabbed my legs, swung them over to the side so I was lying down, and with one hand bracing himself on the back of the sofa, lowered himself onto me. The kiss was the same as the week before. But this time he had me on my back and pinned me with the full weight of his body as he ground his erection into me.

Holy shit. This seduction, or more to the point, pouncing, was met with absolutely no resistance on my part and was fabulously delicious but also clearly insane. It was happening in my apartment, on my couch, which faced the front door. An unfortunate situation should Andrew decide to come home unexpectedly. In an attempt to pull me back onto the straight and narrow, the minuscule part of my brain that was still working, what was left of my superego, was wildly semaphoring from the sidelines. Not only was it beyond the pale to be carrying on like this in my marital home, on the easily visible couch that Andrew and I had picked out together, but I was getting dry-humped like an easy prom date in the back of a Suburban. I loved it, I hated it, I was terrified, but I wasn't stopping it.

Gideon's hand migrated from my face to my chest to my waist and then finally to my thighs and then up my skirt. That's when I snapped back to reality. I was not going to third base with a man I barely knew. Oh dear. I really was living a teenage fantasy. What thirty-year-old says "third base"? I clearly needed to give myself a time-out.

I grabbed Gideon's wrist and shoved his hand back down to the general area of my kneecaps and struggled to sit up. We were both panting and red in the face and he looked confused. "What's the matter? That was so hot. Why did you stop?"

"Gideon, this is ridiculous. You know I'm into what we've got going on here, but I feel weird. This is my home, not an alley." I sighed and wiped the sweaty strands of hair that had stuck to my face out of the way. "I'm fucking married! You know I want you but falling into an involvement like this is nuts. I don't know about the other people you're with, what your other students do, but I can't just dive into whatever this is so fast, if at all."

He gave me the eyebrows-up look of innocence and gave the matching palms-up hand gesture. "That's no problem. You just really turn me on. It's hard to stop." To illustrate his point, his left hand had been slowly making its way up from my shin to the hem of my skirt. I swatted it back down.

"Gideon. Do you have a girlfriend, or anything serious going on? Are you dating a lot of people now? What's your real story?"

"Why do you want to know?"

"Because it will affect my decision about what I want to do about this."

He smirked and said, "What exactly is *this*?"

"Oh come on. Unless you carry on like this with all your students, *this* is *this*. So do you? Is this your normal thing to do?"

Gideon managed to look offended as he stood to buckle his pants back up. When had he gotten unbuckled?

"Truth? There have been students I've gotten together with. But no one at the moment. You're it. And I don't have a girlfriend. Just some girls I'm friendly with."

Nice obfuscating, dude.

"Okay, so what do you want from me?"

Again, Gideon looked simultaneously shocked and insulted. "Um, you started it. Come on, you know you did. I could read you a mile away. You wanted me the second I walked in the door. And you came to my gig. I'm not saying I don't feel it too, but don't put all of what's going down on me."

I considered this moment of unexpected clarity from what I had previously, and erroneously, assumed was an unlikely source. "Fair enough. But tell me what you want from me."

"I have no idea. This is just fun. You're so fucking uptight, preppie girl. Relax. Just go with whatever it is that's happening. Enjoy yourself."

I swung my legs off the couch and onto the floor. I considered my obsessive desire to lick Gideon every five seconds. I considered his near inability to keep it in his pants. I considered Andrew. My chest tightened at that last thought and I had to grip the arm of the sofa just to get ahold of myself. My fingertips turned white. I was suddenly cold and clammy but had no intention of having a full-on case of the vapors. Nonetheless, I had no idea of what to do with the emotional mulch he was churning up. I needed to think.

"Gideon, meet me for lunch or something this weekend. I have to think about what we're up to. Can you swing that?"

"Sure. There's a diner on the corner of Twenty-third and Sixth Avenue. Meet me there on Saturday at two."

And with that the lesson was over. I didn't pay him. That would have just been too gigolo-tastic for me to bear. Gideon didn't bring it up so I assumed he felt the same. He packed up his unused guitar and left no more than ten minutes before Andrew returned home. Again, I brushed my teeth, straightened myself, and washed my face. I felt decidedly off-kilter for the rest of the night. I didn't eat more than a few bites of the General Tso's chicken we ordered. This was not normal behavior for me, a person who ate with gusto and was always trying to lose that last ten pounds. Andrew either didn't notice my sudden self-restraint or chose not to comment on it.

The rest of the evening passed by uneventfully, barring the hysterical self-flagellation and hair-shirt wearing that was going on in my head. I was a creep. Andrew was so goddamned nice. He was boring but that's not a crime. Adultery is. Or once was. I was on the road to sporting a scarlet A on the front of all my sweater sets. At the very least what I was playing around with was grounds for divorce. The thought of it made me light-headed and heart-poundingly panicked. I was overwhelmed with guilt, not to mention guilt's new best friend who would follow him everywhere from now on, shame. I was a shitty shit and a liar to boot. Andrew went about his business, cleaning up the kitchen and going into the bedroom to lie down and read. I watched him walk away and stayed in the living room to silently brood and have a nervous breakdown.

Saturday finally arrived and at two on the dot I walked into the grubby little diner on the corner of Sixth that Gideon had chosen for our assignation. He wasn't there. Of course. I sat down in the booth closest to the door so I could skulk out relatively unnoticed if he didn't show up and started reading the menu cover to cover like it was required coursework. By the time Gideon arrived about five minutes later, I could have recited the entire list of burgers the diner had to offer, as well as a few of their specialty salads. My dining companion slid into the booth and gave me a big smile. "So you made it. I didn't know if you would show."

"You didn't know if *I* was going to show? You're the one who's late!"

"Well, I didn't want to have to wait if you weren't going to show."

"Okay, well, we're both here. What do you want to eat? I'm starving."

Gideon scanned the menu for about three seconds and put it down, decision made. I already knew that I didn't trust the general cleanliness of the place, so I was ordering the safest thing you can order in any diner, a grilled cheese. Classic and usually E. coli–free. Gideon opted for a plate of fries and a glass of water. The waiter appeared, we placed our orders, and were plunged back into silence, staring at each other across the expanse of Formica that was our table.

"Okay, you wanted to have lunch, so here we are. What's the deal?"

I wasn't ready to dive into my reason for calling this particular summit conference, so I tried to buy a little time by employing some misdirection.

"Why are you only ordering fries? Aren't you hungry for something more substantial?"

Gideon sighed and leaned back in our Naugahyde booth. He rolled his eyes and asked why I needed to know.

"I don't know. It just doesn't seem like lunch."

"You're such a yenta."

"Well you clearly have something to hide. What's your deal?"

Gideon leaned in and stuck his face in mine. "You

know you're making a big deal out of nothing. I'm getting bored. What do you really want to talk about?"

I just stared at him, pissed that he wouldn't answer such a simple question but also nervous about broaching the real topic at hand. During the pause while I was collecting myself and shifting around uncomfortably in my seat, Gideon threw me a bone. "I'm a vegan. That's why I'm eating fries. There really isn't anything else on the menu that I can eat. And I try to stay away from refined white flour too."

"You're what?"

"A vegan. You know what that is, right?"

"Of course I do, I just can't believe that you'd basically condemn yourself to a lifetime of soybeans and lentils. Oh yeah, and endless amounts of vegetables and the resulting horrific flatulence." I was being so caustic in my anxiety that the sound of my own voice surprised me. Gideon looked a little taken aback but gamely answered the question.

"I had a girlfriend who turned me on to it. It's incredibly healthy. Seriously, I can't believe half the crap you must eat. Burgers? Dairy? Disgusting. You're polluting your body. And all of that can't possibly make you taste very good." He waggled his eyebrows in a lascivious version of Groucho Marx.

"Oh please, Gideon. One of my friends is a lesbian who briefly had a thing with a woman who was a strict vegan. Susan swore that all those vegetables made the poor thing taste like mulch. I don't think my dietary habits are a cause for concern. Yours, however, are. I can't imagine how healthy your choice is if you're sticking to fries for lunch."

Gideon drummed his fingers on the Formica table-top and just stared at me with growing impatience until our food arrived. I dug into the greasy sandwich, American cheese oozing between my teeth as Gideon finally exploded.

"Look, I'm going to go if you don't tell me what you want to talk about. All you've done is give me shit about my eating habits. What the fuck is the deal with you?"

He was right. It was now or never.

I cleared my throat, but my voice broke anyway as I finally blurted out, "So, I assume we're on the road to having an affair."

Gideon gagged on the french fry he had just popped into his mouth and took a minute or two to finish coughing up bits of potato and wipe away the tears that were leaking down the sides of his face. "Are you serious?"

I stared at him in disbelief. Could he possibly think that we weren't on the road to hell in a handbasket? Was it lost on him that our sexual chemistry was so embarrassingly palpable that even our waiter was getting a whiff of it? What the hell was he thinking? Oh no. Maybe he wasn't thinking at all. Maybe this was just how adults who hadn't been married since time began behaved. Shit. I was just going to have to plow ahead.

"Of course I'm serious. What do you think we've been doing? Playing canasta? Let me be clear. You come to my house, where I live with my husband; hump me on the couch; play a few chords with me; and leave. Something is happening between us and it's clear to me that we're on our way to something a little more serious than feeling each other up on the furniture. Am I wrong?"

No reply from the vegan.

"Well am I?"

Gideon took a long drink of water. It was obvious that he was at a loss in the face of someone he thought was a hot chick but had turned out to be Torquemada. He kept eyeing me over the rim of his glass, trying to get a handle on just where I was coming from. I imagined that he was weighing the possibility that I was either the most pragmatic person he'd ever met or the most nuts. Possibly both. He was being pressed for a straightforward answer to an uncomfortably direct question. Uncomfortable for anyone, but even more so for a guy like this who clearly liked to play things fast and loose while still keeping his cards close to his chest. He decided to defuse the situation by laughing a little and throwing his hands up in the air. "I don't know what to say. No one's ever asked me that before. You're the one who's married; aren't you the one who's supposed to say if we're having an affair or not?" Good point. Nicely played, Guitar Boy. But not good enough for Lawyer Girl.

"I believe I did say that, if you were listening and not picking through those sad fries. I said that if we continue going down the road we're on, we'll be having an affair. So my question to you is, do you want to keep going? If you do, it's going to get weird. I don't know how weird, but weird. So if you're not up for it, I get it. But I just really want to know what you're thinking. Or at least what you want. I know what I want."

This last bit of bravado shocked the shit out of me. Who says stuff like this? I sounded like I was channeling Jimmy Cagney in some 1930s gangster role along with a dash of Scarlett O'Hara. I knew I was coming off as both shameless and dangerous. My little performance would either turn Gideon on or completely scare him off. I had no idea. The truth was that my heart had been in my throat the entire time I was talking. To the average observer I'm sure I sounded perfectly composed and logical, all of my lawyerly training kicking in at just the right moment, but I felt like I was having a total psychotic breakdown as each word shot from the zip gun that was my mouth. I could feel my pulse hammering in my temples and the base of my throat and swallowed drily, waiting for his reply to my deposition. I was beyond terrified.

Gideon and I both knew that implicit in my question was my own willingness to embark on what I had mildly called weirdness but was for me much more like ripping all my clothes off while standing on the observatory deck of the Empire State Building and then taking a flying leap toward the pavement. It was a raw, naked, and brutally honest moment. Not only because I was telling this person I didn't really know how desperately I wanted him physically and possibly emotionally, but also because I was hearing myself say it out loud for the first time. I was also finally admitting to myself how unsatisfied I was in my marriage. And that this affair felt like the only way to stave off the feeling of crushing doom that came over me every time I thought about all the decades of marriage that stretched out in front of me.

While I was delivering my speech to Gideon, I imagined a third party sitting in the booth with us listening right along. What would Andrew do or say if he knew this clandestine negotiation was taking place? Would he break down? Would he punch Gideon in the face? Would he punch me in the face? Would he tell me to immediately pack all my belongings and get out of the house? Would he dispense with the civility of speaking altogether and just throttle me until my eyes popped out? The thought of Andrew as a sudden addition to the party was in every way just as heart-thumpingly horrifying as what was actually happening in the moment. I hated the thought of hurting him, as well as the idea that no matter how much the marriage was killing me, I didn't want to lose him. But Andrew's physical absence made it easier to push that concern aside to worry about later.

I was too busy laying it on the line to be concerned with or address the everyday realities of my life. Gideon now knew how I felt, and I had manipulated the situation into making the decision his. I knew it was my home life that was in jeopardy so all balls were really in my court, but if Gideon could be forced to say yes or no, then I wasn't going to have to claim full responsibility and shoulder the blame of what I was proposing all by myself. I could pretend that I was just being pushed along an inevitable route by someone else's ardor. I wanted Gideon to be the answer to my most passionate, sexual, outrageous prayers, but I also needed him to be a willing accomplice. For this situation to work for me, he had to be a true partner in crime. He had to play my game.

I turned to Gideon. "So?"

He sighed and ran his hands through his hair. "Look,

Jess, I'm really into you. You know I'm dying to have you. But you're married, man. I don't know what to say about that. It's one thing to have a one-off with some married chick, but an affair? Actually being involved? I don't know. It's so fucking complicated. I don't know if I can handle it."

I took notice of the fact that he had not explicitly said no. There was a chink in Gideon's armor. I could tear it open. I'd finish this situation off with logic that my Zeppelin-loving paramour couldn't deny. Whether I could sanely say I wanted to be in a relationship with Gideon was becoming a moot point. I was hell-bent on winning. He wasn't going to be allowed to say no.

I began a carefully considered oratory. "Gideon, I know it's weird for you. But isn't it possible that it's just because you haven't done this before? New doesn't mean bad. And I'm not really interested in having the kind of affair that's a big mushy love-fest. In fact, I have a set of rules."

"Of course you do."

"Yes, I do. And they will make both of our lives easy. Number one, we will not treat this as a love affair. We'll have fun with each other and finally consummate this thing between us. We'll have affection for each other, but that's all. Number two, I don't want any presents, flowers, love notes, or stuff like that. I want to keep it clean. Number three, we'll keep our assignations to the times of the guitar lessons. So there will always be a logical reason for us to be together at certain times. Number four, you can have all the other women you want, I just don't want to know about it. Number five, I won't talk to you about Andrew." Suddenly my mind was blank. I knew I had another rule but couldn't remember it. It was on the tip of my tongue and driving me crazy.

Gideon was trying not to laugh as I methodically told him in no uncertain terms how he was supposed to feel and behave while in my presence. He waited while I was obviously trying to recall something. "Is there a number six?"

"Yes. I can't remember what it is. Oh yes! I've got it. Neither of us will say a word about this to anyone else. It's just for us. Okay?"

Gideon considered the six-step program for total emotional removal I had laid out before him. "You really think you can do this, Jess? Forget me. Forget what I want for a second. Is this really something you want?"

"I think I've made my position clear."

"Wow! You are seriously all business! Look, honey, if you think you can do this, okay. I'll go along. You're amazing. In more ways than you know. No one has ever spoken to me in my entire life the way you have today. I'm in, but watch out that you don't fall in love with me, baby." He looked up at me with those blue eyes through his thick, dark lashes. "You're sure you can resist all this?"

"I'm not resisting it, you idiot. I want it. I just think we can play it safe."

"Whatever you say. Like I said, I'm interested. But I've got to go back to work, so I'm leaving. Can you pick up the check? I really have to run."

I figured that covering his fries was the least I could do after what I'd hit him with.

"Yup, I've got it."

"Yes you do. You've got it, baby. You're totally crazy, you know that, right?"

Finally, I let out a bark of laughter. "Yeah. I probably am. But we're on?"

Gideon was already putting on his coat and making for the door. He looked over his shoulder and said, "I'll just call you later."

4

WHITE LINES (THE MORE I SEE THE MORE I DO)

It was at around this point that I finally realized that I was doing something strange. This strange thing was something I had never done before and consequently didn't recognize I was doing it until a few weeks had gone by. I had begun compartmentalizing my life. I had always compartmentalized the *elements* of my life in that special way that people who are eternally teetering on the precipice of true OCD do, but I had never done it to my actual, whole, global existence.

As for my usual compartmentalization, it generally went like this: I liked my physical surroundings to be neat and tidy, so it stood to reason that I operated in a neat and tidy way so that my brain would match my environment. I would accomplish this handy trick by visualizing, for example, my career as a particular set of achievements or failures that I could put in a box in my brain marked "career" and deal with it when I needed or wanted to. The same concept applied to "family" and "friends." And even the battier stuff like "health and burgeoning hypochondria." This is a good time to mention that my general anxiety and agitation would every so often manifest as my deciding that I had some horrifying disease. Every few weeks or so I would lie next to a sleeping Andrew, silently weeping and mourning my own untimely demise.

Dealing with the vagaries of my existence by handling everything that came my way as a discrete issue was nothing new. Not only was this neat and tidy, it kept the commingling of my various insanities at bay. It was, however, breaking new ground to lead two lives. Which is what you do if you embark on a serious affair. If you don't, you live in a swampy, stinking morass of guilt that will suck you under and make you either end the fun of the affair of your own accord or do something completely stupid so you purposely get caught, thereby ending the affair as well as your primary relationship. The only way to keep the affair going is to create a split personality, which, if we use my previous "boxes in the brain" concept, means that all the little boxes wind up getting stacked into two bigger boxes labeled "marriage" and "what the fuck am I doing oh my God I can't stop doing it, holy shit I'm having an affair."

The marriage side of your life, I soon discerned, is relatively easy. You just keep doing what you're doing and try not to leave a trail of bread crumbs behind you that will lead to your lover's door. The affair side of your life is more complicated because you don't have a routine yet, you don't really know each other that well, and you don't know what the other person might do or not do that will fuck up the other part of your life. It is essential to note that these are also the elements that make the affair exciting and utterly irresistible. And dangerous, provided you want to stay married. So essentially, what I did to keep my life with Andrew going as I explored having a new experience with Gideon was to divide all of my actions and emotions into two camps and hang on for dear life, ignoring Camp A when I was with Camp B and vice versa.

My General Patton routine with Gideon at the diner had really been an exercise in psyching myself up to pack him into his series of boxes; Gideon wasn't an idiot and clearly understood what I was doing. As with all things related to Gideon, it took me a longer time than it took him to catch on to the realities at hand. I just thought that by cracking my whip against my riding boots and adjusting my epaulets with military precision, I was in total control. Appearances were everything, or so I had been taught. And so I believed. Believing in appearances was my version of whistling a happy tune. If no one would suspect I was afraid, I simply wouldn't be. If no one suspected I was out of control, I wasn't. And that was that. But no matter how hard I tried, my little boxes didn't always keep my Guitar Boy–related shame totally contained.

I chalked the creepy feeling up to the prospect of diving into God knows what with Gideon the Gorgeous, or more appropriately, Gideon the Potentially Ghastly. Andrew, on the other hand, I took entirely for granted, as he did me. I figured that what was good for the goose was good for the gander. Why not let Andrew's laissez-faire attitude toward our relationship work to my advantage? He had never bothered to suspect me of any wrongdoing before, or even being capable of it, so why should he start now? I hadn't been caught making out with Gideon during a lesson, I hadn't been seen at the bar downstairs, and Andrew was so irritatingly content with the perfection of our marriage as I assumed he saw it that it simply didn't occur to him that anything would ever go awry. While this quality of Andrew's was turning out to serve my purposes very well, it was one of the issues that had slowly been driving me bonkers. If we were at a party and I flirted shamelessly, Andrew never seemed to care, much less notice. If I was approached by a drunk guy at a bar, Andrew would leave me to fend for myself. Which I could, but still, nice to have a little backup. And if I had a domestic complaint, he'd correct it, but only briefly. He'd revert to old habits within weeks, confident that I'd always forgive and forget.

Andrew's overwhelming ability to take me, and my interest in him, as a given would be the cloak of invisibility I'd rely on to let me have my cake and eat it too. If Andrew couldn't muster up the energy to consider that I might actually inflame some interest in anyone other than him, he would just have to suffer the consequences, damn it. I was thirty years old and still looked good, twenty-five-year-old good, despite my librarian-from-hell wardrobe. If Andrew wasn't going to bother to treat me like the sex kitten with options I was beginning to see myself as, he would just have to let someone else do it.

With my husband summarily dispatched in this way, I focused on Gideon and what involvement with him would entail. Life with Andrew was a known entity. The world that awaited me with Gideon was thrilling, had its parameters clearly defined (or so I thought) thanks to our pact at the diner, and was infinitely better than another night at home baking bread, arguing with my mother on the phone, doing laundry, or trying to get Andrew to do something with me other than go to a movie or watch reruns of *The Real World*. I was a single-minded burgeoning adrenaline junkie on a mission; I figured that if there was a real world to participate in, I was going to do it and do it big. Breaking out of the perfect-on-paper rut of my life was going to be my way of crashing through the fourth wall of the world I had been trained so well to be contained by and had embraced without thinking. If anything got smashed or a little blood was drawn on my way through that wall, so be it. My mind was made up, but even more significantly, that conversation in the diner and my conviction of Andrew's blindness, or worse, indifference, had set my wheels in motion.

● ● ●

Gideon did call soon. A few days after the diner experience, he called to let me know that he was having a rehearsal with a few guys at a studio on Thirtieth Street, and that if I wanted to meet him after it would be cool. I was giddy. Not only was this clandestine date exciting because it was, well, clandestine, but he actually called! He wanted to do this thing with me! I couldn't wait to get to the rehearsal studio, see what that was like, and meet these guys whom Gideon played with. It was all so alien;

dark and thrilling. Pathetically, it was thrilling because I was meeting him at nine thirty, which was usually when Andrew and I started winding down like a sweet old couple clinging to life in a nursing home. I couldn't wait. I had gotten a few new clothes since the drama of dressing to go to Freddy's, so I put on a short black dress and black suede boots that went to the knee, and as I made my way out the door I simply told Andrew the truth. I was going to see a real live band rehearsal, and wasn't that cool? He said that it was and went back to rereading *A Confederacy of Dunces* for the seventh time.

My nerves were on high alert and I felt jangled and not entirely in my own body from the anticipatory adrenaline rush that kept my heart pounding in my chest as I sat in the back of a cab on my way to Thirtieth Street and Eighth Avenue. I was so distracted and anxious that the overwhelmingly sweet and urinal-cakey smell of the cabbie's air freshener didn't elicit the usual feeling of gagness in the back of my throat that those things normally do. I don't think I even rolled down the windows. I just sat there, silently letting the aroma of cherry-scented ass wash over me and permeate my hair while I sat with my hands folded in my lap, trying not to have a stroke. I was chipper and on a mission when still in the safety of my own home, but the minute I started barreling uptown to the studio, things were getting real. What was waiting for me on the other side of this particular looking glass? I knew it had to be good, partially because it was scaring me shitless before I had even encountered one iota of what it had to offer. There was no going back.

Not because the cabbie and his cherry-ass car wouldn't turn around, but because I knew that going back home to what I had been doing day in and day out for years simply wasn't an option. If I went back, I would die. I'd die of boredom, rage, heartbreak, and disgust with myself for having had the opportunity to try something new and not doing it. So my cabbie and I sped along, weaving through taxis and bicycles, making our way to what would be either a dream or a dud. I was keeping my fingers crossed for the dream.

*   *   *

We arrived at the appointed place, and after throwing a few bills in the general direction of the front seat, I climbed out of the cab and stood on the sidewalk. There was a stiff breeze that I prayed would blow the cab smell out of my hair and off my clothes. After about five minutes of airing myself out and watching a stream of guys carrying cymbals, guitars, conga drums—you name it— in and out of the building, I found the courage to wade into the unknown. I walked into a long and narrow lobby that was entirely clad in linoleum (floors, walls, ceiling . . . someone obviously had an uncle in the business) and made my way to the elevator bank at the end of it. I jabbed at the button with the upward-pointing arrow, which never lit up, praying that the elevator was working so I could get away from the leers of the musicians who had grouped around me and find my way to Gideon and his pals. I was so palm-sweatingly nervous that it didn't occur to me until after I was in the elevator that now I was trapped with these letches in even tighter quarters until I could spring out of that box of vomitrociousness. It was vile not only because the guys were so letchy, but because they all had the distinct pongy smell of BO that no amount of Old Spice can hide. They collectively smelled, as my friend Nikki would say, like a bowl of chili in a laundry hamper. Normally, this would be too much to bear, but after the cab ride I had just endured, weird smells weren't going to faze me. So I just breathed through my mouth, tried not to taste the whole "chili in a hamper" catastrophe, and got out on the fourth floor.

As I sprang from the elevator, gasping for breath and wiping my eyes like I had just emerged from a mustard gassing, I caught sight of Gideon sitting on a bench outside one of many doors that stretched down a long hall covered, not surprisingly, in more linoleum. I adjusted my dress to cover just a little more thigh, as I had an unexpected wave of demureness wash over me in the split second I had at my disposal before Gideon looked up to see me. It was for naught. The second I let go of the hem it sprang back to midthigh. So much for being ladylike. I threw my shoulders back and my boots, which were clearly made for stumbling, toward my fate, strode down that linoleum corridor, propelling me toward what I had no ability to resist. The hollow clacking of my heels on the floor snapped Gideon out of whatever reverie he was lost in. He looked up, registered that the noise was coming from my doing some kind of power runway walk down that mile-long stretch of hallway, and smiled. He didn't grin. He didn't slyly smirk. He smiled. Nice. In that moment I relaxed and knew that the evening would be just fine.

I slid onto the bench next to him and while squeezing my knee, Gideon leaned in close to tell me that rehearsal was over and all the guys were coming out in just a second. He used that second to slide his hand up to my underwear and back again. Game on. Okay. I got it. This was how it was going to be. Sexy, but clandestine even among his own friends. Gideon's timing was perfect. The instant his hand returned to my knee four guys trickled out of the rehearsal room talking about the song they had just finished playing and whether or not they were "in the pocket." I internally rolled my eyes at all the rock-guy jargon I was being exposed to in Gideon's world. This was just more of the Rock 'n' Roll 101 that I had seen at the performance at Freddy's. First it was referring to people as "cats" and "man," and now we had moved on to calling things that sounded really good "in the pocket." If I heard anyone say that the "gig" was "tight" I was going to be forced to leave. Sexy boy or no sexy boy, a girl has her limits.

The band consisted of the following: a tiny bald guy with a pointy beard who looked strangely like a cross between Vladimir Ilyich Lenin and Ming the Merciless. I would later learn that his name was C.C., like C. C. DeVille of Poison fame. I prayed that it was a coincidence. He played guitar by night and was a lawyer by day. Then there was the bass player, who had to be sixty if he was a day. Although winter was beginning to wind down it was still cold out and this guy was wearing shorts with tube socks pulled all the way up to the knee. And, of course, a Hawaiian shirt. This was Ira. A drummer emerged who looked like every other drummer I had ever seen or would see from then on. Which is to say that I have no memory of what he looked like or what his name was. Rob Reiner had it right in *This Is Spinal Tap;* drummers just sort of explode. They disappear. They're interchangeable. Each one is weird in his own way but can be depended on to be odd and unreliable. The final member of the band was another nonentity in that he never surfaced again. The only memorable thing about him was that C.C./Lenin the Merciless was in hysterics for days because this Asian guitarist kept insisting that they tune to the key of B-frat. I didn't know if it spoke worse of C.C. or me, but any time we found ourselves in conversation and couldn't remember what we had been talking about, one of us would bring the other back on point by saying, "You were just saying that we should be in the key of B-frat." C.C. and I bonded quickly, over both our infinite ability to out-snark each other and the fact that we were both English majors who fell into law degrees. Two little jerks to the core, but endlessly amused by each other, which goes a long way.

I was introduced all around, and the drummer and B-frat guy quickly peeled off to do whatever it was they did in the privacy of their own homes. Gideon, C.C, and Ira decided that we should have a drink and immediately pronounced the only acceptable place for our revelry to be Siberia, a bar conveniently located inside the subway station at Fiftieth and Broadway. Conveniently located if you happened to be interested in taking the 1, 2, or 3 line at roughly three in the morning in a drunken stupor, possibly covered in vomit. Vomit that probably isn't yours.

We took a cab to the bar (in deference to me and because I was paying) and descended the short flight of stairs into the station and the entrance to Siberia. Going to that bar as my inaugural run for my new life of wrack and ruin was, in retrospect, perfect. In a lot of ways, it just didn't get seedier or dicier than Siberia, so if I could make it there I'd unquestionably make it anywhere. I have no idea if this occurred to Gideon at the time, if choosing this bar was a test of sorts, but if it was I passed. Siberia was just too interesting to turn your nose up at, no matter how much vomit was on the floor or how many sweating patrons were drunkenly leaning on each other, breathing deeply felt inanities into each other's ears. There was a punk band squeezed into a corner, jumping up and down to the tuneless, rhythm-free din that they were frantically creating. Their sweat and spit flew off them as they whipped their heads around, only to land on the few unfortunates who were clustered around them, not to listen to their musical efforts, but standing in what seemed an optimal place to get the bartenders' attention. The bartenders' attention was, however, only given to regulars or particularly hot chicks. By hot I mean both in terms of beauty and body temperature. The fewer clothes you had on and the more likely it was that your boobs would pop out of whatever was still holding you together, the higher your chances were of getting the Bud you were angling for.

Gideon slid up to the bar and with the wave of one finger had four drinks for us in less than three minutes. Of course. While he was collecting the drinks and paying, a red-faced guy in a tattersall shirt, repp tie, and blazer, all of which were soaked through with sweat and beer, leaned precariously in my direction and boozily breathed into my face that he worked at the *New York Post* and what did I do? Before I could chirp that I too had some experience in publishing, the journo was already sliding off his stool and crashing to the ground in a facedown preppie heap. He was quickly peeled off the cigarette-burned floor by his colleagues and propped up by them against a minuscule space of spare wall. Deftly defying the laws of gravity, he remained erect. This entire calamity took place in the three minutes it took for Gideon to get us our drinks, all of which were served in plastic party cups, and distribute them. By the time Gideon's attention was back on me, the stool next to me was already filled by another patron who stood a good chance of sliding to the floor within seconds of mounting it. I accepted and downed my drink in two gulps, knowing that this was one of those nights and I'd need all the fortitude I could get.

The guys launched into a conversation about the rehearsal, music in general, and people they knew from the guitar store where Gideon worked. I had no place in this conversation, knew it, and decided to set up shop next to a defunct pinball machine that was crammed into the corner not occupied by the punks. I have no memory of whether it was *Charlie's Angels* or *The Dukes of Hazzard* or which other seventies TV show the pinball machine promoted, but it was something in that vein. It was the only thing in that bar that felt vaguely familiar, so I gravitated toward it and stayed put, comforted by its seedy charms. From this vantage point I could both collect myself and get a good look at the insanity that lay before me.

The band had not so much wound down as collapsed in a pile of bodies, self-consciously arranged to resemble the aftermath of a massacre set to their own soundtrack. The bizarre combination of toothless drunks, junkies, journalists, looky-loos, and post-rehearsal musicians continued to talk, sweat, bang into each other, and drink out of their plastic cups, endlessly moving and shifting until they became not much more than a blur in front of me and to each other. Every now and then, Gideon would come over to me and ask if I was doing okay. I nodded in the affirmative as the stereo system had kicked into high gear and there was no use trying to talk to him above the blaring of "Sheena Is a Punk Rocker." Just to make sure I was having the best time possible, Gideon kept a steady flow of tequila shots coming my way, which I drank distractedly yet gratefully. If everyone else was going to be blotto by the time this evening was over, I certainly wasn't going to be the odd girl out.

After twenty minutes or so of drinking and watching the melee, C.C. came over to me and started talking. He had no trouble blaring even louder than the stereo, which had moved from the Ramones to Television. My tequila-soaked brain was probably playing tricks on me, but C.C.'s voice nearly harmonized with Tom Verlaine's as he asked me about myself, drawing closer and closer, clearly hoping that there was an impending opportunity to hook up. Possibly even on the premises, in what must have been the most disgusting bathroom in New York at the time. Ignoring his come-on, I answered C.C.'s line of questioning, and along with figuring out that we had both earned the same academic degrees we found that our birthdays were only two days apart in the same year. In the Wild West atmosphere of that bar, our connection seemed unbelievably significant, and having declared ourselves twins, we spent the next forty-five minutes or so talking about anything that came to mind, including making fun of the drunkest or most belligerent people in the bar. Finally, after enough phlegm, vomit, beer, and cocktails of unknown description had been deposited on the floor or on my boots, Gideon suggested that we go to his place. Excellent idea.

I can't say I regret going to Siberia, but I'll always remember it as the moment that the bar was set for what I could handle and what I couldn't. I know my nonchalance surprised Gideon, but it surprised me even more. Pushing the envelope on what I could tolerate if I framed it for myself as an adventure, and having Gideon around as my tour guide, was clearly going to be part of this odyssey of self-exploration on which I had embarked at first so casually and now so clearly in earnest. I had started the night gagging at a bad air freshener and was now indifferently scraping someone's snot off my boot. And so it began.

It turned out, to my infinite surprise, that Gideon

lived on the Upper East Side, not the Lower East Side, where every self-respecting rocker, wannabe or otherwise, was living at the moment. There was nothing about Gideon that remotely broadcast any bourgeois tendencies, so the cab ride uptown to Sixty-third Street, with all of us piled in the back along with two guitars and a bass, was a bit of a shock. Particularly because I was expecting a night spent in poorly lit and dangerous parts of the city, casting myself as a version of Griffin Dunne in *After Hours*, the film where he couldn't escape TriBeCa and its insane denizens until the sun came up. Instead, I was being whisked right back to my old stomping grounds. When I teased Gideon about his neighborhood, he tensely explained that he had a great deal on an apartment and that I'd see when we got there. I made a mental note: do not question this guy's cool factor. A touchy subject for sure. Perhaps his conviction of his own hipsterdom was not as ironclad as it seemed. I didn't know for sure if that fact would prove to be necessary, but it was worth making the mental note and keeping it flagged.

The taxi made its way uptown and as it did C.C. and I kept talking but Gideon kept his hand possessively on my knee. Ira noted it immediately and flicked his eyes from the hand to the knee to our faces and back to the hand. I thought I saw him roll his eyes slightly but then he returned to his conversation with Gideon about how to pull off performing an all–Buffalo Springfield night at Arlene's Grocery sometime in the next few months. Apparently that had been the subject of their intense conversation at Siberia. Gideon kept repeating, "Yeah, man,

I know, it's a great idea, but we just don't have anyone who can sing like Richie Furay and without that, we've got nothing. We'll just keep looking." I had no idea who Richie Furay was and didn't know anything about that band beyond its big hit "For What It's Worth," so I stayed silent on the subject and talked to C.C. about exactly why I had stopped being an attorney.

C.C. leaned in close to hear me over Ira's nattering. "Yeah, so I was sitting across the conference table from opposing counsel and I looked at this asshole in his crappy suit with this horrifying sense of undeserved entitlement oozing out of his pores, and I had a total Peggy Lee moment."

C.C. laughed. "What does that mean? You teased your hair and started singing from a bar stool?"

"No, but nice one. I just thought, *Is that all there is?* You know the song. The really jaded one that's totally campy and awesome where even her house burns down and all she can say in this totally blasé voice is, 'Is that all there is?'"

"No. I'm not gay. I have no clue of what you're talking about. But I get the point. I don't have that reaction to being a lawyer at all. I agree that most lawyers are douchebags, but I use that to my advantage. I kung fu them. I let them throw all their douchebaggery at me and just when they think they've got me, I bend like the reed out of their way and let their own stupidity boomerang back and bring them down. I never have to land a blow in court. I just let opposing counsel hang themselves. And I love watching it every time."

I listened to this with a mixture of skepticism and

respect. If any of C.C.'s spiel was true, he was getting cooler by the minute. He was the David Carradine of 100 Centre Street. Not bad. Not good enough to turn my attention away from Gideon or his hand on my leg, but still very cool.

We pulled up to a nondescript brownstone on Sixty-third and First Avenue and stayed motionless in the back of the taxi. I had paid for the other cab so there was no way I was paying for this one. After an awkward moment of silence, C.C. broke and gave the cabbie some money. We spilled out onto the street, hauling guitar cases behind us as we got out, and Gideon began his descent down a flight of metal stairs to the basement apartment of the brownstone. We followed him down, clattering on the metal stairs; Ira was familiar with the surroundings but C.C. and I were both taking it in for the first time. The door to Gideon's place was directly under the brownstone's front stoop, so there was dankness at the doorstep that hinted at much worse to come once inside the building. We entered a long hallway cluttered with shoes, guitar cases, and stuff that looked like it had been abandoned on its way to the Dumpster outside. These items had been left in the netherworld of the foyer either out of lassitude or a sudden reconsideration of the wisdom of throwing away something as potentially useful as a broken hamper. Whatever the case may be, it pretty much fulfilled the promise held by the front door.

We passed through another door, which was locked with a padlock, only adding to the general air of NOKD (Not Our Kind, Dear) that these guys and the evening emanated. Gideon wrenched the lock open and we were

suddenly in a large, warm, and cozy studio apartment
that had all the usual bachelor gear set up exactly as it
would have been had it been roughly 1976. Black leather
couch, glass coffee table, big TV and stereo system, bed
tucked behind a Japanese rice-paper screen at one end of
the room, tiny kitchen, and Led Zeppelin posters everywhere. Some of them were even glow-in-the-dark posters, as I would find out soon enough. Throwing caution
(and fear of mold) to the wind, Gideon had even wall-
papered his bathroom with these posters. The bathroom
was surprisingly clean and all the way at the far end of
the room away from the bed area and past the kitchen.
Essentially, the apartment was a long, wide hallway decorated just well enough to make it into a cozy apartment.
I was pleasantly surprised. The best touch was that the
only window in the apartment was over the bed and
was at ground level, lending the whole affair a decidedly
Laverne and Shirley feel. Had Lenny and Squiggy burst
in to announce plans about some ridiculous scheme I
wouldn't have been surprised. Then I looked around the
room at Ira, Gideon, and C.C. and decided that it was
likely that Lenny and Squiggy were already among us.

Jackets were stripped off, guitars were removed from
their cases and carefully set against walls with the rev-
erence usually reserved for religious relics, and Gideon
turned on the stereo. The only surprise about his decision to put on *Houses of the Holy* was that it was so predictable. But truth be told, that's only 20/20 hindsight. At
the time I had never heard the album in its entirety and
was totally swept away by the sexiness of Zeppelin, Gideon's weird but homey place, and the promise of some

kind of excitement now that I was at the epicenter of where the real partying seemed likely to start. We were all buzzed from what Siberia had offered, and the guys were talking loudly among themselves about the various merits of different amps when Gideon turned to me and took my hand to lead me away from the guys and closer to the kitchen/bathroom area. He leaned me against a wall where his friends couldn't see me and quickly ran his hand down my back to my ass, which he cupped with one hand while he leaned in to inhale the general vicinity of the left side of my neck. Just before I could dissolve into a full swoon he backed away and asked me loudly, possibly as a cover, whether or not I wanted to smoke a joint. Then the question was put to the room as though it was a joke. Of course they did. How else could the evening really begin?

Taking my hand, Gideon moved to the black leather couch and threw himself down in the middle of it, taking me down with him. He looked at me with what might have been a mocking smirk, or maybe just his usual cover-up for when he didn't know the answer to a question ahead of time, and said, "Hey, honey, so do you want to smoke or is that not your thing? Have you done this before?" I looked at him in total shock.

"Gideon, I did go to college. I grew up in the city. What the bloody hell do you think I am?"

"I think you're someone who says shit like 'bloody hell,' so I have no idea what you do. So do you want to smoke or not?" I answered in the affirmative. At this point, Ira and C.C. were sitting cross-legged on the floor

on the other side of the glass coffee table and there was
no way I was going to let myself be hazed as the new guy.
Not even if I knew that Gideon was at least partially already in the palm of my hand. Yes, I had been in the palm
of *his* hand no less than two minutes earlier, but I wasn't
going to quibble with myself about it. I was not going to
be the square and that was that.

Gideon got up from the couch, climbed over me, and
went to a tall bookcase in the corner to retrieve an in-
tricately carved wooden box with pretensions of African
origin. No doubt something that was part of his carefully
curated seventies décor. He returned to the couch with
the box and opened it to reveal about an ounce of weed,
a few packs of rolling papers, and a lighter. In record time
(and I went to college in the Midwest, where there was
nothing to do, so I've seen some fast joint rolling), he had
two fat spliffs ready to go and had passed one to Ira and
kept the other for himself. I made a mental note not to
smoke anything that had been in Ira's mouth. The color
of his teeth, beard, and mustache were enough to give
any sane person pause, but the slightly foamy flecks at
the corners of his mouth sealed the deal. Between that
and the socks, Ira, no matter how nice or sweet he may
have appeared to be, instantly went into the "there's
something decidedly off-kilter here, possibly of the Mark
David Chapman variety" category. A bit harsh maybe,
but at least I knew for sure that I wasn't sharing a joint
with him.

There had been no reason to fear. C.C. wasn't put
off by the flecks and he and Ira inhaled that joint so fast

their feat actually deserved a standing ovation. Had they been able to stand after sucking down that smoke so fast I'm sure they would have not only applauded themselves but also taken a bow. As it was, they just stared at each other and then Gideon and me for a minute and then collapsed on their backs, goggle-eyed and tapping their feet to "Over the Hills and Far Away." Gideon was laughing at them and took his time to light our joint. He inhaled deeply and handed it to me as he blew a monstrous cloud of smoke up toward his acoustic-tile ceiling. I took a huge hit too and blew the smoke out of the corner of my mouth so it wouldn't hit him in the face. Gideon teased me for my part–film noir, part-spastic smoke blowing and took another hit. This time he turned my face toward his and very gently put his lips to mine and carefully blew the smoke into my mouth. No stranger to this goofily seductive move, I held the smoke as well as his gaze and then blew it back out through my nose. C.C. and Ira were now rolling on the floor and giggling about something that I kept thinking I could hear but would then escape me. I realized then that I was tragically stoned. Stoned beyond belief. I had to take a weed time-out or there was a high probability that I would either start drooling or say something so inane that it would enter the annals of history as the dumbest words ever uttered. I leaned back into the slickness of the black leather and concentrated on breathing while I watched the lights on the stereo's equalizer hypnotically jump in time to Plant and Page's exertions.

I have no clue how long I sat slumped in the crevices between the cushions on the couch staring at the dancing lights, but I came back to life when Gideon leaned over and asked me if I wanted to stretch my legs. I looked down and saw that I had shifted into a twisted-up cross-legged position. I was cramping up in my Camp Fire Girl pose and said that getting up sounded like a good idea. I carefully unfolded myself, testing to see if either of my legs was asleep so I wouldn't crumple to the ground with a hideously embarrassing case of dead leg. They were awake. Gideon took me by the hands and pulled me up so I was standing no more than an inch from him. I could feel my pulse thumping in the veins in my throat, but I was so stoned that my mind drifted and I started wondering if the thumping I felt was really my pulse or his, because I could see the veins in his neck throbbing in time to mine. Could I possibly feel his pulse without touching his neck? Was I hallucinating? What the fuck was in this pot anyway? I had only had about two hits and was out of my gourd. This was the kind of fucked-up that didn't go away quickly. I would just have to concentrate on relaxing and enjoying the ride. Generally I loved smoking pot, but there had been a few incidents in college when I had freaked out in episodes of major paranoia, all of which culminated with my standing on a piece of furniture and yelling for everyone to get out of my room. I prayed this would not be one of those nights.

While these free-form nonlinear musings were running through my head, Gideon had already started leading me to the bathroom to show me the glow-in-the-dark posters he had in there. I giggled as we walked, muttering something about his being a docent for his apartment. He asked what a docent was, and before I could answer we were in the bathroom with the lights out. It was grown-up seven minutes in heaven. While I was admiring the faintly glowing posters, some of which featured the fuzzy flocking that marked them as true vintage gems, Gideon had closed the door behind us and lickety-split I was being kissed as thoroughly as I had been the night in the alley. My arms were around his neck and his hands were everywhere. I was too stoned to keep track of what he was doing; I could only register that his fingers and palms were all over me, leaving traces of sensation behind them that were so voluptuous it seemed like I was being touched everywhere all at once. I muttered under my breath, "So I guess this is how our arranged affair starts." Gideon didn't bother to remove his mouth from whatever body part it was attached to (there was no way I could identify it at that point) and made an "mmm-hmm" noise that sounded like he was in agreement.

Gideon expertly maneuvered me toward the toilet and kept kissing me as he lowered me down to sit on the lid, all the while spreading my knees open as wide as he could before I squeaked with discomfort. From there he slid down to kneel in front of me, lifted the hem of my dress to my hips, and with the deftness of someone who had done this many times before, pulled my underwear to one side so he could go down on me with abandon. Had I not been stoned, had I not been so turned on by the kiss, had the lights not been out and the loony posters glowing at us, had I had a chance to think about the way he hooked his index finger into the cotton of my underwear and pulled it over without asking, I would have stopped him. I hadn't had anyone other than An-drew down there in almost ten years. The sheer novelty of having another man there alone would normally have been enough to stop me in my tracks. But that night my id was at the controls and my superego was clearly on vacation, possibly back in the Village, where the rest of me belonged. All I could think about was how delicious it felt to have his tongue moving so slowly and languor-ously and hear him say through the haze of my brain, "I've been wanting to do that since you got off the el-evator at the studio tonight. You taste amazing." I must have, because he kept at it until I gave up all attempts at self-control, arched my back, and pushed forward toward him, feeling like I was about to have the best and most fulfilling coronary of a lifetime. Just as I was grabbing his shoulders and getting ready to let loose with a throaty war cry, the doorknob jiggled.

Gideon had forgotten to lock the bathroom door. It slowly opened, and from his crouching position Gideon managed to hold it closed with one hand, as we both screamed, "No!" to whoever it was that was innocently trying to take a leak. The door stopped moving and closed as quickly as it had opened. Gideon looked up at me, and I down at him, and we started laughing hys-terically at how teenager-caught-in-the-act that moment was. The laughter and absurdity of being caught out, and both C.C. and Ira now undoubtedly knowing what we had been up to, killed the moment. Gideon let go of my underwear, gently pulled my dress down, and hauled me back up to my feet. In the darkness of the still-unlit bathroom he washed his face and hands, grabbed my ass one more time, and led me out into the living room.

Our entrance into the living room went completely without comment. Neither C.C. nor Ira said a word. They glanced over in our direction but immediately started complaining that the weed was too strong and they were just too high. They pestered Gideon for the antidote. I didn't know there was an antidote to being high other than eating a huge amount of Cheetos and watching either *Spinal Tap* or porn. Apparently I only had half the story. The antidote they sought was blow, and Gideon had that too. It had been hiding beneath the Zig-Zag papers in the wooden box, a Ziploc plastic bag about one inch square, filled almost to bursting with cocaine.

Gideon expertly chopped the coke with a razor blade (now I knew why he had a glass table), set up four lines, and produced a dollar bill, which he rolled up for us to use to snort the table clean. He went first and handed me the dollar bill next. Let me be clear about one thing. This was not the first time I had seen coke or done it. I grew up in New York in the seventies and eighties. You had to basically be chained to a radiator in a basement not to see or experience coke if you were a teenager or older at that time. But I had always been a good girl. I had only done it once before but had done such a tiny bit, just to create the appearance of fitting in, that it didn't have any discernible effect on me at all. This time was different. Snorting a tiny bit was not what was being offered. What I had in front of me was a giant rail, staring me in the face and taunting me. That line knew it was going to get the better of me, and I knew it too. There wasn't a shred of doubt that this experience was going to be something totally new and different.

I didn't know what to expect, how I'd feel, or what I'd do. I did know that all three guys were watching me to see what my next move would be. Was I with them or against them? This was yet another moment of envelope pushing. I could walk out right now and beg off, saying that their recreational style wasn't for me, and hail a cab to go home. Or I could decline the offering and stay put, steeling myself against late-onset peer pressure. Or I could do the line and see what happened next. This was like one of those *Choose Your Own Adventure* books. Which road would I choose? Where would it take me? I knew the answer in my gut before I consciously made the choice, as with all things Gideon-related. I leaned forward, holding a few strands of my hair out of the way, and with that dollar bill delicately placed inside my right nostril, snorted that table clean. I whipped my head back, my hair landing perfectly in place, and handed C.C. the dollar. Gideon threw his arm around me, grinning as the coke swept the pot cobwebs from my brain, and a strange bitter drip slid its way down the back of my throat. I instantly felt naughtier than I had ever been and had somehow joined a club I hadn't known existed until that first line went up my nose. Within the space of a minute, I began to feel like a master of the universe. I felt invincible, audacious, and in total control of myself and my situation. There wasn't a doubt in my mind that I liked what I had just done. A lot. More than a lot. And there was also no doubt I would do it again. And I did for the remainder of my time at Gideon's that night.

I got home at about three in the morning. Andrew was sleeping peacefully with *Confederacy of Dunces* on the bed next to him. It was only when I slipped into bed next to Andrew, still grinding my teeth a little from the coke, that I realized he hadn't called to check on me once that night. I hadn't touched base to tell him where I was either. Clearly, it didn't matter.

5

THIN IS IN

While I was busy exploring the delights of Bolivian marching powder (or yeyo, or candy, or star-spangled powder, or whatever other cute name you like to use to refer to cocaine), the executives at beenz.com were also entering a new era. An era in which the company didn't exist anymore. After several years and ninety-six million dollars had been expertly squandered, those brilliant tacticians and developers finally decided to call it quits. They had to. If they didn't, it was likely that everything in the office, from beanbag chairs to giant bean-shaped conference table to possibly a few of the high-ranking executives, would be seized by some government agency.

So the shoe finally dropped and Brynne and I were about to be out of jobs. The upside of the squandering of all that money on the part of the company was that our salaries had been absurdly bloated. While it sucked to be unemployed, we had enough money saved up to play for a while without any serious negative financial repercussions. Edward's dot-com started to show signs of terminal illness at the same time.

I heard about Edward's dot-com, which was conveniently located about three blocks away from mine, running into trouble the day before beenz.com finally let us go. My office phone rang and I picked it up to hear the sounds of what resembled nothing so much as the Watts riots emanating from the earpiece. There were a few screams of "Grab it and get out as fast as you can!," crying, and someone desperately trying to restore order by yelling ineffectively, "Can we have some professional behavior here please?"

"Edward, what the hell is going on over there? It sounds like you're at ground zero for some kind of mass-hysteria-induced looting fest."

"I am. I truly am. I'm a little scared for my life. I think someone just stole my stapler."

"Oh come on, how insane can it really get over there? What's happening?"

"Honey, prepare yourself. Your stupid company is probably only days away from the same thing. You think these people you work with are normal, and then the minute they smell trouble they're stealing computers and margarita machines. This is no place for a sane person to be. I'm going to get out of here. Meet me in the lobby of your building."

I turned to Brynne and reported what was going on at Edward's company. She stared at me blankly and finally the light came back in her eyes.

"They had a margarita machine? Why didn't we think of that?"

"Oh I don't know, we were too busy stealing each other's work and blaming each other for failed products. Margarita machines were a frivolity that wouldn't ever occur to dyed-in-the-wool professionals like us."

Brynne rolled her eyes and started packing up her gear. "Let's get out of here."

"Fine, but I'm meeting Edward downstairs."

"You got it, sister."

And with that we were dashing past the corporate offices with our messenger bags held up to screen our faces and diving into the elevator. We found Edward looking shaken and irritated.

Brynne and I debated where we should go and what we should do in our usual noncommittal way. Our nattering was too much for Edward, who rolled his eyes at us and decided to go on his own not-so-merry way. Brynne and I hopped on the 6 train and made our way to Bleecker Street so we could go to Temple Bar. Everyone I knew had been going to Temple Bar since we graduated from college, so it was a familiar, although at times slightly prohibitively pricey, hangout. Thanks to our collective decision to ride the dot-com wave, cost wasn't such a concern for us at that moment. Temple Bar's other draws were the bowls of free popcorn with little crispy strips of yellow and gold beet chips that came to your table in a steady stream, borne by silent waiters and waitresses all dressed in black, for as long as you loitered over your drinks. It was also a major plus that it was one of the darkest bars in New York. You never knew what time it was and what was going on outside when you were at Temple because its romantic gloom hung over you in a state of perpetual midnight that was so soothing it was positively transporting. Being there was like being on vacation for as long as you could keep drinking or paying the bill. As long as you were in residence, you were guaranteed to be totally checked out with no idea what fresh horrors might be waiting for you on the other side of Temple's heavily curtained walls. This was just the environment we needed on a day when jobs were being lost and the end of an era was staring us in the face. So we settled in at one of Temple's tiny cocktail tables and placed our usual orders: vodka dirty martini for me and bourbon on the rocks for Brynnie. Some serious drinking was about to begin. So was some serious gossip.

I removed the top layer of my martini while Brynne slipped into an unaccustomed silent reverie, staring into the depths of her glass. Finally she spoke. "You do know we're going to be unemployed any second. The HR bitch is just itching to call us."

Of course my cell phone rang at that precise moment. A little bit of the bourbon Brynne had just sipped flew out of her nose, landing on my leg.

"See? See? I'm right. There it is. We're toast."

I didn't pick up the phone because I had a sneaking suspicion she might be right. I just couldn't deal with hearing the HR hag's voice if it was indeed her on the other end of the line. If it wasn't her, I didn't care who it was. The only person I felt like talking to was with me at the moment.

Brynne kept speaking even as she held the bourbon glass to her lips. She drained it in two gulps and started sucking the ice. "Don't answer that shit. They can fuck themselves until tomorrow." This was salty language from Brynnie. Clearly she had not eaten enough before embarking on this particular bender. Nonetheless, she motioned to the waitress for another drink. Then she raised her eyebrows and asked if I was ready for a second round. Why not? I nodded my assent.

"Okay, let's talk about something other than work. I have some gossip."

Brynne tried to hide her smile as she munched on the popcorn, bursting with curiosity. Finally, something to think about other than what on earth we were all going to do with our lives.

"What is it? Who is it about? Did someone do something violent or just inappropriate? How well do we know this person? Is it a guy or a girl? Have either of us slept with them?"

This rush of words came out of her in a torrent of rumormongering glee.

"Actually, it's about me."

This statement deflated Brynne instantly. She snorted in disgust and began her journey through Maker's Mark number two. She paused for a moment and directed her slightly blurry gaze at me.

"Jessica. You know this already. If you're telling me something about yourself it isn't gossip. It's just news."

"Generally that's true, but this is kind of out there. It may break new ground and make the leap from news to gossip."

"Okay, shoot."

"So you know our guitar teacher, Gideon?"

Brynne slapped the table and said just a little too loudly, "Oh shit. I knew this was going to happen."

I was already annoyed. I couldn't get a word in edgewise. And she was right to be horrified, but definitely not before I even had the chance to share the news of the night before.

"All right, what went down? Oh wait, I bet it was him. On you." She snickered and crunched on her ice. Thanks, babe, nothing like being judgmental *and* smarmy.

I had a moment of clarity burst through the cloud of the day's weirdness and realized that this best friend of mine could not be confided in—at least not yet. Not only was one of my basic "how to have an affair" rules to tell no one, but Brynne wasn't going to be able to share any of the giddiness I felt about the illicit thrills of what Gideon had done to and for me. She was just going to be pissed off at my overage rebelliousness and, admittedly, incredible irresponsibility with Andrew. I briefly and silently argued with myself that she didn't know or wouldn't acknowledge how benignly neglectful Andrew was and maybe I should preface my story with that. That would get her softened up and on my side. Then I realized that it was a fool's errand. Everyone loved Andrew. They saw him as this sweet and innocent mild-mannered person who had suffered through my earlier wildness and occasionally still had to put up with my aggressive behavior and outbursts of frustration, which they had no clue were built on boredom and even loneliness in my marriage. Sometimes, just to tease me, my friends would refer to my husband as "poor Andrew." I hated that like poison but kept my mouth shut so I wouldn't embarrass him by spilling how I really felt. They should have been saying "poor Jessica." I was in an emotional prison with him. After last night I had come to what I thought was the incontrovertible conclusion that living with Andrew really was like living in a retirement home and that what relationship we did have was completely powered by my steam, anger based or otherwise. Poor Andrew nothing. Even so, I saw in a flash that Brynne would not respond well to the tale I had to tell. So I edited out everything that was going to tip my hand too quickly. Which was most of the story.

"So I went out with him and these guys he plays in a sort of side band with, not Love Craft, last night. We went to this really gross bar called Siberia, and it was fun. I had fun. It was weird to hang out with new people but it was good. You know, new blood. It was like the old days, when we used to go to Larry T's Love Machine or some insane club and get all fucked-up. But this time I was watching other people get fucked-up."

Liar. I'm a big fat liar.

Brynnie stared at me and slowly picked her way through the new bowl of popcorn that had materialized on our table. She chewed, sizing me up.

"Yes. I remember going clubbing. I also remember hearing about you tripping your face off at Larry T's and dancing with three drag queens at the time. You, my dear, have lived. So the best I can say about today's offering is that it is underwhelming. What you have just told me is not gossip. It barely merits being called news. The real question is, what *aren't* you telling me?"

"Come on, it's news. I met new people. I went to a rehearsal studio and saw how the other half lives. It was a fabulous slummy hang. Excuse me if I think that's interesting." I feigned huffiness and prayed that my elitist twist about "the other half" would annoy Brynnie and distract her from the giant liar who was sitting in front of her.

"So, you're telling me that getting out of the house with some musicians to watch them get drunk was a big event for you. That this is a big deal."

"I guess so. Fine. Whatever. Never mind. Pretend I didn't say anything."

Brynne waved down our waitress and ordered another round of drinks for us. She then turned her attention back to me.

"I know you're lying. You are the worst liar on the planet. Something happened. Either you're going to tell me or not, but you brought it up so you clearly want to unload some sordid little rock 'n' roll story on me."

Brynne was getting bizarrely caustic. I chalked it up to the bourbon but was getting annoyed. She continued leaning in so close to me that our noses were almost touching. "You know I love you, right?"

I assured her that I did.

"Then why would you waste my time with your wicked lies, you filthy, filthy girl?" She started cackling and slapping the table again, totally amused by herself. "I know all about what that Gideon does to you when he just looks at you. You wet your fucking pants. Did you forget that you told me that? Well, you did. So if you're not ready to tell me what you did, that's cool. But do not lie to me. I will always know. I'm like those fucking psychics the army trained for cold war mental warfare. I know what's in your head and I'll take you down.

"Here's what happened. You went out with some guys and had a semiwild night of watching other people get fucked-up. My guess is that you got just as fucked-up as they did and topped it off with some kind of snogging with Gideon. Who is a guitar teacher. Which is like fooling around with the pool boy in your elitist little mind."

I kept my head down so my red face, a mixture of shame at my transparency as well as fury, couldn't be seen in the fuggy gloom of the bar. I cleared my throat and as I did threw two twenties on the table. "Thanks. Okay, well, you've got me all figured out so I'm going to go home and let you enjoy how brilliant you are all alone. See you around." I was furious. Furious that she was right, that my actions had been so predictable, that my excitement had been deflated so quickly, and that my friend, who was only trying to protect me, was doing it in such a jackassy way. It's not that Brynne didn't have a point, it's that she was almost smug in her censure and intimate knowledge of how I worked and what was making me tick these days. Fine. If she wanted to be smug about my potentially bad behavior, I'd give her something serious to deal with. Anything I had done in days gone by would pale in comparison to what was next on the menu. I stomped out of Temple Bar and started the short trek home to West Thirteenth Street.

I got home and immediately started pulling stuff out of the cupboards and fridge to make a batch of cookies. Today required something far more indulgent than bread. I wanted Toll House cookies and was on a mission to bake them as quickly as possible. The process of putting them together helped to calm me down, and I was betting that eating them in a steady hand-to-mouth stream of butter and sugar would also help to get me down from the ceiling. By the time the cookies were all stirred up, dolloped onto the baking pan, and in the oven, Andrew's key was turning in the lock and he was walking into the apartment sniffing the air and asking what I was baking this time.

"Cookies. I don't have it in me to make or eat a real dinner. I'm in a foul mood and am going to eat chocolate chip cookies for dinner or until I pass out. So if you want real food, call the diner or the Chinese place."

"Wow. You're torqued up, what happened?"

"I'm about to get laid off. I have no intention of quitting because I want every bit of unemployment insurance those assholes owe me, which works out fine because I know that I'm definitely getting shit-canned imminently. The worst part, to be totally honest, is that I have no clue what I want to do with myself now. I have no concept of what the right next move is, considering the career I've cobbled together so far. The HR bitch hasn't called yet, but there's a message on my cell phone voice mail and I'm convinced it's her, so none of this is conjecture. I've got to come up with answers. I don't know if I should go back to publishing, be a lawyer, be a literary agent again, start working the pole . . . no clue. So I'm freaked out. And I'm royally irritated beyond all human comprehension." I elected to leave out the part about how Andrew's laissez-faire attitude toward me and our marriage, and his just being mentally absent in general regarding our relationship, was driving me out of my mind. I also left out that I couldn't get the image of Gideon kneeling in front of me in his psychedelic bathroom out of my mind, nor did I want to.

"Well, why don't you check your voice mail before you get hysterical? But you knew that this whole dot-com thing was winding down, so just relax and think about it. You've made enough money for that not to be an issue; that's why you took the job in the first place. You've got more than enough of a cushion to give you the freedom to take some time to figure out your next move. Just try to relax."

Andrew's "don't worry, be happy" attitude set my teeth on edge. It was completely emblematic of his whole "why deal with a difficult issue today if you can sweep it under the rug and pretend there isn't a huge lump in the middle of the carpet?" mind-set. Other people might see him from the outside as just being a mellow and sweet dude who looked for the upside of things and minimized the bad, which could be construed as a good thing. In my book, it wasn't. It was, in fact, pretty much one of the most annoying qualities he had. He wasn't being a chilled-out dude, he was committed to totally avoiding dealing with anything big, which led to my basically having to act out both sides of our relationship in order to move us forward in any way. It was exhausting. Andrew was so passive it was like trying to have a serious conversation, or even an argument, with a wet sponge. If I feel the need to talk about something, I want some push-back, a challenge, anything to give me a solid entity to bounce off of so I can hone my thoughts and figure out my next step. I needed a wall from a squash court, not Andrew's evasiveness and soft acceptance.

I've always believed that if you've got an issue, you should deal with it head-on. My whole life I have been combative and painfully forthright. Which, admittedly, has won me some friends but has also lost me others. If there was something that enraged me or I didn't think was going to work out, I spoke up and let my feelings be known. There were, however, a few rare exceptions to my rule of thumb where I felt that the recipient of my feelings would crumble if I really let loose on them. Andrew was one of those people, and as much as he could annoy the shit out of me, I also felt like I would break into a million little pieces if I seriously hurt his feelings. So I worked unbelievably hard to keep myself in check and accept that he would never be that hard wall I could bounce ideas off of in my quest for answers to anything at all. Nonetheless, his modus operandi was antithetical to my very being. So it took Herculean effort on my part not to pinch him as hard as I could when he displayed this particular trait, or yell at him like I would an unruly or willfully dim child. I frequently failed. If, however, I was being honest with myself, which I most decidedly wasn't that night while I baked cookies for dinner and acted like a grade-A asshole thanks to my complete lack of perspective, I was sweeping a massive issue under the rug myself and pretending that it wasn't there. Andrew was by no means the only one who was living in a dream world.

Even though I was staunchly sticking to my guns in the monologue that I had raging in my head that said that everything sucked, that Andrew was useless, and that my friends were traitors for not buying the bullshit I was trying to make them swallow, I had to concede that Andrew had a point. I should listen to my voice mail. Maybe what was waiting for me wasn't as bad as I was making it out to be and my penchant for catastrophic thinking was raising its warped little head for no reason. To my infinite lack of surprise, it actually was as bad as I thought. The HR hag had left me a message that I should call her back as quickly as possible before the end of the workday. That was all she said. The workday was long over, so she'd have to wait to drop the bomb on me until the next day.

The weird thing about losing a job is that even if you know it's coming, it's still a shock when you finally get the boot. It's not unlike the rejection of a lover who has moved past their need or love for you, or the horror of finding an eviction notice on your front door. No matter how much you hate the job or have the financial means to take care of yourself in other ways, that moment of "move along, now, nothing to look at here" that is thrown your way when your company gives you the sack is horrible. You get a sinking feeling in your gut and a simultaneous sensation of floating outside of your own body. You've been let loose from the life you know and are desperate to moor yourself to something stable and solid that will define your role in a new life as quickly as possible.

At least that's how I normally felt, because the embarrassing truth was that I'd been fired a fair number of times. True, this new scenario was technically not a firing. I was being laid off. Nonetheless, the feeling is exactly the same. There was the store I worked at in high school that fired me when I forgot to open the place because I had gone shopping instead at Bloomingdale's with my mother; there was the market research firm that wasn't pleased with how much time I spent on the phone, not interviewing people about clients' products but loudly yakking with my friends about the shenanigans we had gotten up to the night before. Then there was my stint at a temp job one summer during college where I was so bored and zoned out that I couldn't get up the energy to answer the phones, and when I did my messages that were written in triplicate in a giant phone message book were totally unintelligible. So they politely told me after one week that they wouldn't need me to come in the next Monday. My temp agency was not pleased. I was appalled, not because I got fired but because it was from a *temp* job. That's pretty hard to do. Provided you have a crumb of education and can actually get in on time, losing a temp job requires work. I thought it required something as outré as being found in the ladies' room with a needle hanging out of your arm. Apparently, it took much less.

So there I was, financially okay for the time being but completely adrift in terms of how I was going to dive into my thirties. The question was so huge and open-ended, and I was so ill equipped to answer it, I might as well have been shaking a Magic 8 Ball and asking it the meaning of life. The only answer at the moment was to eat the cookies, possibly while lying on the floor.

I did make one decision, although it didn't address any of these life-determinative issues. I called my best friend from prep school, Alex, to tell her everything that was going on. She hadn't judged me once from the time we met in detention when we were thirteen and I knew she wasn't going to start now. I could tell her anything and she would be able to take it in stride and possibly even provide valuable feedback. Even if she was horrified or grossed out by what I was doing, she'd tell me and then move right on to focusing on how I felt and what should be done about the situation. And I faithfully did the same for her. If neither of us had any good advice to share with the other, at least we'd have a laugh. Not surprising, considering this was the woman with whom I had been kicked out of chemistry lab, English class, morning prayers, and glee club.

Alex knew the joys and agonies of being an occasional miscreant during our teenage years and early twenties due to her commitment to underage drinking, questionable sexual conduct in public, and teaching anyone in her orbit how to French inhale. She was, without a doubt, the coolest girl in our class of forty-two girls who spent their days studying maniacally in kilts and loafers and their nights in a teenage confusion of how to find or create our own illicit fun. Even though Alex had grown into a responsible adult and mother of two, she was and would always be the girl with whom I had to polish the brass handrails of our school's staircases as punishment for laughing uncontrollably during assembly, teasing another girl just a little too mercilessly, or getting caught cursing loudly on the front steps of the school. This was the person to whom I knew I could divulge every dirty detail and get a thoughtful reply.

Alex had moved to Connecticut and was usually at home after work, juggling two kids, making dinner, and keeping an unruly dog from tearing the house apart. I moved from the living room to the bedroom so I could close the door and speak openly. I rang her up and got her answering machine. I left a message and told her to call me back immediately. I lay back on the bed crosswise with my feet hanging off the side and stretched my arms over my head until my fingertips were almost touching the other side of the bed. I was still in a bad mood and had the beginning of a hangover forming at the base of my skull, my penance for drinking two martinis far too early in the evening.

Andrew was puttering in the kitchen, making a more sensible dinner than a plate of chocolate chip cookies, and from the smell that was creeping under the bedroom door it was some kind of pasta with red sauce. My mouth watered. Clearly, Andrew had made the better dinner choice. I wanted in on what he was having and reflected on the fact that while I was busy trying to find a friend to talk to, I had a friend in the other room. I was being a fool. Andrew was a good egg and time spent with him was never time poorly spent. Of course I couldn't share any of my angst about Gideon with him, but there were zillions of other things we could talk about. There always were, but lately it just seemed kind of useless to try. Andrew was in his own world, zoned out, unless he was responding to something I was throwing at him.

As I lay there on the bed, smelling the bubbling marinara and stretching my arms and legs as far and as hard as I could in an attempt to get some of the tension out of my body, I forced myself to think about how I really felt about the weird encounter I had had with Brynne and how cranky I was with Andrew and came up with the very unsettling truth that I was just confused. I didn't have an answer to exactly why I was doing what I was doing and why I was so pissy, and I hated that. I wanted so badly to be on top of what I had let into my life, but lying there on the bed that evening, I knew that I wasn't on top of anything more significant than the duvet and knew next to nothing about what my next move would be.

Maybe I was making some horribly dreadful mistakes, but I was having fun. I felt like I was coming back to life and wasn't willing to give up that new spark that provided the only rush I had gotten in way too long. So how could I do what I wanted to do to feel real and alive and young and vital and excited to be in my own skin, but not suffer bouts of crippling guilt and self-doubt for betraying Andrew and behaving in a way that I knew would scandalize my family and at least a handful of my friends? How could I have my cake and eat it too? That's what I needed, because the thought of living without Andrew was inconceivable. It simply didn't even register with me that it was an option. Andrew had been in my life for so long, being without him would be like sawing off a limb. But I was too stifled by Andrew's presence and the responsibility of dealing with it to feel anything but suffocated. I still cared deeply for him thanks to our history and his innate goodness, but the guy was holding a pillow over my face.

Long before Gideon had arrived on the scene I had complained to a friend that I wanted to "kiss a boy." And I didn't mean Andrew. I didn't really mean that I wanted to kiss some random guy either. It was my shorthand for "I have to do something wild and exciting and unexpected so I don't wither into a tiny shriveled crone in a matter of seconds as I stand here before you." I hadn't understood how serious I was about needing to do that at the time, but there was no escaping the whole "I want to kiss a boy" phenomenon now. As of several weeks ago I had indeed begun kissing a boy. And while it was like being presented with an enormous chocolate buttercream cake to eat all by myself with a spoon (with no caloric repercussions), I wasn't quite sure about eating the whole thing yet. I had taken a bite, so technically I had my cake and was eating it, but I hadn't committed to finishing it down to the last crumb. That would entail abandoning the life I knew and the discomfiting comfort it provided, which I needed. There was no way I could pursue that option. As I continued to lie there on the bed, conjuring these images in my mind, all I could think about was that eating all that buttercream would be disastrous and lead to nothing better than heaving nausea and a giant ass. But then Gideon's face appeared, blotting out the image of the cake like a giant boy-pastry eclipse, and thinking about what he had done to me in his dark bathroom with its glow-in-the-dark posters, I had a full-body shudder that left me rattled and covered in goose bumps. I was definitely confused.

I went into the kitchen to see what was up with Andrew and give him a hug. I crept up behind him, slipped my arms around his waist, and squeezed the stuffing out of him. Even with Gideon still lingering in my mind, hugging Andrew's warm body made me feel a little better. I felt briefly normal and comfortingly humdrum. He patted my hands, which were crossed on his stomach, and asked if I was feeling a little better. I leaned my head against his back and relaxed into his body while nodding my head.

"Yes, I'm feeling better. I was just having a meltdown."

"Do you want some dinner? I know you've got your cookies but I made pappardelle with marinara. I think there's salad stuff in the fridge. Interested?"

"It smells amazing. I might have a little, but only if you made enough for two."

"There's enough. Take what you want."

• • •

Soon enough, another Thursday rolled around and it was lesson time. But I couldn't bear having the lesson at my place. My guilt had grown to full-fledged intermittent anxiety attacks based on my envisioning a horrific marital denouement. I imagined that Gideon would be in the middle of struggling to yank my pants down just as Andrew walked in the door unexpectedly early. It would be the worst kind of hackneyed scene from a romantic farce and I wasn't willing to play one of the roles. So I told Andrew that I was going to try to learn electric guitar instead of acoustic, and Gideon had tons of guitars and amps at his place so the lessons would be relocated from now on.

Andrew had no problem with that. Didn't say a word or raise an eyebrow. Had it been me in his shoes, I would have put up at least a little fuss about his going to a strange woman's apartment. But no, not a word came from Andrew. Did he not care? Was he that trusting? Was he possibly so lost in his own world that he couldn't see past the tip of his own nose? I had no earthly notion what was going on in that silent man's impenetrable mind. I wasn't going to bring the issue up because stirring the pot might put an end to my time with Gideon. But if I gently, subtly asked Andrew what he was thinking or if something was bothering him, he'd have just smiled at me and said something like, "It's all good." So I went to Gideon's.

Since the dreaded HR woman had had her way with me and work was now a thing of the past, the usual mad dash from office to home was over. I was also no longer in need of changing into jeans or anything less formal than my usual skirt, sweater, and boots for the lesson. My time was my own now, so I spent my first few weeks of unemployment lounging around the apartment and gossiping with my friends on the phone. I finally got Alex on the phone and told her what was happening. Gideon would have been livid about how regularly I was breaking my own rules. But who knew what he was saying and to whom? Predictably, Alex had no judgment but was practically stern in her demand for every detail, sordid or otherwise, so she could get a clear picture of what was going on for future analysis. It was an awkward if mildly hilarious scene as she was trying to pull licentious information out of me while speaking in code so her six-year-old son wouldn't clue in to what we were talking about and later ask in a loud voice at the dinner table, "Dad, what's a blow job?" Just imagining that scene had us giggling enough to make the download lighthearted and easy. As I had suspected, Alex was the best confidante possible. And as a married person, she understood the difficulties inherent in keeping a long-term relationship fresh. So she shared some of her own challenges, and for better or worse I was instantly catapulted from ingrate to normal person in my own estimation, thanks to her.

My lessons with Gideon had been moved to five o'clock so I could see him as early as possible and stay a little later. At four thirty on the first day that my lessons were to take place at Gideon's underground lair, I got myself into jeans, ballet flats, a sweater, and a light jacket and hopped into a cab to go to the Upper East Side. I was still preppie but a little less uptight looking.

While the cab made its way to the portal to the seventies (I had begun to think of Gideon's apartment as the wardrobe that took the children to Narnia, only his pad transported all who dared to enter to 1973), I did a little personal inventory. I really was struggling with my attraction to Gideon and the growing recognition that my attraction to Andrew was so low as to be nearly nonexistent. It wasn't just guilt that was getting to me, but also the confusion I had felt from day one over the fact that I was such a willing moth drawn to such an unlikely flame. Gideon was everything I would normally have made fun of, much as I did for Andrew's amusement after the first lesson. He wasn't nearly as well educated as I was (not even the same ballpark), he wasn't particularly witty, and he really did look alternately like an especially beautiful extra from *Saturday Night Fever, The Song Remains the Same,* or possibly *Joanie Loves Chachi.* What the hell was it that was making me into such a morally questionable dimwit when in his presence or just thinking about him? Was it only sex or something more? Was he the type of guy that I should have been looking for all along and not an aberration? What did liking him say about me? As I sat in the back of the weaving cab, holding on to the door handle for dear life, I laughed out loud. Once again, in the midst of thinking about someone else, his qualities, his merits and failings, it all came back down to me. Even as I pondered whether or not this was normal self-examination or raging narcissism, I couldn't escape the conversation in my head that took place between me and me and never gave me a break.

I tried to focus on the positive as we hurtled down Fifty-seventh Street, almost at the final destination. The only thing I could drum up was that all this hysteria over what I was feeling about Gideon and what we had done, and would most likely keep on doing together, had continued to affect me the same way it did the night that Andrew made his pappardelle. I wasn't able to eat and was losing weight. Rapidly. It was an enormous ego boost to look better by the day. I loved it. But I also hated myself for being one of those women whose sense of self-worth would ride on something like that. I was sure that somewhere on the island of Manhattan, Betty Friedan could hear my thoughts and was throwing up.

I arrived at Gideon's apartment, paid the driver, and got out fully expecting to barrel forward and fling myself at his front door. Instead I stood on the sidewalk and did a few breathing exercises to steady myself. I reminded myself that this could very well just be a guitar lesson if that's all I wanted it to be. Walking over the threshold of Gideon's apartment didn't constitute a compact that required me to follow through on continuing the affair we had barely begun, just as much as it didn't hold him to that standard either. We each had absolute authority to exercise our individual free will and do as we chose, no matter what had been done or said before. Freeing myself up this way from a sense of obligation, destiny, or anything else that would render me powerless to keep what we had started from rolling forward quieted the turbulent cumulus that was flashing thunderbolts through my nervous system. One more deep breath and I trotted down his loud metal staircase and leaned on the doorbell.

The door swung open nearly the moment I touched the button. The clattering of my shoes on the staircase had been warning enough to Gideon that I was on my way down to invade his home. He stood in the doorway and for once looked less cool and on the make than usual. As I stood there scrutinizing him, I realized that his mask had slipped and the expression on his face that I hadn't identified at first glance was a look of anxiety. Or maybe it was a glimmer of uncertain anticipation. Thank God he was human. Gideon was as aware as I was that this visit to his home, just the two of us alone, was a shift in our dynamic and we would both be wise to be a little scared of it. Who knew where it would take us?

This time it was my turn to walk around inspecting his joint the way he had mine the first time he gave me a lesson. The night of the drug taking and oral sex making was such a blur of fun and dementia that I hadn't really taken the place in the way I wanted to. You learn so much about people from their apartments.

What I learned in that quick first sweep through was that nearly every book on the bookcase in the living room was music related, while the place wasn't the cleanest it could be it was definitely very tidy, the kitchen was in a bit of disarray, and the stove top definitely needed a cleaning. So he cooked for himself. Interesting; not a usual single-guy thing, but if you're a vegan I supposed you have to break out of the mold. I also noticed when the closet door was open and Gideon's back was turned to me that he had something in the vicinity of twenty guitars in that surprisingly huge closet. This was not someone who was really interested in anything beyond what he was already doing. The guitar selling and teaching wasn't a side gig while he wrote the great American novel. Playing guitar, and playing in a band, was his life, and his selling guitars and teaching kept him as close to what he liked as possible.

I concluded that Gideon was perhaps a little more one-dimensional than I might have initially thought. But what did that matter? His role in my life was to teach me guitar and have a physical relationship with me. I already knew that the first task was right on track for him, and I didn't need him to have a second, third, or fourth dimension to deliver on the second task. Ergo, all was well. Now I knew a little more than I had before and would be more than capable of second-guessing whatever he might present me with, emotionally or otherwise.

By the time I had finished inspecting his place, Gideon had set up two guitars and plugged both into amps. We were, finally, ready to rock in the way that Brynne and I had initially imagined. All thoughts of kissing Gideon flew out of my head and I stared at the guitar that was meant for me with a mixture of excitement and fear. I was totally psyched that this was my first real opportunity to make some serious noise. The only downside was that my previous lessons had been so frequently interrupted with our make-out sessions that I wasn't sure I could actually play any of the simple tunes he had been teaching me, particularly on an unfamiliar guitar.

Gideon handed me one of the guitars and waited to see what I would do. I clutched the neck, made the shape of a G chord with my left hand, and with my right hand clutched the pick, which was already slipping around in my sweaty fingers, and strummed through all six strings so hard it was as though I was trying to get past them to hit the front of the body of the guitar. The noise that came out of the amp was amazing. It would have been totally insignificant to anyone who actually played an electric guitar or had already taken a real walk on the wild side and had already felt the power of loudly declaring that they were there and to be taken seriously. For me, it was a revelation. I felt the reverb in my stomach, and the wailing crunch of that G chord made the hairs on the back of my neck stand up. So this is what it was about. The power of that noise transferred its energy to me and I knew that this was something Brynne had been right about. Sex with Gideon was a thrilling idea, but repeating *this* feeling over and over as frequently as possible was a necessity. If sex with Gideon could mimic this thrill, then all the better. The noise I made with that guitar was so ballsy I knew that if I kept doing it I'd have to live out the rest of my days playing in a band and wearing a skintight black leather jumpsuit. The look of satisfaction that Gideon gave me when he heard the chord ring out and saw the stunned look on my face assured me that I was on to something.

We worked through all the basic chords and did a few scales and Gideon showed me how all the gear worked. I still felt out of my element around all the equipment, but that first G chord made me pay attention because I knew that I would need to soak all of this information in. Eventually, the lesson was over and the problem of handing over his fee came up again.

I gave him the cash and felt a little bad about it because he had given me an extra half hour but wasn't asking for any more money. I made an offer to give him more but he refused. The money was also problematic because I knew what was going to come next. There was no doubt that we were going to get busy, but I needed a little lag time after paying him so I wouldn't feel like we were in a cheap(er) version of *American Gigolo*. I asked Gideon what he liked to read, which was the only thing I could come up with considering that I was pulled tight inside with tension, anticipation, and my old friend guilt-ridden anxiety.

Gideon didn't say anything. In lieu of providing an answer, he just waved in the general direction of the bookcase as he rifled through his CD collection to find something that he really wanted me to listen to.

"Remember that conversation we were having that night about Buffalo Springfield?"

I said I did and that they couldn't find someone to sing who had the right sound.

"Listen to this and tell me what you think. I bet you've never heard it. Tell me if you like it."

He started up the CD and chose track three, "Sit Down, I Think I Love You," initiating me into the world with which he and Ira were obsessed. I had no idea what to expect and for some reason thought it would sound like the Grateful Dead. Maybe because the bands were contemporaries; who knows? What I heard was lilting and melodic. I loved it. It was groovy pop music by way of folk and bluegrass. Or at least what I thought bluegrass sounded like. I told Gideon that I thought it was fantastic and I wanted him to play it again.

"I'm going to. I want to try something. You told me once that you were in glee club in high school, right?" He managed to make the words "glee club" sound as flattering as "fat camp," but it was true and I admitted as much.

"Cool. So you can sing. I'm going to play this two more times and then I want you to try to sing it. You've got a low voice so you're probably an alto. Which could be in the same range as the guy who's singing."

"You mean Richie Furay?" I was showing off that I had been listening through my weed haze to his earlier discussion with Ira.

"Yes! Very good!" Mocking tone aside, I knew he was pleased that I was exhibiting at least a glimmer of interest in his grand experiment.

We listened to the song two more times as promised, and then Gideon picked up an acoustic guitar to accompany me along with the recording as he launched into a third playing of the track. The lyrics were simple so I managed to hang on to most of them as I closed my eyes and leapt into the abyss of actually performing, albeit to an empty underground living room with Gideon as the sole member of my audience. I got through the song in my usual low alto register, which is like your average tenor who occasionally takes a leap up into falsetto. I matched Furay note for note, but who knew what Gideon thought of my abilities. I hadn't looked at him for one second as I sang. Instead I concentrated on my reflection in the television set and focused on the music coming from the speakers and Gideon's guitar. When the song ended, Gideon sprang up from the couch to hit the pause button and whipped around to stare at me.

"Holy shit! Why didn't you tell me you could sound like that? You can actually sing. More important, you sound exactly like Richie fucking Furay. This is insane. Ira is going to freak out. Do it again."

So we did. I sang the song three more times, each time Gideon grinning wider and wider, the answer to his prayers for a gig at Arlene's with a night of Buffalo Springfield (that would never come to pass thanks to a combination of Ira's innate disorganization and Gideon's fruit fly–level attention span) sitting next to him on the slippery black leather couch. Gideon moved on to another track, "Flying on the Ground Is Wrong," to see how I'd do with that, and the response was the same. Hours passed this way, my usual lesson hours were long over, and I remembered Andrew and home and dinner with a jolt. I had to call him. This sudden disappearance was beyond the pale. I fished my cell phone out of my bag and called home. It was eight o'clock and I had lost myself entirely in this experience, which was steeping me in affirmation as well as the sheer fun of singing. I had nearly forgotten about all those years of singing Fauré and Handel in high school and how much fun it had been, even if our choral conductor was a total douche. I got Andrew on the second ring.

"Hey, honey, I'm still at Gideon's. We went from playing guitar to having me do some singing and I know it's really late but we're not totally finished yet. Should I come home? Are you set for dinner?"

Andrew's voice was light and unconcerned. "No, no, everything is great. If you're having fun, just keep doing what you're doing. Come home whenever you're ready."

"Okay, thank you so much. I don't know when I'm going to be done but I'll take a cab home the second I'm out of here."

"No problem."

It was in that moment that I realized Andrew's behavior was both gratifying and baffling. I was glad to be on such a long leash and not have a hulking jealous husband breathing down my neck over every move I made, but his total lack of concern still struck me as bizarre and, underneath the weirdness, actually a bit hurtful. Not wanting to be an aggressive guy is one thing. A total lack of concern is another. Had I been in Andrew's shoes I would have politely suggested that I get my little ass home immediately. For all his sweetness and affection, Andrew just didn't care. And if Andrew didn't care, I could do whatever I wanted, whenever I wanted, and however I wanted, anytime, day or night, without feeling any responsibility to Andrew or our marriage. I could rebel in a way I never had before. The rebellion would be just as much against the set of rules that I had imposed on myself as it was against the life that Andrew and I had created. I would launch my rebellion by staying late at Gideon's that night without having to keep my eye on the clock. And as every revolutionary knows, once you start your rebellion, you've got to finish it. If you don't, you're guaranteed to be the first casualty of war. I closed my phone with a decisive click.

Gideon had been quietly listening to my conversation and when I got off the phone he asked if I was going to stay. We were both standing at the end of the couch nearest his bed. I answered in the affirmative.

"Great, then Ira can hear you sing too. He's on his way over here in about forty-five minutes."

"Oh, okay, cool. So do you want to go back to playing guitar for a while?" In a flash, I was back to being nervous and focused entirely on Gideon. The magic of singing and playing had been sucked out of the room, leaving a vacuum that desperately needed to be filled. On top of that, I was back to inhabiting the role of architect of an unconsummated affair, which held much promise but about which nothing serious had been done. I had no idea whose move it was in that moment. Was it mine because of my speech at the diner, or was it his because we were on his turf? We had forty-five minutes to kill and there was no question in my mind that he was not going to choose trying to teach me "Blackbird" again as a diversion until Ira's arrival.

Gideon surprised me. The next words out of his mouth weren't "Take off your clothes." All he said was, "Wait a second."

He retrieved the same stash box I had seen the night of the bathroom shenanigans and got out a little amber vial and all the other accoutrements he had used that night. With practiced speed he laid a line out for himself without a moment's hesitation on a piece of a mirror that he'd placed on top of the glass-top coffee table. Despite being fascinated, his actions did give me pause. Gideon had blow on hand both times I was in his apartment as well as a clearly designated stash box and could get himself set up to get high in under ten seconds. Was this an occasional thing, like my relationship with pot, or his primary avocation? Did the coke rival music for his affections? As I was pondering this vital question, he asked me if I wanted to join him. All concern about how deeply Gideon was into hard drugs vanished the second he made the offer. It was too enticing to reject outright, so I did a little quick thinking.

I didn't want to do a huge rail and get jittery and fucked-up since I was a little nervous about doing drugs already, with my heart knocking around in my rib cage like a rogue Super Ball. I definitely wasn't interested in doing enough drugs to endanger my health and having to be carried off to the conveniently located Lenox Hill Hospital. On the other hand, I didn't want to miss out on an experience that I hadn't had before, just the two of us getting a little high and seeing what would happen, before Ira arrived. I also knew that the coke would kick any trepidation I was experiencing out of the way and replace it with that irresistible Master of the Universe feeling I had enjoyed so much the last time I had indulged. So, like Tom Cruise's little pal in *Risky Business*, I finally said, "What the fuck." I told Gideon I'd do the blow, but only a little.

He gestured for me to sit next to him on the couch and obligingly handed me a tiny silver spoon fit for a doll's tea party and explained that the spoonful would be just enough for a little bump. It would get me exactly where I wanted to be. I dipped into the little vial, thinking that it looked like I was daintily preparing to add sugar to the dolls' teacups, and holding my left nostril shut with my left forefinger, I snorted the contents of the spoon directly into the recesses of my right nasal passage. It only took a moment and then that familiar bitter drip ran down the back of my throat. Another moment passed and my brain and entire nervous system sprang to life. I was acutely aware that I had gone from nervous rabbit to predatory wolf. Well, "wolf" might be an overstatement. Maybe "ferret" or "stoat" was more accurate at that point. Whatever the case may be, I instantly had an appetite for flesh and sharp little teeth with which to dig into it.

After snorting the mirror as clean as humanly possible, Gideon delicately sniffed and ran his finger first across the mirror and then around his nostrils, making sure there wasn't any residue to miss out on. That finger went into his mouth, and it seemed like the thing to do so I did the same after wiping my own nose. I felt Gideon's gaze on me so I turned to him again, slowly this time, and locked eyes with him. We stared at each other long enough that we became no more than two sets of blue eyes looking at mirror images of themselves. Nothing else in the room held my attention, just his blue eyes reflecting my own blue irises back to me. I was like a tiny rodent caught in the gaze of a snake. Or was he the rodent and I the snake? If I was a snake, was I a cobra or a deadly black mamba? Was this the coke talking? Was I making any sense, even to myself? How long had I been letting this insanity run through my head? I glanced at the clock. Only five minutes had passed since I joined the dolls' tea party. Gideon finally broke the silence.

"You're liking this, aren't you?"

"Of course. It's amazing. It feels incredible. You look incredible. Did you know that we were looking at each other for so long? Did you know that it felt like an hour but it was only five minutes? What's the deal with wiping your nose and sticking your finger in your mouth? I know you get all the coke you can that way but it seems a little unsanitary . . ."

I went on this way like I had an Evinrude motor attached to my mouth that had the power to propel me across the room if I chose to do so, headfirst. Gideon laughed and said, "Wow, just a bump and you talk this much? Come here, I'm going to fix that."

I slid closer to him on the leather love couch. Gideon silenced my manic chatter with a heart-stopping kiss. Maybe it was the coke enhancing the sensation of the kiss, maybe not, but that was the best kiss I had ever had in my life. It topped our first kiss near my building and every one that came before it from Gideon and every guy I had ever known. My nerve endings were blazing and the slightest texture of his lips, tongue, and teeth were exquisite as they met with mine. The coke imbued every sensation with crystalline lucidity, ferocity, sensory over-load, and desire.

It was in that state that Gideon, who really was a wolf, and I, who was still at a nascent ferret-like stage, attacked each other. We kissed until our mouths were swollen and our faces were raw from rubbing against each other. We mumbled to each other as we kissed that this or that felt great, and I vaguely caught him saying that I felt skinny. That offhand comment distracted me for a nanosecond as vanity overcame desire and my attention drifted from the magnificence of our kissing to the mag-nificence of my own ass. I must have slacked off in my duties as make-out queen for a bit too long because Gideon bit my lower lip a little too hard, probably a sig-nal that I had to get back to work. I did, and soon I had beard burn from the top of my nose down to the base of my neck and he had tiny scratches and bite marks on his face that were light enough to stop just short of being full-on hickeys. Which would have been mortifyingly teenybopperish of me, but in the moment I didn't care how I marked him or how he marked me. I just wanted to devour him and be devoured, while contemplating how fabulous I was looking.

It was in this spirit that Gideon peeled my shirt up to my neck to continue his rampage across my chest and down my stomach to the top of my jeans. I had my hands up his shirt and the contrast of his almost girlishly smooth skin and silky chest hair was too much to bear. We had been kissing so intensely that we had forgotten to breathe. Gasping, we took one second to come up for air like South Seas pearl divers who could hold their breath for insanely long periods of time, looking for treasure, but who would still occasionally have to rise to the surface to survive. We locked eyes with a mixture of surprise and glee at the crazed desire we inspired in each other and wordlessly told each other that we were both doing fine. And then we leered at each other and plunged our hands into each other's pants. The coke dulled the strangeness of encountering a penis that wasn't attached to my husband, so I could enjoy the smooth, hard, and rather flattering enormous erection that was pulsing in my hand without being weirded out by it. I stroked it, not with the intention of getting him off, but just to enjoy the sensation on the palm of my hand.

Gideon had been doing the same to me and his hands were slick with the results of his efforts. He unbuttoned and unzipped his pants and started to unbutton mine. Out of nowhere, the God of fire-and-brimstone paintings from the 1800s appeared to me. It was the image of

God's hand reaching out of the clouds, pointing at some poor unfortunates who had fucked up mightily and were about to pay for their misdeeds in a manner too odious to consider. It was with this image in my mind that, like God's hand, a thought beamed out of the clouds and into my head. That thought was simply, *No*. It wasn't until Gideon reared back in surprise that I realized I had said that solitary dick-wilting word out loud.

"You've got to be kidding me."

I raised myself up from the prone position I had settled into on the slippery couch and tried to pull my clothes back into place, raking my hair out of my eyes so I could restore some semblance of order. "It's not that I don't want to, you know that. Come on, you can feel it. You can tell."

"Exactly. This has been going on for weeks. We've got another twenty-five minutes before Ira gets here and you're wasting it with I don't know what kind of freak-out. Come on, you wanted to do this and now you don't. Either you will or you won't, Jones. Pick a fucking side already." Gideon was frustrated and upset, and although I felt like I was in an after-school special where someone like Willie Aames is peer-pressuring Melissa Gilbert into having sex with him before she's ready, I knew that saying no was just the way it had to be. For now. Because holding this guy's junk was one thing, but actually doing the deed was another thing entirely. I just wasn't ready. But how to explain this to a coked-up guy with a hard-on he was trying to stuff into his pants while retaining a shred of dignity?

"Gideon, I want to. I will. I know I will. I just can't right now. I don't know why, but I can't. I promise I'll be ready soon." I heard the words come out of my mouth and was a little confused. How had I gone from being General Patton at the diner to Melissa Gilbert on the couch, reassuring her overeager boyfriend that she'd eventually bang him so he wouldn't dump her? This was not the way I envisioned the Gideon scenario playing out. My need to keep him engaged was winning out over my need to remain cool and in control.

Gideon was silent with his back to me as he pulled himself together. He finally turned to face me and composed himself, going from frustrated sex fiend to reasonably normal person. I knew the coke was still doing its thing to both of us and assumed that my anxiety-ridden, overly apologetic response had to be the result of the drug. I also decided to assume that Gideon's sexual aggression was the result of snorting those lines and was not a window into his soul. Oh my God, who says "window into his soul"? Jesus, I was still high.

Eventually Ira showed up and I sang for him, with Gideon showing all the enthusiasm for the songs and my singing that he had earlier. It was as though nothing had happened. I noticed that Ira took in the drug paraphernalia that had been left out on the coffee table but that he chose to say nothing. He listened to me sing and silently nodded his head as I did so, tapping his sneakered foot in time to the recording. Once I had finished both songs Ira looked at both of us and said with all the gravity of an elder statesman, "Yeah, man, she's got it. Jessica, you've definitely got it. We can try to get this show done now. We have a voice." He smiled at me and grabbed my shoulder, lightly shaking it like a proud coach. Gideon grinned broadly and wrapped his arm around my shoulders. My previous cock blocking was forgiven. I was relieved but also uncomfortable. I didn't want his approval to mean something to me, but it did. My protective bubble of dominance and control was popping in slow motion and I couldn't think of a damn thing that could stop it.

6

THROES LIKE A GIRL

After a few weeks of being unemployed I got a call from Drew, an old friend from summer camp who was working at a small publishing concern in NoHo. He knew that I had been an agent and a book packager as well as the director of business development at the dot-com and had already recommended me to his boss as the much-needed rainmaker they'd been trying to find. I was eager to get back to publishing, which had always been my real love, so I went to the interview with a spring in my step and bubbling optimism. My can-do attitude and brash display of total self-confidence sealed the deal. By the time the week was over, I had received an acceptable offer and was employed once again.

The only problem with this new job was that I had to be sitting at my desk (the boss very obligingly gave me the corner office, which cheesed off a lot of people who had been there for years and instantly saw me as the enemy) by nine A.M. I am and was many things, but I have never been a morning person. I had finagled a schedule at beenz.com where I could push my arrival to ten A.M.

or ten thirty thanks to my reasonably high rank, but even that was difficult. So working nine to five was not exactly in my wheelhouse. It took effort, even under the best of circumstances. And unfortunately, I was not operating under the best of circumstances.

In the weeks that preceded my appointment as director of business development and visionary at Rook Publishing, I had been spending an increasing amount of time at Gideon's place. Once a week became twice a week, then three times. And the hours I kept with him steadily crept further and further into the night and early morning. I was singing more, getting into the Dusty Springfield and Delaney and Bonnie catalog, and doing coke with the guys as a normal part of my new lifestyle. The regulars at Gideon's place were C.C., Ira, Gideon, me, and a revolving cast of other rum characters, including Gideon's new bandmates who had come onto the scene once he was no longer with Love Craft, which had imploded after a few years together, as most bands do. There were also a handful of women I was sure Gideon had slept with or was sleeping with at the time. Those women bothered me enormously, but I wasn't putting out and I knew the laws of the jungle. I couldn't claim Gideon for myself until we had done the deed. Which certainly had not happened thanks to my Hand of God moment. We had come close but no cigar, figuratively or otherwise, to date.

As for Andrew, he never mentioned my odd hours and generally careless behavior. So now instead of being completely angst-ridden about my life of deception, I decided to just be as blithely carefree as he was. I set my mind to it and tried extremely hard to be cavalier about my late nights, drug use, and, oh yeah, cheating, but it was easier said than done. Andrew was a good guy and a part of me couldn't help loving him even though my romantic impulses were reserved exclusively for Gideon. So I ping-ponged between defiant bad girl and freaked-out guilty shithead from hell. I was either totally elated and zinging with the thrill of being completely emotionally and physically present, or having panic attacks and crying in the bathroom of my apartment, my office, a restaurant, wherever. All this emotional insanity had cut my appetite down to nothing. I had gone from a size eight to a size two in record time. Even if I was crazy as a fucking bedbug, I was finally smoking hot.

And my parents were thrilled. They had always wanted me to drop the extra pounds I had picked up in college and never managed to let go of. I firmly believed that it pained them to have what they considered a fat daughter. I was, for the record, not my best weight just prior to meeting Gideon, but by no means truly fat. That didn't matter. In my family, thin was in. And if you were thin and generally looking good, you could get away with almost anything. This was proven when I attended a family dinner in my Gideon-inspired newly purchased skintight black leather pants, black boots, and clingy white tank top with hoop earrings and wild hair almost down to my waist. I looked hot but I also looked like there should have been a neon sign flashing over my head that screamed, TROUBLE! Or perhaps the sign might have read, YOUR DAUGHTER HAS ENTERED AN ALTERNATE UNIVERSE AND LOVES DRUGS, MUSICIANS, AND EVERYTHING YOU TOLD HER TO STAY AWAY FROM! Instead, in front of my aunt, my uncle, and a bevy of cousins, my parents oohed and aahed over my newfound svelte beauty. Then the rest of the peanut gallery joined in. All I could think was, *Screw Weight Watchers, let me introduce all of you to my new physical fitness regime: fucking (sort of) and snorting.* I was a ball of hot, diagnosable action and my family was applauding the results. This was totally bizarre behavior, right? Unfortunately, not in my world.

My new look of skintight black leather pants, black boots, and clingy white tops got a thumbs-up from my new friends, but it wasn't scoring me any points at work.

I was making every effort to play by the rules at Rook. I came in at nine on the dot, even if I was totally incoherent due to either lack of sleep or just my usual aversion to early hours. I learned what the company's strengths and weaknesses were and tried to figure out how I could bring in more money. I attempted to forge friendships with my coworkers, but except for the other two women who worked at the company and my friend from camp, no one was biting. That corner office really had done me in. And showing up in leather pants and wraparound shades mumbling incoherently about needing coffee until about eleven A.M. didn't help much either.

But I tried, every day, throwing myself into the midst of that semihostile but opportunity-laden environment to see what I could do for Rook and what it could do for me. It seemed like I had an open invitation to invent new lines of business and new projects, and for someone who had just come from the stultifying world of a dying dot-com, this was like getting a glimpse of the promised land. Ergo, I hauled ass into Rook Publishing every day, on time, and tried to think of new books to create, new publishers to cuddle up to, and new ways to use our resources to make money. Not only was it an interesting intellectual challenge for me, but the job also provided the structure that I so badly needed. Rook Publishing was the perfect nerdy and familiar counterpoint to the rest of my increasingly disorganized, drug-and-passion-fueled life with Gideon and his motley crew.

On my off time I was still singing with Gideon and Ira, having the occasional guitar lesson, and hanging with C.C. These reasonably wholesome activities were regularly interrupted by our penchant for ricocheting between smoking pot, doing blow, and swallowing the handfuls of painkillers C.C. liberated from his grandmother's medicine cabinet. And while I still hadn't gotten past my Hand of God moment with Gideon, any time we had alone was spent in a sexual frenzy of "everything but." I was also trying to find time for my college friends, who were doing their best to be supportive of this new version of me they were being asked to accept. Some had an easier time than others. My guy friends, like Larry and Jake, seemed torn between total confusion, uncomfortable titillation at my new look, and amusement that the least likely person on the planet was finally taking a walk on the wild side. Edward remained unamused. They didn't exactly know about Gideon, but anyone with half a brain was able to see that there had to be a male catalyst behind my sudden transformation. The guys kept an eye on me and would listen to any of my kvetching or oblique references to my "involvement" with my guitar teacher, but they didn't seem too worried about my welfare. Not yet.

The women in my life were a different story. Aside from Alex and Brynne, who knew that a big part of my personality was that no matter how crazy I might get I had an internal "off" switch that would serve me in good stead, my girls were nervous. They understood that when a woman starts to act weird, something is definitely weird. Where there's smoke, there's fire. In this case, where there was a runny nose there was coke, and where there were constant references to a new man who had popped up out of nowhere, sex was possibly on the horizon, if not already happening. Alex and Brynne managed to keep from thinking that I was just one step away from turning tricks and shooting up. Their faith in my innate good sense and upbringing was unwavering, and many of my friends who were more prone to catastrophic thinking actively suspended their mounting hysteria for the time being. They thought I was playing with fire but could also acknowledge that maybe it was high time I did. They had been party girls earlier in their lives while I was busy studying and getting married. Alex and Brynnie knew that I needed to go a little crazy but were hoping that "a little" was where it would stay, merely for my emotional sake and safety.

Despite all my pals' concerns and reservations, they were still dying for all the juicy details of my exploits. I couldn't blame them. Who could resist the urge to live vicariously and gossip madly when a close friend has obviously gone a little haywire? What my pals worried about was that I was careening down a Slip'n Slide filled with lube, drugs, bodily fluids, and God knows what else. But only Alex and Brynne (to whom I had finally spilled the beans) knew the whole story. Until I had a better handle on how I felt and where I was going, I stuck to the rules I set in the diner. It was getting harder to stay quiet, but I did, primarily for Andrew.

Although I was glad to have people who cared about me, the nagging knowledge that there was probably judgmental gossip going on behind my back irritated me no end. I knew that my muckraking friends thought something was wrong. Duh! Of course something was wrong. Everything was wrong, but only if you defined right as everything I had been doing prior to my decision to dive into Gideon's world. As far as I was concerned, there was no way I could subscribe to that view anymore. I had been miserable when things were "right"; now I was giddy and nervous and sometimes scared, but I wasn't miserable. And that seemed more "right" than anything I had known to date.

My sampling of Gideon's world, so far, had been all about pushing the envelope I had been tightly sealed in for thirty years. While I had been all about order, control, and propriety, Gideon was the polar opposite. Though charming, he was combative. He kept odd hours and rarely got to his job on time. He flirted shamelessly and clearly had sex with multiple women. I'd see it on their faces when I met them. And then there were the drugs and alcohol. Whatever Gideon did, they were always in the background. And the better I knew him, they were less background noise and more the steady drumbeat that kept him, and most of his circle, going.

Even with the dark and thrilling fear Gideon inspired in me, no matter how ominous my friends might have thought he was, whenever I let something about him slip, I never cast him as the architect of anything that was happening. I was the sole planner behind the mission on which I had embarked. Gideon had merely provided me with the tools and resources I needed to fall through the looking glass I had stayed on one side of so studiously for so many years. I wanted to push past what I had always thought sex and passion were like to see if there was something much more outrageously heart-stopping and moving than what I had experienced so far. I wanted to go beyond my self-imposed creative limitations and sing again, maybe even finally start that band with Brynne, or anyone else who would play with me. I certainly wanted to get past the idea of what "nice girls" did and figure out exactly how nice or not nice I really was. And as I contemplated all of these issues when they came to me, usually in a mad rush at the most inconvenient moments, like during a meeting with my boss or a prospective client, I had to admit that I had never considered any of these questions before. And if I hadn't considered them, I had no ready-made answers. And if I had no ready-made answers, how well did I know myself anyway? I was starting to feel like a stranger in a strange land.

The only way I could think of to make order of the

swirl of anxieties and unfulfilled fantasies that were competing for attention in my increasingly overwhelmed mind was to approach problem solving the way I usually did. I made a list. I made a list of everything that I wanted, everything that was freaking me out, and tried to identify what I thought would be achievable or solvable. What I came up with was pretty simple. The things I wanted were as follows: I wanted to meet new people, I wanted to be in a band, I wanted to sing, I wanted to play guitar, I wanted to know what it felt like to be really and truly sexy, I wanted to have crazy sex, I wanted to keep my job, and I didn't want Andrew to be devastated. I didn't know what to do with my feelings about him yet, but my almost fifteen-year-old instinct to protect Andrew remained firm. The majority of the items on this list added up to one thing. I wanted to keep Gideon in my life. He was the key to all the new experiences I knew I both wanted and needed, and was also the embodiment of every carnal and visceral urge I had ever wanted to explore and had yet to experience. So he was staying. Without him, there was no sure path to finding out what I really wanted and what I was made of. Without him, I'd be back to square one: wearing tweed; playing by arbitrary, boring, self-imposed rules; and taking my marriage—which was increasingly unsatisfying the more I looked at it—as a nonnegotiable given.

Having a band was seriously important and getting more important as every day went by. True, it was a way to stay connected to Gideon because I knew that he'd be into my ballsy move to play guitar or sing, or both, right out of the gate. But having a band was also a way to genuinely express myself and really do something fun and totally outside my definition of who I thought I was, just like Brynne had originally planned. But I wanted my own band. Enough with singing what Gideon liked from the seventies. I wanted to be in control and to own something that made me feel as powerful and badass as I did when I hit that G chord for the first time on Gideon's electric guitar. I wanted the thrill of passion and sex and just being loud, but it had to be rooted in something. It had to be connected to a creative outlet, not just a guy. I knew I was way, way into Gideon and was becoming absurdly obsessed with him, possibly more because of what he represented than who or what he actually was, but he couldn't be the sole reason behind my feeling alive. I wanted my body to vibrate and my heart to race because of what I was doing, not what someone else was doing to me.

When I was in law school, my friend Amy from high school called me up and told me that I had to listen to this album that totally blew her mind. It was Liz Phair's *Exile in Guyville*. After hearing it, I became obsessed with Liz Phair and would play her song "Flower" over and over, shocked at how a woman barely older than me had the balls to write a song about her drippingly lusty desire for a fresh young creature she had in her sights. Equally mind-blowing was that a major record company thought it was a good idea to release this song on a commercial album. Liz was what it was all about. She knew the score and every time I listened to *Exile in Guyville* I knew that pretty soon I'd find something equally bold to say. That album guided my mission and helped me to add to my checklist of things I wanted and how to get them. I had to write a song as outrageously true and raw as "Flower," or at least try.

So those were the things I wanted that fell into the "pro" category of my list. But then there were the cons. I had to figure out who the hell this new person I felt I was becoming really was. So far, I was in transition without any resolution in sight. I was like an Eleventh Avenue tranny who looked great from the outside but still packed a surprise when her skirt went up at the crucial moment. I was betwixt and between and didn't know who I'd become when I was finished with all my exploration. But I knew it wasn't going to be anywhere near who I was when I started. Admitting to yourself that you're not really sure who you are is terrifying and sucks. So I tried very hard to do it as little as possible.

Another con category was the whole Andrew situation. I knew that every late night, every kiss, every fumble on the couch, every lie—whether outright or of omission—was bullshit and not worthy of either of us. Being a jerk to him was horribly unfair. But I knew that if I held on to the life Andrew and I had been leading I would never change or grow. Even with that deep desire to flee, I also desperately wanted to hang on to Andrew. He was still the person I trusted most, the person I had made a comfortable home with, and he was constant, unchanging, and accepting. He was a calming port to return to when I needed a break from the hurricane I was making of my life. Everything I was doing regarding Andrew was selfish but I did it anyway.

The other, and possibly biggest, con was Gideon's love of drugs and drug culture. I knew that I'd never do as much as he and his friends did because I just wasn't interested in losing total control of my life, much less my mind. I had a lot of fun and played along, but I knew that there was a limit to how much and how many drugs anyone could do without doing serious damage to themselves and others. I was pretty sure that Gideon's crowd didn't know its limits but nothing bad had happened yet, so I chose to ignore the scariest possible outcomes. I could take care of myself and that was good enough.

Now that I had had my "want" list and my "pros/cons" list, I came up with a to-do list of four items:

Number one: Keep it going with Gideon and cowboy up to have sex with him. I wanted it, he wanted it, and I'd already transgressed so badly with Andrew that it wasn't like this final act would make a crucial difference. Or so I told myself.

Number two: I had to start a band immediately. It might include Gideon, it might include Brynne; I didn't know what the makeup would be. But the band was happening.

Number three: I would go along with the drugs but only tell a select few friends what I was doing. If things got bad, they'd know enough to get my back. I just had to decide who they would be. Alex would know for sure, Brynne too, probably Larry, and definitely my older brother, who had seen it all already.

Number four: I would keep up every charade possible to insulate Andrew from any indignities he might suffer while I made these life changes. I would do my best to help him live in ignorant bliss. I'd keep things this way until I knew if I wanted to make a serious life change and alter or end our marriage. I just needed some time—and for Andrew to stay passively accepting.

The only problem with these carefully planned life changes was that I have the worst poker face on earth and didn't stand a chance of keeping the status quo for long. I'd have to push my agenda as rapidly as possible. I would, however, really try to keep things together for Andrew's sake. And, truth be told, for mine too. Selfishly, I just didn't want everything to blow up and have even more drama to deal with.

· · ·

I began with the band. I thought it was the easiest thing to do first. Brynne, who had elected after much internal debate to keep up with her lessons, was the obvious first choice as a bandmate. But I knew that somehow my life with Gideon would blend into whatever the band would eventually become and she wasn't exactly a fan of what she knew was developing between us so far. She knew about my drastic lifestyle change and, while she accepted it, didn't love it. So that ruled her out.

I kept thinking about other options, running through the Rolodex in my head, considering friends from high school, college, camp, even law school, and nobody seemed like a good choice. Basically, it boiled down to my gut instinct not to mix my various worlds together. For now, things had to remain separate. There could be no crossing of the streams. Allowing anyone outside of the circle of musicians, maniacs, and miscreants who hung around Gideon's apartment to know too much about him, our attraction to each other, and any of the excesses we indulged in together seemed too risky. I didn't know exactly how I felt about any of it yet and I didn't want anyone I loved, respected, or relied on to form an opinion of their own before I had formed mine and potentially influence my decision-making process about anything on any level.

And then it came to me in a flash. There was a perfect person in my life, thanks to Gideon, with whom I could form a band: C.C. We had already established that we shared everything from what we studied in college and law school to taste in books, taste in music, even our nearly identical birthdays. We were perfect for each other. And he was also desperate to play in a band, having voiced that sentiment several times but with no serious response from the revelers of Sixty-third Street, so he was likely to say yes. I found his information in my PalmPilot and after a few fortifying spoonfuls of coffee ice cream, one of the few foods I could stomach, I screwed up the courage to make the call.

I was terribly nervous, as though I was about to ask him out on a date. Which, I suppose, I was. But this was a date that, if all went well, would last a very long time and would let us live out the sort of rock 'n' roll fantasies that only two pent-up lawyers—one active and one former, but certainly two people with real professional lives—could have. I dialed his number and waited for his voice mail to pick up. I prayed his voice mail would pick up. For all my extroversion, I had never been very good at asking guys out on dates. Oh Lord I hoped this wasn't the case, but maybe that's why Andrew and I got married. I just couldn't imagine having to pursue and date people and he was lovely and already there. Was my whole marriage based on the fact that I was afraid to date?

As this cyclone of psychosis blew through my brain, I heard C.C.'s voice on the other end of the line. I waited for a few seconds so the voice mail message could finish and I'd leave some cryptic message about calling me. It was only after he had said, "Hello?" a few times that I was snapped out of my nutty navel-gazing and realized that I had the man himself on the phone.

"Hey! Oh! I didn't think you'd pick up. Hi, C.C., this is Jessica. From Gideon's place?"

C.C. laughed and said, "Of course I know who you are. How are you? What's up?"

"Well, I have a weird question that you probably won't be up for but I thought I'd give you a try. I've been wanting to do this thing for a while but couldn't think of who would be a good person to try it with and then you came to mind."

"This sounds so cryptic that I don't think I can say no to whatever you come up with. Try me. What is it? Grave robbing? Eating sushi and not paying for it?"

"Nice *Repo Man* reference, my friend. No. Ummm . . . well, I thought it might be kind of cool to try to start a band. Gideon's got that new weird gender-bending band forming with that guy with the Mohawk, so he's not around, and I thought you might be up for it. I think you said something at Gideon's about wanting to play more, so, anyway, that's the idea."

I delivered this little speech all in one breath, petering out at the end like a fully inflated balloon that has been let loose to fly around the room and then land in an empty little stretched-out heap on the floor. Great. This invitation to come over and play (it really did feel like a grammar school playdate invitation more than an opportunity to rock) left me feeling like nothing more than a wrinkly flap of rubber. Lame. If he actually said yes, how much more neurotic would I get? I had only sung in front of Gideon and Ira. What if C.C. hated my voice and my song ideas? I was getting ahead of myself. There were so many other things to be hysterical about. Why choose this? Steady on, Jones.

"That sounds awesome! I'd love to. Perfect. I've been dying to play and I have a bunch of song ideas but I don't think our friends who are stuck in the seventies would be into them. I'm more of a rockabilly kind of guy. I don't think those guys would care about Buddy Holly if he rose from the grave and bit one of them on the ass."

He had said yes. Oh my God.

"Great! Yes, rockabilly is totally cool. I'm sort of into Liz Phair and the Breeders and every kind of bubblegum pop you can think of. How does that sit with you?"

"Great. Totally great. Let's just get together and bring whatever we've thought up so far and just jam a little and see what happens. Sound good?"

"Definitely. You just have to know that I'm not really a very good guitar player. Gideon's been teaching me but I'm nowhere near being anything close to competent. So you'll have to do most of the playing. But I do have some musical training and a really good ear so I can sing stuff and you can figure out how to play it on the guitar. If that's all right."

"Yes. Enough with the caveats. Let's get this scheduled. What's today, Wednesday? How about Sunday afternoon?"

"You're on."

"Great, e-mail me your address and I'll see you at around noon."

"Done."

"Done."

And we hung up.

With that, I had the beginning of a band.

. . .

The next and most obvious question was what I wanted to call the band. Andrew, who has a wicked and insane sense of humor, suggested that I call it Diesel Pussy Hound. I thought it merited consideration, but when I mentioned it to Drew, my camp friend who had recruited me to Rook, he gave me a long, hard look and then said with total assurance, "You should be called Throws Like a Girl." I was impressed. Drew was on to something. It was catchy, sounded subversive but not for any discernible reason, and was true. Drew had seen me attempt to play softball at around the age of twelve with horribly embarrassing results. I did throw like a girl.

"Drew, you're right. That's totally brilliant. But what if we spell 'throws' with an 'e,' so it's Throes Like a Girl, so it's more angsty and a little more riot grrrl–ish?"

Drew gave me a blank look. "No one will get it. You're being too brainy. Just do what I said. And it sounds exactly the same, so it only matters if you make flyers, so you're way ahead of yourself." Conversation over. The oracle had spoken.

Nothing more need be said. It was the perfect band name. Now I had to convince C.C. that it was what we should be called. And try to write at least one song by Sunday.

C.C. had said that he'd bring some material he was working on and I'd be damned if I didn't have something to show for myself. The only chords I could comfortably play without having to look down were G, A, and D, so those were the chords I had to work with. No reason to stretch if I didn't have to. It was pretty easy to come up with a melody that worked over the simplest chords on earth. So that was done. It was the lyrics that were holding me up. What did I really have to say? I certainly wasn't going to write about anything that was going on in my life at the moment. That was just too personal and risky. Not to mention stupid. I tried to think about what girls wanted or would relate to. What did I want? I managed to come up with the most mundane concept in the history of the universe: the idea that all girls wanted was a guy to be nice to us. Yuck. Where was Joan Jett or Suzi Quatro when I needed them?

With only Sandra Dee and June Cleaver as my inspiration, I wrote a song called "Nice to Me," which not only put out the groundbreaking notion that it would be a good idea to be with a guy who was nice to me but went so far as to reference a cherry pie. It was a song that sucked beyond belief but was something that I could show C.C., who might be able to make more of it than I had been able to. I asked Andrew to listen to a little of it and he politely nodded along and gave it a thumbs-up as a good first effort. Knowing that he was lying didn't bother me; it was still nice that he supported my debut attempt. Oh, hey, look. He was nice to me. I guess I had all a girl could want. Jesus. My song was shit.

The next day, Thursday, was guitar lesson day. My time with Gideon certainly wasn't confined to guitar lessons anymore, but we kept the lessons going so that there would be some structure to our burgeoning romance, which we still tried to consider "just hanging out," as well as my weekly schedule, and there would be a slim chance that Andrew might buy that my relationship with Gideon was still based on learning how to play. It most certainly was not and was getting more complicated and intense as every week went by. We had increased the frequency of my "lessons" and two nights per week or so I "went out with friends." Gideon had landed on my doorstep roughly four months prior to that particular Thursday, and we had been steaming forward increasingly rapidly in our bizarre non-love affair. Our attraction to each other was careening out of control and we took every chance we got to maul each other, giving that couch of his a regular and vigorous workout.

Gideon's dangerous and totally foreign vibe had me completely in his thrall and I had gone through weeks of soul-searching, wondering if I was enraptured by what he represented or if I could actually be disobeying yet another one of my own rules and be falling in love with him. I had no idea if it was sad, normal, or simply the way things were in this particular case, but I really didn't know how to tell the difference between being infatuated and being in love. The more attention he gave me, the more I thought I was in love and talked about him glowingly to the few friends who knew about him as well. The less attention he paid me, and during those times I'm sure he was lavishing attention on the other women who flocked around him at his gigs or bars we'd hang out in, the more I chalked my feelings up to infatuation. And even then I was equally obsessed. It didn't really matter at that point if what I was feeling for him was love or something else. I wanted to be around Gideon all the time. So that Thursday was a day I was looking forward to, to say the least. And I definitely had plans to make the most of our time together.

I arrived at Gideon's place right on time and after a few minutes of catching up and opening beers, we started making out on the couch. Business as usual. It always struck me that no matter how many times Gideon and I fooled around, the first kiss every time we were together always stopped my heart for just a second. The experience was unwaveringly the same: my chest would seize up and then my mind and body would melt away into whatever it was we were doing. I loved feeling his body through his shirt, running my hands over his ribs and stomach, feeling his long legs running up and down the length of mine, and letting our hands slip into each other's waistbands to feel as far down as we could go with our pants still on. I couldn't bring myself to un-buckle his giant Led Zeppelin belt buckles to get to his goods, but Gideon usually got my pants off. Or he would hike my skirt up and go down on me and I couldn't seem to get over the thrill of the way he expertly and swiftly exposed me and got to work. Gideon was absolutely the first person who really made me understand why people used the phrase "I ate so-and-so out." He really did go after me like he was hungry and drank and gnawed at me like I was his last meal. Gideon had a crazed urgency to him when he did that and his passion was part of the incredible turn-on.

I liked to think at the time that there was an emotional element to it for him, but maybe not. Maybe it was just need and desire, but it didn't matter because he was ex-cellent at getting me off, and watching him, seeing his pretty face between my thighs, was like nothing I'd ever seen before. His flushed cheeks, long and dark eyelashes resting on the tops of his cheekbones when he closed his eyes, and silky hair falling forward that I would push back as he went to work for what seemed like hours was one of the most gorgeous things I'd ever seen. Gideon was a handsome guy, but in those moments his face would go soft and almost girlish and he looked younger and more vulnerable than I think he would have liked to know.

Perhaps it was because he struck me as so lovely that day, or maybe he had just tipped me past the usual point of arousal, or maybe it was just a day that had to be arbitrarily chosen or else this ride would come to its inevitable end, but I took his face in my hands and pulled it up to mine. He looked disoriented and confused and became even more so when I tried to speak but my voice was so husky nothing intelligible came out. I cleared my throat and tried again.

"Gideon, I'm ready."

It finally dawned on him what I was saying and his eyes went from dreamy and hazy to clear as a bell and what seemed like a little scared.

"Really? Now?"

"Yeah, now. Do you want to? With me? Now?"

"Yes, yes, of course. Yes."

In the course of about three seconds, cool Gideon had gone into a panic. He yanked my pants back up so I could walk over to his bed but first pulled me up to a half-lying-down, half-sitting position on the couch. He kissed me very softly and very deeply like a lover, not like the maniac he normally became when we were together, which had to be partly born of frustration. His sudden slowdown told me that he was deciding how to go about this with me, the only woman in his circle of admirers who wasn't a slightly weird fringe-y person. I wasn't a career partier or musician or any of the things that he was used to. To Gideon, I was something different, particularly due to our pact that I had made him agree to in the diner. I had formalized something that day that had never been consummated and now it was going to be. I forced him to agree to a relationship that had remained undefined until now. The occasion had weight for him, but more than anything his behavior and facial expression told me that I fundamentally made him a little nervous. And it was that nervous tension that had turned him on all these months. Now it was time for him to perform and he'd have to live up to what all the anticipation we had built up promised.

As for me, I went from being totally turned on to emotionally and physically numb. Even though I had known that I wanted this all along, wanting and doing are entirely two different things. I couldn't believe what I had said. I couldn't believe what I was about to do. I was having an out-of-body experience. I had the eerie feeling that I was watching myself embark on this next phase of our relationship from someplace else, someplace outside the me I understood and identified with. I watched the physical me kissing Gideon, getting up from the couch, and walking behind the shoji screen to get to his bed. The emotional and intellectual part of me watched the scene play out, wondering how I was going to make the leap across the huge gap between fucked-up naughty wife to full-on adulterer. It was easier than I thought, thanks to my being so dissociated and numb. Up until now, everything about Gideon had made me feel vibrantly alive. But this was different. I knew in my bones that what I was doing was generally considered morally bankrupt and wrong. To do what I wanted to so badly, I had to leave so much of my ego behind that all I had to work with was my body and what it could do for me.

I had a few brief flickers of fear as we started peeling off our clothes, and while I momentarily reconsidered what I was doing I didn't stop for a second. I would be remiss if I didn't pause briefly at this juncture to give Madonna her props. "Like a Virgin" turns out to be filled to the brim with genuine sentiment and possibly even instructional advice. Because the anxiety I felt as Gideon stripped both of our clothes off was remarkably similar to the first time I had sex. I had gone about it in a slightly numb state then, blanking out so I could do what I knew I wanted to do but was absolutely terrified of. This felt the same. I had no intention of slowing down this freight train, but I had to go on autopilot to do it. So, Madonna, thank you. You were right; it is possible to feel like a virgin again. Having that confirmed was, later on when I had my wits about me again, comforting and helpful in explaining why I had rocketed back to being seventeen again the first time I had sex with Gideon.

I lay in Gideon's bed, Christmas lights lit and tacked up all around the bed (which I have found a lot of guys favor as an attempt at interior design; guys, stop it, it's tacky and is not a convenient replacement for candles), with Gideon finally totally naked and stretched out next to me. It was hard to look at him. He was gorgeous, but I was on sensory overload and looking at all that flesh at once was too much for me. I remember him that day as a collection of body parts, not a whole person. I chose to focus on his face, which was still flushed and scared enough to be soft and boyish. That scared and boyish face clinched the deal for me. In that moment I went from questioning if I was in love or lust to deciding it was love.

And as if that wasn't heartrending enough, the wild rumpus did not begin. Gideon was conscientious enough to have a condom handy, but he took a while to get hard enough to put it on. So there we were, two giant tangles of anxious nerve endings, one with willing flesh and weak mind and the other with willing mind and weak flesh. To stop Gideon from having a total seizure, I held his face in my hands and kissed him as sweetly as he had kissed me while we were still on the couch. That did the trick. In no time at all the flesh was willing and the condom was on and before I could say "Hester Prynne!" he was inside me.

Everything about having sex with Gideon was different from the sex I had had before with Andrew or anyone else during my college years. I didn't know that some people just fit you better than others. Gideon was built so that all he had to do was lean forward very slightly and he was in me. This new little factoid was both shocking and delightful. Kinky and weird, true, but it did cross my mind later that night. And while he was certainly well endowed, it was that mind-bending body shape and fit that really worked to his advantage. He was hitting all the right spots and had me flushed and, to my enormous embarrassment at the time, screaming after about five minutes or less. I think he was as shocked as I was at how electric and perfect the experience was turning out to be.

The shock wore off for both of us quickly and we lost ourselves in each other, whispering sweet nothings to each other that we had never dared to say before. The new intimacy threw an emotional door open for both of us and a litany of tender sentiments we had both been harboring flooded out. From that moment on, that was the primary way and place that we would truly connect and reveal how we really felt about each other.

As for the sex itself that first time, while it seemed to me to be as physically and emotionally explosive as sex could be, it was the tamest encounter we ever had. But that didn't matter at all. It was possibly one of the most exciting times we ever had together because it was so new and fresh and scary. We had been instantly drawn to each other the first time we met, and the way we fit and moved together now that we were finally doing what that first meeting had promised months before, we were smitten all over again. We didn't stop kissing throughout the whole thing, which took no more than ten minutes. We looked at each other for a long time after, not moving and quietly staring into each other's eyes. Everything would be different now. I was praying that at the very least, we'd keep doing it and he'd be nice to me.

•   •   •

I had crossed the Rubicon, but what exactly I had crossed over to was uncertain. I didn't know if Gideon and I had sealed our diner pact and were now in a seventies-style key-party-ish no-strings-attached affair, or if we had both fallen hard and were in a love mess. Perhaps we had simply had sex and I had cuckolded Andrew but had gotten my ya-yas out and could now return to a slightly more normal, less sex-crazed life with significantly fewer drugs involved. The music could stay, but the rest would go. I had a suspicion that grew stronger day by day that there was no way that I had gotten my ya-yas out, so it looked like I was going to keep pushing this thing I had with Gideon forward, and whatever that relationship would turn out to be would define, or perhaps just reveal, my path. Because of Gideon I had started finding new parts of myself that were surprising, exciting, and frequently flat-out scary.

The most notable of these new elements were my abilities to compartmentalize, lie, party very hard, hang with some rough people, have sex with someone I absolutely shouldn't have been having sex with, and most disastrously, have powerful feelings for that person. Who knows what else I'd discover? My long-buried unconscious desire to build a new life was finally busily floating into my consciousness and forcing itself to become an acknowledged priority. And while I was having a lot of fun, divesting myself of so much that I had believed and relied on for so long was the source of continuous pain. It felt like I was in a constant state of slowly ripping off scores of Band-Aids, only to be soothed by satisfying the same new parts of me that were causing all this trouble in the first place.

I would keep up the charade as best I could. I was

unwilling to stop my behavior, so I piled on more and more lies. The only way I could imagine keeping Andrew safe was to keep him in the dark, and that required a level of lying that was so extreme it almost rivaled my infidelity for the title of what would devastate him most. The fault line that we lived on shuddered and crumbled a little more every day. I didn't have a clear notion of why I couldn't just tell Andrew everything as an act of mercy. I considered it whenever my guilty nausea got too bad or I caught myself playing him for a fool. Of course he deserved to know what was happening in his own life and marriage. In the middle of the night, I'd wake up with that knowledge bouncing around the inside of my skull, driving me insane. But I couldn't tell him. During those same middle-of-the-night panic attacks I would eventually acknowledge, although dimly, the truth behind my reticence. I didn't want to lose him. My fear of losing Andrew while not knowing what lay in store with Gideon kept Andrew hostage in a morass of duplicity he may or may not have been aware of. I was afraid to be alone, I was afraid to be without Gideon, and I was afraid to set Andrew free. It was true that hurting Andrew was the last thing I wanted to do, and that kept me from telling him. But even more potent was my need to keep everything just as I wanted it while I was figuring myself out. It was all totally self-serving. I was so unintentionally and casually cruel that thinking about it will always make me cringe. But I did it out of abject fear, confusion, and a horrible brand of self-preservation.

I became increasingly abrupt with Andrew, while he

treated me as he usually did, without any trace of suspicion or bile along with his general passivity.

Then we were told by our landlords, who sublet their apartment to us, that we needed to find a new place within a month. With work and my extracurricular activities, I had no time to try to find a new place. But because Andrew was so accustomed to my taking care of big stuff like this, the job fell to me. I looked for an apartment for two weeks, using brokers, newspaper listings, leads from friends, anything, but had come up empty. I was exhausted and frustrated and scared that we'd be forced to put everything in storage and stay with my parents while we continued to look. That was not a satisfactory solution. I felt the way I frequently did when dealing with serious real-life situations where I could have used a partner's help: alone and solely responsible for providing answers to each and every problem Andrew and I encountered. Andrew generally had no problem doing whatever I directed him to do, but the fact that he never took the initiative enraged me.

This time, after two fruitless weeks of apartment searching in New York (which anyone who has ever lived in any borough of New York City knows is one of the worst experiences you can possibly encounter due to crooked brokers, a general shortage of space, and apartments that more often than not make you want to throw up when you walk in the door), I wigged out. All my pent-up irritation, incredulity, and anger blasted out of me and hit Andrew full in the face. I started screaming at him about how fed up I was with his inability to take

the bull by the horns, ever, and that I was finished looking for a place. I continued my rant by swearing (I think I
insanely said something like "on a stack of holy Bibles")
that if he didn't want to live on the street in a refrigera-
tor box, he would have to take over looking for our new
apartment.

To my infinite surprise, Andrew did it. He relieved me
of the task 100 percent and looked everywhere he could
think of for a reasonable place to live. The vital question
was whether or not I was willing to leave Manhattan.
Anyone who knew me knew that the question was absurd. No, I was not willing to leave Manhattan. The idea
of living in Brooklyn, a place my parents had worked so
hard to flee, was like moving backward in the history of
my family's immigrant tale. Furthermore, Brooklyn was
boring and required going to Manhattan to do anything
fun. Which meant taking the subway late at night, which
I did not relish. Queens was out of the question because
I had been there so infrequently that I was barely able to
acknowledge that it existed. Ditto for Staten Island, and
having grown up in the seventies, I still thought of the
Bronx as the burned-out gateway to hell it had been during the Koch administration.

In what I remember as being a matter of no more than
one day, Andrew came through with a solution. Which
both infuriated and delighted me. I was enraged because
he had proven that all it took was minimal effort on his
part to take care of vital issues, but he never took the initiative to do it. I was, however, delighted at his solution,
and my delight was a surprise to both of us as it violated

all of the rules I had set for the search. At the time, Williamsburg, Brooklyn, was not the built-up overdeveloped hamlet for hipster wannabes that it has become. It was reminiscent of SoHo in the seventies and early eighties. There were tons of industrial buildings that had been roughly modified to accommodate residents, and some of these buildings had been altered by the pioneers who wanted to live there. Those pioneers tended to be artists, musicians, and general square pegs, because the rents were cheap and the available spaces were big enough to paint, rehearse, or do whatever the hell you pleased in them. The most favored buildings used to be bakeries, factories, sweatshops, etc., so the living spaces were huge and open. They were true lofts like you'd see in documentaries about Andy Warhol's Factory and other cool but now gentrified parts of Manhattan.

The downside was that there were few amenities in the neighborhood at all. There were barely any dry cleaners, laundries, normal grocery stores (only a collection of bodegas and an Italian specialty food store), shoe repair places, or anything else that New Yorkers take for granted as part of their landscape. There also wasn't a tree or a blade of grass in sight. Just grit and broken glass. Williamsburg was a pretty stark place in 2000 and Andrew knew that he was really taking a shot in the dark when he made his bid for us to live there.

The day that he found our new place, Andrew burst in the door and was grinning ear to ear.

"I found the perfect place. It's totally insane. You'll love it, and we can rent it from this bizarre, nutty little guy who's an artist and he doesn't care about credit checks or anything. He just liked me, showed me the place, and it's ours."

I was skeptical. There was no way he found the perfect apartment that quickly. There had to be a catch. "What's the catch?"

"Well, I know how you feel about Brooklyn, but please try to think about it differently. I'm not suggesting we move to Park Slope or any other yuppie hangout where you have to hike back and forth to the subway."

This was not sounding promising. I remained silent and made an impatient motion for him to continue.

"Okay, look, I know you always wanted to live in a loft but that we could never afford one in Manhattan and all the really cool ones don't even exist anymore. Right?"

"Right. True. Okay, so what did you find? Where is this incredible place?"

"It's in Williamsburg. It's one stop out of Manhattan on the L train, which you can get in Union Square. The walk to the apartment takes five minutes. And it's a real loft. And it has a washer and dryer in the apartment. And it looks totally fucking cool."

Andrew was bouncing on the balls of his feet as he delivered this speech. He was really excited and it was cute. I had to admit, he was adorable and his excitement was infectious. What was even more important was that he had taken me seriously about getting off his ass and doing something, because once he did he achieved results that made him so happy. True, it wasn't totally proactive on his part, but looking for and finding that apartment wasn't more of the same old pattern we had sunk into. Finally he had made me feel a slight flicker that I was in a relationship with another person for the first time in a long time. Hope for our future bubbled up in my chest a little.

I prayed that the place was really as good as Andrew thought it was. I wanted to be seduced by this apartment as well as the totally new lifestyle that living in Williamsburg would force on us. We'd have no choice but to break out of our rut. Maybe I'd see Andrew in the new light of Williamsburg and magically fall for him again. I knew that I couldn't and wouldn't wriggle out of Gideon's grip, but I also knew that it would have been so much easier to desire Andrew again and settle back into married life. Everything would have been simpler if I had been able to, because while I didn't lust for Andrew, I still loved him. I loved him in that "I can treat him like shit but anyone else who tries will lose a limb" way. We had too many years together for me not to feel an intense love for him, which was made all the more potent because I knew he still loved me. And the cool factor of finally living in a loft and pioneering in the SoHo of the '00s was winning me over by the second.

"Okay, let's go tomorrow to check it out. Call the guy and let him know we're coming."

"Sweet! Great. I can't believe you might actually live in Brooklyn. Awesome and hilarious. Love it. But seriously, this is cool. You're going to like it. And what's also cool is that there's a bakery right across the street so you smell bread baking all the time. Nice, right?"

"Yup. Sounds good. Thanks. Thanks for finding something so fast; I just hope it's as fabulous as you say it is and that the L train isn't a big deal. I want to like it, believe me, but if the place is great and the neighborhood is scary, we'll really have to talk."

"Don't worry. It's going to be okay."

And with that, Andrew drew me into his chest in a bear hug, still rocking a little on his toes with what I assumed was excitement about coming up with a solution for us so quickly. Whatever else he was thinking was, as usual, a bit of a mystery to me.

The loft was in a single-story building that had once been a glass factory. The area around the building looked totally bombed out. Not a tree in sight and tons of broken glass and graffiti everywhere. But there was something cool about the street that kept it from being scary. Maybe my enthusiasm for change eradicated my usual distaste for that level of urban grit, but I was digging Andrew's find and just stood on the sidewalk for a while looking at the front door. It was steel, with the building number painted on freehand. I assumed our landlord the artist had added that little bit of panache to the building. Directly to the right of the front door was a huge window, but to protect the privacy of the inhabitants of the apartment, the window was made of glass bricks. I got it. Light in, but no opportunities for looky-loos. Nice touch.

Andrew knocked on the door and then had to bang on it to get our landlord's attention. When he finally came to greet us, I found myself face-to-face with someone right out of central casting for "downtown artist." He was a perfect storm of white messy hair, deep dark

Bain de Soleil tan, black Buddy Holly glasses, and elfin features, dressed all in white, splattered with paint, and looking befuddled but pleasantly so. His eyes drifted over to Andrew and the crazy little painter came to as if out of a dream.

"Ach! Yes! You are back for the place, yes?"

"Yes! Can we come in? My wife wants to see it too."

"Of course! Come in, my name is Heinrich. I hope you like it. Your husband is so pleasant. I only want to rent to pleasant people, you know? It has to be easy for me."

I liked hearing this. Andrew had been right. If we liked it, the loft would be ours for the taking.

We walked into a huge space by New York standards, about twelve hundred square feet. The apartment was slightly U shaped, with a curve at either end and a long space running down the middle. It was painted white, so Heinrich had clearly extended his aesthetic to his vision for the place when he built it out. There were white walls, white floors, a white ceiling, white cabinets, and white kitchen appliances. Everything in the bathroom was white too, including the washer and dryer. If the enormity of the space hadn't sold me, that washer and dryer did. That's another luxury that's hard to find in a standard New York apartment and I had no intention of letting that slip through my fingers. The final gorgeous detail was that all the light that flooded the apartment came from five enormous skylights that ran down the length of the apartment. It was incredible to be in this white spaceship of a place, looking up at blue sky. I loved it.

"Heinrich, can you let us talk for a second?"

"Of course! I'll go next door to my apartment. You

knock on my door when you're ready." And with that he skipped off to throw paint at canvases or whatever it was that he did in his lair, which shared the front door to the street with what could be our place. Thankfully, we each had another in a foyer once you entered the building.

"Andrew, we have to rent it. What's the price?"

"Same as what we're paying now. Maybe two hundred or so more. We can totally swing it."

"I am so fucking in love with you right now. This place rocks. Let's do it."

"The neighborhood doesn't freak you out? Heinrich is okay as our neighbor? You can tell he's sweet but a little nutty. I don't want you to go mental after a month or two and start screaming about going back to Manhattan."

"Look, we'll sign a one-year lease and if we hate it we can always try someplace else. I really want to do it. I want the change."

"Great. I'll go get him back in here."

And with that three-second conversation, Andrew and I changed the setting of the next chapter of our marriage. And turned our visions of ourselves upside down. We were no longer the preppie couple in the Village. We were officially hipsters. It felt right to me. I figured the reason that Andrew was so down with the change was because he had once had a tendency to try new things with a faddish zealotry that might have been raising its trendy little head again. In our earlier days, he had taken karate lessons, learned to cook, become obsessed with wine . . . trying on the hipster lifestyle was probably his new long-awaited project. And that was fine by me; we would both get a little of what we were looking for but I prayed that his zeal wouldn't fade before the lease was up.

Andrew got all the forms we needed to sign and initial from Heinrich, and right then and there we executed all of it and gave the elf our down payment. Mission accomplished. Now we just had to pack up everything we owned and figure out how to schlep it all over the Williamsburg Bridge.

●　●　●

Andrew and I spent Saturday planning the move and decided to beg our friends to help us load up a U-Haul to save a little money so we could buy anything new we'd need for the loft. We made calls, figured out how many boxes we'd need, let our current landlords know that we'd be out at the end of the month, and generally got things in motion. All of our friends were in stitches that we were moving to Brooklyn, or more accurately they were in stitches that I had agreed to it. But my true inner circle got the whole "in for a penny, in for a pound" mentality I had adopted toward my ongoing life change. Frankly, I didn't care who laughed so long as they showed up to help us move our stuff.

The next day was band day with C.C., which was a welcome relief after the real estate whirlwind that had become my life. I was still horrified by the song I had put together for our first attempt at playing together, but

I'd survived more embarrassing moments. Like having to eat a sleeve of saltines and whistle "Yankee Doodle Dandy" as my competitive contribution to Color War at camp in the "athletics" category. It was a searingly clear statement by the rest of my bunk about their estimation of my physical prowess. Yeah, go Blue Team. With that kind of self-exposing dorkdom in my past, presenting this song would be a piece of cake.

C.C. arrived at our apartment at the appointed time and the first thing that struck me was how normal he was. I had only spent time with C.C. while with Gideon and the rest of his crew of dangerous revelers and had lumped C.C. in with them as a bit of a wild card even though I knew he and I had a lot of similarities. Once he was on my turf and unpacking his guitar, chatting about his workweek, the vagaries of being a lawyer, and how I was smart to have gotten out of that racket, I saw that C.C. was real friend material. He was normal and, most importantly, smart.

I had my doubts about exactly how intelligent the crowd I'd been hanging with really was—even Gideon was still under review—and smart mattered to me no matter how out-there and rebellious I wanted to be or not. I just couldn't abide dumb. I knew so far that Gideon was street-smart, wily, and definitely excellent at reading people. That added up to something, but not necessarily smart. The jury was still out. It wasn't out for C.C., who was a breath of fresh air in this respect. So I found myself warming up to him and trusting him instinctively from the get-go. The more we talked, the more I got a bead on him and came to the conclusion that he was going through something very similar to my need for a walk on the wild side.

C.C. and I talked for what seemed like ages about what music we liked and what we were listening to at the moment. I reiterated my whole "strong woman plus the Archies" vibe for him and C.C. played a few Buddy Holly riffs and some rockabilly stuff for me. Then he launched into a few Stones songs and T. Rex and I saw where he was coming from. He was pretty much into every way any musician or songwriter had ever packaged the blues. Which was good. I told him that I thought that we might be able to do something cool because my stuff was so light and he was able to be all crunchy and rock 'n' roll–ish even on his acoustic in my living room. Without further ado, C.C. demanded that I present my song. I did, Donna Reed insipidness and all. I held my breath after I delivered my drivel and waited for C.C. to wordlessly pack his guitar back up and walk out the door.

I knew I was blushing madly because my face was in flames and was even hot to the touch. But to my happy surprise, as I was busy monitoring my blood pressure, I noticed that C.C. was not only still rooted to the couch but reworking the song with an up-tempo blues shuffle. His new version was 800 percent better. We grinned at each other, blissed out that with very little preparation we had been able to pull a viable little tune together in roughly two hours.

"I know the lyrics are shit, but the way you bounced around with the chords through my melody was amazing! Tell me the truth, what do you think? Good? Not good?"

C.C. looked at me like I was high as a kite. "Have you taken your meds today? That was great for coming out of nowhere! The lyrics are a first go but I've heard worse. And words can always come later. For me, it's about the music. Let's do it again." I cared more about the words, but what the hell.

We played the song a few more times at different tempos and with a few extra flourishes thrown in by each of us either vocally or with the guitar as we noodled with the song. After another hour or so had passed, C.C. looked at me with a gleam in his eye.

"I think this could be fun. Want to do it? Want to start a band together? It'll be cool, and we're practically a novelty act: professionals by day, rock badasses by night. Want to try this again next week?"

I said I did, we shook on it, and I knew that not only did I have a band coming together, but C.C. seemed like he could actually become a real friend. Which was excellent, considering I'd probably need one in the crowd we were hanging with. I told him so and he gave me a giant hug before he started packing up.

"Jessica, I do have a question. Do you mind if I ask?"

"No, go right ahead."

C.C. was standing in the foyer and asked the sixty-four-thousand-dollar question point-blank. "If I'm not mistaken from looking around this place as well as at your left hand, you're married, right?" I nodded that he was correct. "And aren't you with Gideon?"

"Sort of." I wasn't going to give up more than I needed to. I liked C.C. but I didn't know if he was going to freak out if he knew exactly how duplicitous my life was. I knew that my conduct would draw a very deep line in the sand for a lot of people, particularly now that I had done the deed with Gideon. I didn't want to alienate C.C. and send him packing before we had a chance to get our venture off the ground. I wanted to be able to make the choice about how our friendship would develop, and at this point lies of omission were acceptable in my world.

"Look, it's no big deal to me. I'm just a little, you know. You don't seem like the type. But hey, you do your thing. It's just that if we're going to hang, I want to know the score."

"Yup, you've pretty much got the score."

"Thanks for being so up-front. Like I said, no big deal. On another note, do you have any ideas for band names?"

"Yes. Throes Like a Girl. And 'Throes' is spelled with an 'e,' not a 'w.' So it's a pun, which I know is the lowest form of humor, but it's a joke about how angsty girls are. You know what I mean." I was suddenly a little defensive. "I like the joke."

C.C. chuckled, put his gig bag over his shoulder, and opened the front door. As he walked out he said, "I like the name. It suits you. Let me think about it. But that is definitely the perfect band name for you."

Now C.C. had to be my friend. I couldn't afford for someone who had gotten my number so quickly to be anything but.

* * *

Two weeks later, Andrew and I packed up a U-Haul with our friends' help and moved to the white spaceship that was waiting for us in Williamsburg. We pulled up to the metal door with the painted-on numbers on North Eighth Street and got everything inside in short order. Our friends drank a few beers and left, exhausted from the lifting and still puzzled by our decision to move to this new place considering that we had gone from yuppie-hood to hipster-hood in the course of approximately two weeks. Hearing about our big change was one thing; seeing it must have been another for them. Even so, they had helped and we were grateful. Andrew and I were excited about our new adventure. I was on a major quest for life change, and Andrew was probably delighted by the novelty of a potential new fad dropping in his lap. Whatever the motivation, things needed to be mixed up if we were ever to be saved, if there was to be any hope of a "we" in the future. Even though that motivation directly contradicted my need for Gideon, I couldn't ignore that I still cared deeply about Andrew and couldn't conceive of a life without him.

After our friends left and the metal door slammed behind them, I felt like I was in the last scene of *The Graduate:* Elaine Robinson sitting in the back of the bus after fleeing her wedding with an expression on her face that clearly says, "Now what?" I had no idea.

All I knew was that I was already deep into the task of checking off the various points on my eight-point "want" list. Numbers one through six were in play, but numbers seven and eight were looking like they would become or continue to be, to put it lightly, tricky. And even though

I had more than half of my "want" list in the bag, I still had no clear answers to "Now what?" or its uncomfortable bedfellow "Who are you really?" The only way to find out was to stick to my list and keep doing what I had set out to do. Maybe if I did, a lightbulb would finally go on over my head and shed light on all the answers I was looking for. If that lightbulb did appear, with all the chaos I'd kicked up, karma would probably make it fall on my head and light my hair on fire.

7

HAVING A GOOD TIME, GLAD YOU'RE NOT HERE

sex, drugs, and rock and roll is not the same as Sex, Drugs, and Rock 'n' Roll. On the surface, the distinction might seem like no more than a grammatical quirk. It's not. Here's the thing: when it's only sex, drugs, and rock and roll that's being spoken of, what you're discussing is no more than a list. You're identifying and describing individual activities: a physical act, illicit substances, and an aural experience. Each one of these items can stand on its own, not needing the other two to prop it up to provide it with meaning. Hedonist or not, anyone can partake of any one of these three individually listed items and enjoy it on its own merits.

Sex, Drugs, and Rock 'n' Roll, on the other hand, is another beast of an entirely different stripe. Sex, Drugs, and Rock 'n' Roll isn't a list; it's a lifestyle. Each element is inseparable from the others; they all hold one another together and each imbues the combination with deeper and darker meaning. Think of this (un)holy trinity as the giant triliths at Stonehenge, two upright slabs (although it might be argued that there isn't much that's upright about any one of these three elements we're pondering at the moment, depending on who you're talking to) supporting a lintel lying across them. If you remove one of the three elements, you've got nothing. All together, when made of stone and sitting in a field in England, they create mystical structures arranged in a circle that have lured people to them for aeons. When not made of stone but instead of three distinct visceral experiences and linked by the proper grammar and mythic lore of televisions thrown out of windows, groupies, and mud sharks used for nefarious purposes, the lure is no less potent than the stone version, perhaps even more so.

For a large portion of the American public, from the day that Ed Sullivan kept them from seeing Elvis's hips swivel suggestively in time to his own music, those TV viewers knew they wanted what the King could supply and stodgy old Ed elected to deny. Those people glued to their tiny black-and-white screens could suddenly point at something completely new and tantalizingly illicit that flickered briefly in their own living rooms and say, "I want *that* and all that comes with it." In that moment, with Ed Sullivan acting as a stern and withholding paterfamilias, American kids, teens, and adults (whether that last group admitted it at the time or not is irrelevant) were turned on and intrigued by what they couldn't have. And like most human beings who are told they can't have something, they went after getting it in droves. On that fateful day in 1956, the Lifestyle was born. Well, almost. The Drugs part was going on, but most people didn't know about it. Even the King needed a little time to incorporate that into his act. But soon enough, the trilith of decadence and wild personal expression came into existence and grabbed innumerable people by the throat. It didn't matter if the people being drawn in were rock stars, rock star wannabes, or just fans who, without being able to sing or play a note, decided to emulate their golden idols. They were all powerlessly drawn in to living fast and possibly dying young.

This little discourse is not so much meant to serve as a history of rock but to explain what happened next in my ongoing plummet down my personal rabbit hole. The thing is that once you've decided to embrace the full lifestyle package, Sex, Drugs, and Rock 'n' Roll can most decidedly fuck with your head. Whether you're next in line for VH1 to do an episode of *Behind the Music* about you or not doesn't matter. If you get sucked up into the tornado of a life that anyone who subscribes to the trilith is offering you, you're toast. You may not know it at first, but you are, with all apologies to AC/DC, on a highway to hell. After enough time has gone by and, limp with your overexertions, you've pulled off that highway and are on your way to the nearest rest stop, you can look back at the speeding artery you've just left in your rearview mirror and breathe a sigh of relief. And you can try to remember what you did when you were flying at top speed, and in what order you did it all, but you'll be sorely disappointed because you won't be able to do what was once a simple task. You will not be able to say exactly what happened and when it did. And you will feel profoundly dumb, or more accurately like you've just emerged from a fugue state that has left you disheveled, disorganized, and massively disoriented.

If you're reading this and don't feel like the above statement is true, more power to you. But I'm wagering that if you claim to know exactly what went down, and how and where it did, while you were associated with Sex, Drugs, and Rock 'n' Roll people and playing their reindeer games, you're full of shit. Jimi Hendrix is frequently attributed with nailing what this phenomenon is all about when he said, "Of all the things I've lost, I miss my mind the most." But if it was someone else it's no less spot-on a statement about living a life of S, D, and R 'n' R. Which is why I call bullshit on anyone who says they can give you a blow-by-blow accounting of what they got up to during that period of their lives. Because there is no doubt about the fact that I can't.

I can remember a huge amount of what happened in the two years that followed the day that Andrew and I moved to Williamsburg, but it's more a series of memories that float independent of one another than a chronological story that remains fixed and static in my head. Those memories manifest as emotional impressions or physical sensations that roughly organize themselves on the three tracks of Sex, Drugs, and Rock 'n' Roll, but those three tracks have the annoying habit of winding around each other and overlapping. As the three tracks cross and weave around each other, something resembling a coherent story emerges, and then just when I think I'm safe and my memories are tidy and manageable, a tangential thought will worm its way in and ruin what I thought was the linear story of my life.

While I found it disturbing to think about my exploits during this period, all these little individually wrapped vignettes that took up residence in my head (even as the events themselves were taking place) did serve a purpose. For years after my time spent as a quasi-edgy, sort-of rock chick and definite sexual nutcase, I would tell all about my experimentation with sex, adultery, singing, going to dicey clubs, doing drugs, and consorting with people who were decidedly off-kilter (and a few possible criminals) in an offhand way as cocktail party banter that was designed to either shock or amuse. The reality was that when all of the psychosis of those two years was happening to me it was certainly exciting and shocking but only occasionally amusing. Nonetheless, it is a crime to throw away good cocktail party chat, particularly if you can raise a few eyebrows in a stuffy room. And, as the old joke "Time plus tragedy equals comedy" goes, as more time passed, my fugue state was less a terrifying head trip and more of a life-changing transformation studded with moments of unbelievable humor, so those stories got funnier and funnier. I eventually came to see, and describe, the funny moments as the petrified fruits and nuts that studded the Christmas cake of my life experience. And believe me, the crowd I wound up grasping to my bosom like a newfound family was made up almost entirely of fruits and nuts. So, clearly, I fit in perfectly.

● ● ●

After Andrew and I moved to Williamsburg, there was a short period when I thought that maybe, just maybe, the move would solve our problems. It's a common mistake. If you're thinking about moving or doing something equally disruptive to get yourself out of a rut, stop right now. It won't work. External stimuli do not solve problems. I learned this the hard way when a month or so had rolled by and Andrew, who had taken the reins so admirably with orchestrating our relocation, slipped back into his usual pattern of passive behavior and being emotionally checked-out, though he was still sweet to me for the most part. His behavior pushed every button I knew I had and located a few I hadn't been aware of. I found myself growing less and less tolerant of Andrew and would scream at him like a harpy over the dumbest things, living in an uncontrollable rage that I was too crazed to analyze and too fired up to stop. Poor Andrew, who did remarkably badly in the face of personal conflict, would silently suffer through my crazed flip-outs, or occasionally yell back when he couldn't stand to hear the sound of my voice anymore. It was in these moments that I found a shred of relief, because at least he was responding in a normal way to having *his* buttons pushed.

I have no memory of what specific occurrence or event precipitated my insistence that Andrew see a therapist, but such a thing did indeed happen, because he found one and started going. From my point of view at the time, he had so many suppressed issues that caused him to be repressed, emotionally distant, and mute that he had no choice but to get professional help. If he didn't start dealing with his shit, I knew in my bones that we did not stand a chance of having any kind of life together. On the other hand, I did not think I had a problem. I felt that if I did have a problem, he was a big part of it. It's easy to foist your issues onto others, isn't it? Active foisting was my preferred coping mechanism at that juncture. Even so, Andrew didn't appear to think I was off base. In fact, he seemed to agree that therapy would do him some good because off he went to find out what made him into the zombie I had taken to accusing him of being. I was delighted by this turn of events. I thought that maybe my life would take on some of its original shape and structure, and my need for Gideon and his lifestyle would evaporate. If it did, my life would be infinitely easier. I thought that maybe Andrew's therapy would change him and, by proxy, me into people who could answer that "Now what?" feeling that struck me the day we moved to Brooklyn. I thought wrong.

The final denouement in my decision making, both conscious and unconscious, about what to do regarding my commitment to Andrew and my attraction to Gideon and all he had to offer came after Andrew's third or fourth therapy session. He came home that evening and was obviously mulling over what he had covered with his therapist. I had already been to enough therapists at that point in my life to know the signs: silence and a contemplative but slightly puzzled look. That was fine by me. If he was processing his thoughts and feelings the therapy must be doing him some good. I hadn't seen any changes in him yet, but I was willing to be happily surprised. When Andrew did finally speak, I was definitely surprised.

"Can I ask you a question?" he said.

"Sure, honey, what is it?"

"Well, actually, it's something that my therapist asked me to talk about with you. To ask you."

This was going to be interesting. Finally, a window into what they were talking about! "No problem. Shoot."

"She wants me to ask you why I'm in therapy."

If I was a cartoon character, in that instant I would have morphed from a normal human to a person whose eyes were popping out Tex Avery style, to an erupting volcano, to a steaming kettle, to an exploding atom bomb complete with mushroom cloud, finally settling in as a ten-foot-tall Gorgon with a stony gaze and taste for blood. Andrew had unwittingly uttered, without exception, the dumbest and most infuriating question I had ever heard in my life up to that point. There I was, thinking that my husband had willingly and thoughtfully gone to a decent psychologist. Instead, in one split second he revealed the most mind-blowing information possible. He was as passive and checked-out as ever, he had gone to therapy only because I had told him to, the therapist who sent him on this fool's errand was most likely a quack, and as usual, the big questions and work that needed to be done for him and consequently the two of us was being thrown in my lap. Andrew was in therapy and I was the one being quizzed by the therapist. Give me a break.

I went absolutely fucking nuts, screaming for what seemed like hours about how stupid the question was and how ridiculous he was to bring it home to me. Why hadn't he tried to answer the question himself? Why hadn't he told the therapist that he had to take responsibility for himself? Why hadn't he told the therapist that even though I had suggested therapy he was the one who agreed to go, ergo, he was qualified to answer the question without me? Those were some of the issues I covered while shrieking myself hoarse and getting crazed enough to threaten popping a vein in my eye. Which would have been gross but a lasting symbol of my disgust for Andrew to mull over. But no vein popped and the screaming eventually subsided and Andrew defended himself by saying that he was following what the therapist told him to do, what was the big deal? I said something infantile, like, "If you don't know at this point then you never will," and called it a day. I tried to stay away from him for the rest of the night, but in our spanking-new wall-free loft, there was nowhere to hide. Well, there was the bathroom. I think I must have spent some time in there.

The upshot of that charming domestic scene was that I wrote Andrew off that night. I didn't write off my love for him, but I did throw away any last clinging shreds of hope that we could have what I considered to be a marriage that was normal and fulfilling. I know it wasn't fair to dismiss him so thoroughly in a moment of anger and frustration. It was bad form and not worthy of him, because no matter what his personality was doing to my nerves, he was always a good guy with good intentions. Everything that had been driving me crazy with frustration and resentment in a slow build for years finally gelled when he asked that question, and I snapped. Not only did I outwardly act like a monstrous nightmare, but inwardly I just let go. I couldn't imagine that Andrew would ever understand how I saw him and our relationship and that I understood it to be rife with failures to communicate and power inequalities. Those power inequalities kept me in the driver's seat so relentlessly that the responsibility and necessary energy required to keep things going had worn me down to a nubbin.

Once that huge part of my heart that had been reserved for loving only Andrew had officially let go and set him out to sea to fend for himself, there was an empty spot desperate to be filled. Gideon slid into that spot at the same moment that I pushed Andrew out. I upgraded Gideon without any serious thought from lust object and possible love to dyed-in-the-wool true love. I did it with lightning speed; it was so fast I barely knew I was doing it and the deed was done before I had a chance to talk myself out of it. I became the George Mallory of love. Like Mallory, who famously explained his decision to climb Mount Everest with "Because it's there," I started loving Gideon for the same reason.

In retrospect, that was a grade-A fuckup moment on my part. Not only did I write my husband off in a fit of pique (even if I was going to write him off, doing it in anger was a jerk move), but I then devoted myself to a cipher with a guitar. I was so wrapped up in my own needs that I didn't bother to contemplate the obvious fact that the cipher had his own feelings and issues and was about to be overwhelmed by a tidal wave of ardor that was towering above him. I was a love tsunami and the poor guy didn't stand a chance. Neither did the women I suspected him of sleeping with. I was going to dominate his world and make those women run for the hills or die trying. I wasn't just in love, I was also faced with the challenge of making Gideon love me back, and nothing rings my bells like a challenge. My competitive dander was up and all I could think about was winning Gideon and getting what I thought I wanted.

I'd be lying if I didn't admit that in the midst of these emotions, and what can only marginally be described as a thought process, I fell into what was now becoming my usual state of feeling guilty and horribly sick to my stomach. I was nauseated by the erosion of my feelings for Andrew, my mission to live a life that couldn't include him, and that I was going to have to ramp up the life of deceit I had already begun in order to achieve my dubious goal. Insanely, I was still hell-bent on keeping Andrew close because I didn't know a life without him. From a logistical standpoint, it didn't even occur to me to tell him I wasn't happy with our marriage. Being married to Andrew was my status quo and it was beyond my imagination that I would or could change our situation in any way. We were stuck together and that was that; there was nothing that could be done. Nonetheless, I felt that Andrew had screwed the pooch. I firmly believed that his emotional disengagement and its result, that I was essentially in a relationship by myself, left me no choice. I responded by embarking on my mission to run Gideon down and bag him.

•   •   •

The focus of my life shifted that day. My daily to-do list now consisted of: go to work, do some actual work, lie to Andrew, go to Gideon's place, have sex with him or play guitar or do both, lie to Andrew some more, go out to some bar or club with Gideon and his pals, get home late, and possibly write lyrics or a melody to work on with C.C. I would occasionally manage to add "eat something" to my list. Gideon was indeed warming to me more and more and showing that he was taking an interest in me beyond my status as bedpost notch. I warmed to him too, and lo and behold, we became friends. Which was bizarre.

Despite the *Mean Streets,* Martin Scorsese veneer that Gideon worked hard to affect, he was a very sensitive person. I understood how it was to live with your nerve endings so close to the surface and could communicate effectively with him as a result. I could listen to his problems and he to mine without it being an exercise in pulling teeth. And Gideon was witty. I had been wrong about that. It totally threw me for a loop. When he was relaxed and didn't have to deliver his tough, sexy guy performance, he was hilariously funny. He would remain enigmatically silent during any random encounter we'd have or experience we'd share and then deliver a one-liner that was pure Borscht Belt and have me on the floor. Sometimes Gideon was intentionally hilarious and sometimes he was not, but we laughed a lot.

One time we were driving around New Jersey, under circumstances that are too bizarre to bother getting into, in a pickup truck that his father owned. Gideon was next to me in the front seat. He didn't have a driver's license and was in a panic with me behind the wheel, convinced that my lackadaisical driving style would surely get him killed. After a few minutes of grousing, Gideon punctuated his argument by waving his arms in the air and pointing out that I was driving practically on top of the yellow dividing line in the road. The road was deserted. I explained that we weren't in any danger. I did this all the time and I was still alive, so no problem. Unable to keep himself from being the yenta he really was, after accusing me of being Evel Knievel, Gideon unintentionally slipped into a Yiddish accent and wailed, "Why? Why? Why do you always have to be different?" I had to pull over to stop laughing so I could continue driving without actualizing Gideon's worst fears and really getting us killed. Being funny is the quickest way to win me over, and Gideon was and did. Between the sex, the emotional connection, and a shared ability to laugh at the world and each other, we frequently had a great time.

But we always connected best in bed, and after our initially awkward but sweet inaugural love-fest, we set out to work on perfecting the act. We were so attracted to each other that it was impossible to have bad sex, but each time we did it, it got better and better. With that kind of return on our investment, there was no reason to do anything but continue boinking each other's brains out on a steady basis. It got to the point where, once our relationship was in full swing, we had sex every day. Sometimes more than once. We were awash in hormones, bodily fluids, and a sense of amazement that no matter how much we did it, it never got old. At least not for me, because while the sex got better and more adventurous with the passage of time, so did our ability to talk to each other and emotionally connect while in the sack.

It's a heady combination, so heady that most romantic comedies heavily feature the kind of pillow talk that we engaged in as the ultimate goal of the main characters' relationship. Harry and Sally had nothing on us.

At one point, when things weren't so great and I was lamenting that my relationship with Gideon was taking a turn for the worse, a friend told me to get over it and just get him into bed. When I asked why, she said, "That's where the two of you always find each other. You lose each other in the mess of a life that the two of you lead, but you find each other in bed. Get over yourself and get him there. You'll be fine." And while nothing was ever really fine, she was dead-on about how to locate Gideon's heart and mind when I thought they had taken a permanent vacation in unknown parts.

The result of the combination of our burgeoning friendship and relentless attraction to each other was that I got further away from my "because he's there" Mallory point of view and really started to fall in love with Gideon. As for Gideon, he did what I'm sure was the unthinkable for him and became protective of me. Well, if not genuinely protective, he certainly wanted to look after me a bit. This was a strange development. I absolutely wanted him to have that impulse but didn't expect him to bond to me so soon after we started sleeping together. I assumed that he was such a player that he couldn't possibly get attached to any woman in what seemed like no more than a nanosecond. In only the few weeks since I had grown so horribly fed up with Andrew and decided to turn my attentions to conquering Gideon, he began looking after me in the best ways he knew how.

One way was to harangue me to become a vegan. I made it clear that was never going to happen, but I did meet him halfway just so we could eat out together by becoming mostly vegetarian. Which was fine with me because I barely ate anyway, but there was not a chance I was giving up ice cream or cookies, so vegan-hood was out.

Gideon also took to opening doors for me, making sure I had a seat on the subway if we traveled together, shielding me from obnoxious drunks in bars—basically keeping an eye open for my personal safety at all times. He hated the way I always crossed the street against the light and even took to holding my hand when we crossed, making sure I wouldn't be flattened. The most appealing and fun way that Gideon initially displayed his desire to look after me was to encourage me to buy an electric guitar of my own and then take me shopping for one. I was thrilled. I was inching closer to my rock chick aspirations, and I was going to buy a shiny new toy in the company of another shiny new toy.

I met Gideon at his place to begin our shopping trip. He was a bit nervous, or maybe he had snorted a little toot before I arrived. I had no idea because I wasn't very good at telling the difference at the time, but he was in good form and very sweet to me. (See? I was taming a bad boy. I was a genius.) We hailed a cab and he bounded over to yank the door open for me before I could do it for myself. No matter how often he did this, I was astonished. Someone had once taught Gideon proper manners beyond how to share his stash and which spoon to use for coke and which for soup. Who knew? I slid into the cab and he pushed in next to me, giving the cabbie the address of the first guitar store we were going to hit.

I was all girly and mushy over his excellent behavior and took a moment to look over at him adoringly. He was wearing glasses that day, which I had never seen him do, but I wear contacts every day and when I wear my glasses people are always surprised. So I figured he was secretly as blind as I was and just couldn't bear to put in contacts that day. I sidled up to him to kiss his cheek and thank him for the shopping expedition. As I did, I caught the view through his glasses out of my peripheral vision. Damn, that was one weak-ass prescription. Why bother wearing them if he barely needed to? I took another sly look by kissing him again. I was wrong. There was no prescription; the lenses were clear plastic.

"Gideon, are you nearsighted? Are those glasses for distance?"

"Um, why do you ask?"

I had a creepy feeling that made my skin shrivel up and my stomach drop. It was a cringe-inducing moment. I was embarrassed for him but couldn't say why. If he thought they looked good on him, why not? My senses came back to me. Why not is because the only people who wear fake glasses are in sixth grade and are trying to look smart. I was back to cringing on the seat next to him.

"Oh, nothing. I just glanced through them and they seem like a really weak prescription."

Nothing from Gideon.

"Are you wearing them to look cool?" I poked my finger into his ribs as I kissed his neck. I figured the only way out of this was to tease him and make the discovery of his embarrassing choice into something cute.

He was a little sheepish. "I thought they looked good. Do you think they're dumb?" He whipped them off his face and stashed them in his shirt pocket.

Shit. Here was this person trying to do something nice for me and I was crapping all over him. Probably because I saw an opportunity to be the alpha of the cab and took it. I was being not only lame but aggressive and bitchy as well just so I could establish my dominance over Gideon. While I was at it, I might as well have peed on him.

"No! I think they're cute. You should put them back on! Come on, they're adorable on you."

Gideon wasn't buying it. The glasses stayed in his shirt pocket and I spent the rest of the afternoon sucking up to him and acting like I was made of spun sugar. Gideon must have wordlessly forgiven me my behavior, because he didn't reveal a moment of irritation as he schlepped me from store to store, finally finding my perfect guitar somewhere around Thirtieth Street on the West Side. The day ended with me as the proud owner of a gorgeous black-and-white Rickenbacker semi–hollow body guitar, the same kind that Tom Petty used. I had "American Girl" playing in my head as I fondled the thing, cowed by it because there was no way that I could eke out anything that sounded like that song, but delighted that if I ever could I now had the equipment to do so. Gideon carried the guitar in its case for me, because all packed up it must have weighed forty pounds, and got me a cab to take me back to Brooklyn. There was no way I was going to be able to carry that thing around on the train. He kissed me good-bye as he settled me in the cab.

"Don't forget to practice. I'll call you later."

I wanted to say something to redeem myself for being such a tool earlier but couldn't think of anything that would sound right.

"Okay, I hope so. And thank you so much for this."

"No problem. Later."

He closed the door and I was whisked back to my own borough. In my mind's eye, Gideon was off to find solace in the arms of one of the other women he was playing around with because I had been powerless to keep my big trap shut and had driven him off. The upside was that I did learn a few things from the outing. First, I was coming out of the gate playing a power game with Gideon by being obnoxious and challenging him, mostly because his lifestyle scared me a little and made me feel like I was at some sort of disadvantage. Second, he liked me enough to go soft on me and take me on a little outing where he could help me. Third, it was possible that I unnerved him a little, just as he unnerved me. His bad-boy persona made me a little jumpy, but my egghead good-girl side had gotten to him. Why else would he make an attempt to look more bookish with those crazy glasses? So, in essence, I now had a handle on where we stood. We wanted to get in each other's pants nonstop, we were soft on each other, and we were locked in a power struggle. It wasn't a wholesome relationship, but it was certainly interesting.

Even though I came out swinging in our ongoing

battle of the sexes, Gideon was no slouch and had me on the ropes on a pretty constant basis. While my weapon of choice was intellect, Gideon's were emotional manipulation and his harem. After the shopping expedition, we continued to get closer and more intimate, sometimes simply hanging out and watching a movie at his place or having a drink instead of just hooking up and jumping into his bed. Gideon and I would sit on the couch holding hands, talking, and cuddling, doing a terrific impression of normal people. This kind of relaxed intimacy would go on for a week or so and then Gideon would freak out, demanding to know what I wanted from him because I was married and shouldn't be coming over to his place so much. Directly on the heels of these outbursts, which sent me reeling out of his orbit and into a state of despair since he was the closest thing I had to a proper intimate relationship at that point, Gideon would pull me back in again by calling me and wooing me and sulking a little with complaints of "You don't love me." He knew these would always elicit a knee-jerk "Of course I do!" from me in my desperation to keep him by my side. So we'd do that dance until Gideon knew that he really had my attention and I wasn't planning on going anywhere. But if I rebelled and ignored his pouting sulks or was too busy at work to respond quickly enough, he'd pull out the big guns. He'd flaunt his liaisons with the rest of his women.

I never knew exactly how many other women Gideon slept with while we were together, but there were three I was sure about. One was a sweet and terribly fragile hippie named Rachel, who worshipped Gideon and appeared to have the same intense need for him that I did.

I don't know what her need stemmed from, but it was there and it made her a sympathetic character I could relate to.

The second woman in Gideon's harem was a caustic creature named Sophie who never really understood the man she was dealing with. I was dementedly attached to Gideon and adored him but always knew that he, to put it kindly, had issues. I couldn't help myself when it came to him and could be hurt at the drop of a hat, but I knew that trying to make him behave like a normal boyfriend would be like trying to make a house pet out of a raccoon you find snacking on your garbage at night. Don't get me wrong; I tried to do it. But when he failed or rebelled I would be forced to reconnect with the notion that it was his dangerous lifestyle and smooth, manipulative charm that had attracted me in the first place. The conundrum of Gideon was that what made him so magnetic was also what made him so alarming. You had to accept his yin to get to his yang. So to speak. I was able to do this when I felt that I was in total command of his affections, but when one of the other women became too present in his life for me to ignore, it did drive me nuts. Sophie never found any balance with Gideon's other women and would pop up at inconvenient moments shooting daggers with wild eyes at any woman he laid a finger on in her presence.

The third of the third wheels was a woman who was only referred to by her last name, Fiore, who would do blow with Gideon and occasionally screw him. I never got the sense that there was any profound relationship there so her presence didn't make me nuts. Fiore was actually kind of a good egg, and we even hung out a few times during my stint as Love Interest Number One. Fiore didn't make me crazy; it was Gideon's decision to have sex with her that bothered me. What bothered me even more was that he was possibly doing it to get free coke. Which took his behavior from callous to gross. It's not a proud moment when you find yourself seriously considering if mentally referring to your lover as a coke whore is fair or not. But I put up with all of it to keep Gideon close. I was as addicted to him as he was to getting high and getting off. And I even managed to create a strange friendship with Rachel that was a comfort to both of us whenever dealing with Gideon became too draining. It was weird, no doubt about it. We were a harem, and while we tolerated each other's presence, none of us was thrilled about the situation.

Although I eventually came to begrudgingly accept Gideon's complex love life, I had a total meltdown when I first realized that these women were always in the background, not occasional flings. The first one I twigged on to was Rachel, and it was in a ridiculous way. Gideon and I had been seeing each other seriously for more than six months but less than a year. I can't remember exactly how long it was, but it was short enough for me not to know all his dirty little secrets and long enough for me to believe that he was my boyfriend in the traditional sense. I thought we were serious about each other because he knew that I had stopped having sex with Andrew and logically expected the same behavior from him.

In addition to my assumption that Gideon and I had a

mutual unspoken understanding of exclusivity, based on my status with Andrew, I had a set of keys to his place. You'd assume that if a guy was seeing multiple women, he wouldn't give his keys to one of them because she might stumble in on him having it off with one of his other paramours, right? Wrong assumption if you're dealing with Gideon. He happily offered me the keys to his castle and I happily accepted them and waltzed in whenever I felt like it. On one such occasion I arrived at his underground lair before he did and let myself in without a second thought. The place was a little messy and I thought I'd have myself a nice little OCD moment and straighten up. The last thing I did in my sweep of the apartment was to make Gideon's bed. The sheets and duvet were all crumpled down at the foot of the bed, so I climbed in to pull everything up and out in order to start from scratch. In doing so, I felt a little lump in the tangle of sheets that I dislodged by snapping the top sheet out flat. That little lump was a pair of women's underpants. They were minuscule. Rachel was a teeny-tiny person and those lacy underpants would have fit her as perfectly as a glass slipper on Cinderella. It goes without saying that I was not pleased. It would be more accurate to say I went totally bananas.

The process of going bananas went like this: I sat on the edge of the bed for what felt like an eternity but was more likely about ten minutes. As I sat there, my mind went from numb and blank to raging inferno of hatred for both Gideon and Sluterella, she who couldn't manage to keep track of her underpants and apparently had no problem going commando. As my rage was roiling to the surface, Gideon had the misfortune to come home. He took one look at me on the bed holding those petite panties and knew he was in for it. But I didn't yell at him and at first he was relieved. Then I became the Clarence Darrow of sexual intrigue. I slowly and carefully walked toward Gideon, who had set up camp on the other side of the room, deposing him with carefully worded questions about how he thought the underpants got in his bed and who they might belong to. I continued my line of questioning even though he brazenly insisted that he didn't know whose they were or how they got there. My queries were so finely crafted that, in fairness, if he had attempted to answer a single one of them he would have hung himself. My slow approach finally landed me about six inches away from him and we stood there in a silent standoff. He broke the silence with a statement that should have alerted me to the fact that I was dealing with a seriously twisted mind. The conversation that followed went something like this:

"I don't know anything about those. You probably put them there."

I was still deadly silent. I quietly asked him to repeat what he said. Gideon became more agitated as he had to repeat and stick to his incredible lie.

"You put them there! You want to prove some point or something. I have nothing to do with those."

That was my breaking point. My silent menace dissolved and was replaced by screaming at a decibel level that bordered on supersonic.

"You motherfucking piece of shit! Why the fuck would I put them there? Why would I do that? That's something you would do, you fuckhead! You are a cheating, lying fuck of a human being."

It took me a few seconds to realize that as I delivered this eloquent speech, I was hitting Gideon with the underpants. More accurately, I was whipping him with them. He had one arm raised to protect his face from the panty-whipping (as my friends later dubbed that episode) and was backing away from me for fear that I would actually do him some serious damage. I would have, had I been holding something other than underwear. If there was anything that I wasn't going to tolerate from Gideon, he who had a stranglehold on my heart, it was cheating and lying.

The irony is not lost on me.

To his credit, Gideon never wavered from his blatantly ridiculous story. He knew better than to allow for a chink in his armor. If there was even one weak spot, our dynamic would move from a power struggle to total dominance on my part. He could hurt me and I could hurt him and we always teetered on that edge, keeping each other in a constant state of desire and distrust. It was irresistible.

That particular encounter was a great example of the "Sex" portion of the Sex, Drugs, and Rock 'n' Roll program. It perfectly encapsulates how sexually charged everything was with Gideon and how sex with him was frequently about something other than the act itself. A lot of it was about individual struggles regarding trust, fidelity, need for attention and affirmation, and definitely a need to feel dominant and in control of our relationships and lives. I tried to face and address all of those issues in the highly charged dynamic I was creating with Gideon. He acted out his struggle through creating complicated entanglements with multiple women, with me getting the brunt of his effort to deal with power dynamics. Add to all of that the unfailing rule that for every action either of us took there was a reaction, and you start to get a picture of the complex knot of psychopathia sexualis twisting around Gideon, his women, and me.

After C.C. and I had that first musical encounter that wound up being Band Day number one, we met at least once a week. We'd each bring more songs to the table and learn how to work with each other well enough to form something that resembled a band. My specialty became writing lyrics and producing lilting melodies to go over C.C.'s bouncy guitar riffs. Most of my songs, unsurprisingly, were about love and heartbreak.

The drama that Gideon brought to my table made writing heartfelt lyrics a piece of cake. If I didn't write down what was happening in an effort to purge my demons, I would have been driven even madder than I was.

The one song I wrote that perfectly encapsulated how I was feeling during this whole transformative process was "Fallen." It was raw, sexual, angry, flirtatious, and seriously profane. I loved it and so did C.C. Amazingly, so did Gideon, who turned out to know the lyrics by heart but never acknowledged that he was the primary inspiration for the song. Which was a major act of restraint as the first verse was

Can't believe how you move me
shocked by how you use me
amazed by how you rule me
[spoken] but I love the way you fuck me
and I hate, I hate who you are.

And if that wasn't revealing enough, later on comes

So now I've got you in my clutches
can't escape you're caught in the rushes
fallen victim to my gentle pushes
[spoken] now you're always begging to fuck me
and you hate, you hate who you are.

The first time I sang it with what would become our full band we recorded it. I later listened to it and was both horrified and elated. I sang it like my life depended on it. I was a short step away from screaming the song, sounding like I would eat any man whole who got within ten feet of me. It was an awful, scary sound but it was the beginning. When I heard it, I knew I could and would say anything. Knowing that I had to make the song fun to listen to and not something that made an audience run for the fire exits, I later modified the way I sang "Fallen" so that it sounded lilting, teasing, and sweet. It always got a laugh and appreciative round of applause, particularly from male audience members, and once, when we played it at Freddy's, one guy got to his feet. I love that guy.

Although "Fallen" wound up being what I can only loosely call our breakout hit, it was powerful because it was so visceral. And it was visceral because it was about my indispensable but devilishly fucked-up muse, as was almost every song I wrote during that period. It was totally unavoidable. He was the catalyst for so much of the change I was going through, there was no way to write about myself or what I was feeling without including him. The funny part was that most of my lyrics were really dark and angry or dark and sexually charged, but C.C. loved bouncy rockabilly, so if you weren't listening carefully you wouldn't know that what I was singing was pretty raw. It was not unlike primal scream therapy.

Gideon liked what we were writing, which was very gratifying. As time went by and the band came fully into being, with Gideon and Ira stepping in on drums and bass respectively, C.C. and I would frequently hear Gideon humming the tunes to himself as he set up his drum kit or even when we were out at night. C.C. and I would wonder out loud to each other if Gideon knew any of the lyrics or had even noticed that it was remotely possible that they were about him. And that they were frequently not very complimentary. We got our answer one day when we were practicing and Gideon heard me go totally blank during the second verse of a song about how awful it was for me that he slept with multiple women. Without missing a beat, Gideon piped up with, " 'Being number one in a list of three just isn't me . . . the things we had were great but I don't want them now.' " C.C. and I were stunned. Gideon just smirked.

●　●　●

But sex with Gideon was definitely not all about insanity and heartbreak. It was also about the constantly deepening connection between us, louche and unapologetically debauched fun, and pushing our boundaries to see how far each of us would go and if either of us would admit to having limits. For the most part, neither one of us did. I know my willingness to do just about anything shocked Gideon, but I expected it of him and assumed that whatever we did was already old hat to him. The majority of it probably was, but the emotional component of what we had was what tripped him up and threw him into uncharted territory. I wouldn't have been so clear about his feelings had Gideon not told me, which he did. Often. Whenever we were in bed and he became aware of his own tenderness or aware of his love for me, he'd tell me. And always include how much it surprised him. I was used to being connected to people but craved experience and finding something that would finally shock me into slowing down. I don't remember that ever happening.

There wasn't a single bar or club in the East Village that we went to where we didn't wind up sneaking off to the bathroom to get it on. We made out or had some variety of sex in so many places, it's hard for me to talk about any location in that neighborhood without wanting to blurt out, "I had sex there." I don't want to say it to prove anything to anyone, it's just that it still surprises me that we had that much energy to constantly go out, be turned on by each other, and maul each other into the wee hours of the morning.

Oh, wait.

I forgot.

There was the coke.

Everything we did was fueled by cocaine: giant lines for him and a steady stream of bumps off of keys, Bic pen caps, and the odd coke spoon for me. I never bought it from a dealer myself, but I financed a decent amount of what we consumed. For some reason I managed to keep my wits about me regarding buying drugs. I refused to do it under any circumstances, convinced that I'd be the idiot to wind up behind bars, not to mention being disbarred. I wouldn't do well in prison. I was never good at arts and crafts and I seriously doubted my ability to make an effective shiv. So I insisted that Gideon or one of his new bandmates, all of whom now were a major part of Gideon's social life as well as mine, do the buying.

For those of you who aren't familiar, here's a quick overview on what hanging out with people who do drugs is like. Not to mention doing it yourself. There is a huge amount of time dedicated to the procurement of your drug of choice. First there's the talking about it. Everyone involved wants to know if someone is holding and there's a lot of conversation about who has some, had some, where it went if they no longer have it, and whether or not someone might have some elsewhere. Once it is determined that no one has any drugs any-more, the dealer is called and the waiting begins.

Calling and waiting for a drug dealer is very similar to dealing with a contractor. If you've ever had anything done to your house or apartment, you know that finding a reliable contractor is hard, getting him on the phone is harder, and waiting for him to arrive (which always takes much, much longer than you ever anticipated) is hardest of all. Same exact scenario goes for drug dealers. You make the call and then spend an eternity waiting for some shifty guy to show up. And while you're waiting, all that anyone can concentrate on is when the drugs are going to arrive. Feeble attempts at conversation are made, but the discussion always reverts back to frustrated queries about when the dealer said he would show up and how late he is.

Finally, the dealer arrives and the person who made the call, who presumably knows the dealer and can vouch that he's not a narc (and the dealer is sure the customer is not a narc), hands over the cash. There's an awkward moment when the customer and dealer pretend that they are interested in having some kind of conversation with each other in an attempt to legitimize the relationship. I don't know why that happens, but it always does. The dealer then jumps back into his Escalade and the procurer divvies up the purchase according to who contributed to the cost of the purchase and in what amount. Then the drugs are consumed and everyone is too stoned or hopped up to have a real conversation.

In essence, doing drugs is mostly boring with a payoff at the end when you get high, and then the cycle begins again. The saving grace for me, and the reason that waiting on the man wasn't so horrendous, was that doing coke with Gideon meant that if we stayed in we had sex for hours, which was thrilling. If we went out, we'd do it wherever we landed, which was also thrilling. They weren't kidding with the "Coke is it" campaign. It was the slogan we lived by.

Getting back to the issue of sex, describing our sexual adventures in public places reads almost like a map of the East Village and Lower East Side as it was circa 2000. We would succumb to each other's charms everywhere we went with such regularity that the crowd we normally hung with probably expected it and spent a lot of time rolling their eyes at us and gagging. We didn't care and got off on the cheap thrill of possibly getting caught. Gideon and I, to the best of my recollection, got our kicks at a party space called the Green Door, the Cock (gay bar, obviously), the Boiler Room, Meow Mix, CBGB (RIP), Fez, Walter's and Bellevue (those two were midtown), Niagara, several loft parties, 7A, and Arlene's Grocery. There were others, but the mixture of drugs, adrenaline, and time has whisked them away to the darkest recesses of my brain, never to be known again. The parts that I do remember are fractured and littered with random images like slashes of graffiti written in Magic Marker on stained walls, my hands gripping the sides of a sink to brace myself, and Gideon's face in one of the many bathroom mirrors that reflected our dubious endeavors.

What I can recall with greater clarity are the sex-a-thons that we had at Gideon's apartment. Coke kept us awake and turned on for hours and hours, and we'd keep at it for so long that it was amazing I was ever able to walk again. Crass but true. Those times together were so seductive because Gideon knew how to set the pace perfectly. He created an incredibly wanton environment in which we would go from languid lovemaking to porny fucking to taking breaks during which we would decadently smoke cigarettes, indulge in some kind of narcotic, and inspect one another's bodies until we knew them like our own.

I'll never forget one particular evening when, after a vigorous two hours or so of passionate sex in every acrobatic position imaginable, we took one of those breaks for a while. We were on the love couch and Gideon sat on the edge of it while he smoked a cigarette with one leg crossed over the other, looking at me. He didn't say a word. He just peered at me through the smoke drifting up toward his face. I was lying back on the couch, my head propped up on the arm, one foot on the floor and my other leg bent with my knee pointing up to the ceiling and my foot flat on the couch. I asked Gideon, as all women tend to do, what he was thinking. He said, "Nothing, just looking at you." Then, as casually as if he were lighting another cigarette or leafing through a book, Gideon reached out to touch me with the expertise of a jaded gynecologist and said, "Wow. You look incredible. You're really swollen, do you feel okay?"

I was stunned. No one had ever appraised me with that sense of entitlement and ownership before. And I certainly couldn't remember any man in my past, including my own husband, who was tacitly agreeing to what I was doing at that very moment with his silence, inspecting me so frankly and almost clinically. Gideon's manner, the way he handled me, what he said and how he said it, were shocking. It was a moment of relaxed and unbridled sexual confidence that I had never seen before. What Gideon did utterly changed my perspective on how people can relate to each other sexually. It was so altering that in spite of all our subsequent various activities over a considerable period of time, it's a moment that has stuck with me and most likely will forever.

The sexual world that Gideon lived in and had me living in was fueled not only by drugs but also by the company he kept. When we first met, Gideon's social life was largely made up of hanging out with the guys he worked with along with the guys in Love Craft. The other members of Love Craft were reasonably solid people whom I never really got to know very well, but they didn't give off any crazy vibes or weirdo energy. Once Gideon had moved on from that band and taken up with his new band Ritalin Cowboys, crazy came out to play. Except for Gideon, whose sexual energy was so huge and blasted out in an enormous radius that included anyone and anything he laid eyes on, making me sometimes wonder whether or not he was totally straight, everyone else in Ritalin Cowboys was definitively gay. Or so they said. It seemed to me that they were in a constant state of sliding around Kinsey's sexual orientation scale, which wasn't a problem except when it affected me directly. Which it did on a few occasions. Gay is more than okay in my book. It's just that I hate surprises. I've never wanted a surprise party and I nearly die of fright at horror movies that operate on the "boo!" principle. Therefore I wasn't overjoyed when someone I thought was gay suddenly shot his hands up my skirt to cop a feel. Or when an avowedly straight person (like Gideon or a few other revelers in our group) decided to fool around with a pretty boy in a not-so-private place in a bar. As time went by and I saw how nimbly the members of Ritalin Cowboys glided from zero to six on Dr. Kinsey's scale like Brian Boitano on a freshly honed pair of skates, the "boo!" factor diminished and the rampant sexual ambiguity affected me less. What did affect me was that there was so much sex swirling in the air around the band members and Gideon that it became a chokingly thick smoke that threatened to asphyxiate us if we weren't careful.

The first of the new players in our sexual psychodrama was the lead singer of Ritalin Cowboys. Morgan was a charismatic, handsome, and sweetly charming guy who wore whatever damage he had survived right under the surface of his skin. He was avowedly gay but stole kisses and copped feels without any gender bias. I assumed that his need to gather love from his audience as the front man came from the same place as his desire to gather love in its myriad forms from whoever would supply it. But Morgan was fundamentally a good person, so it was easy to brush off whatever he did that might have been a little left of center. As far as I went, he entertained himself by doing mountains of blow with his friends and then thrusting his hands up my skirt or down my pants at odd moments. Funnily enough, Gideon minded Morgan's wandering hands far more than I did, and he loved Morgan. It was another tip-off that Gideon had fallen for me harder than I ever thought he would. I was delighted that he was jealous and possessive; in an embarrassing tribute to Cheap Trick, I have to admit that I wanted him to want me. Mostly because I wanted quid pro quo. Every time Gideon went nuts, it was a reminder that I had him, to some degree, in my control. Which I assumed bothered him. Which I liked. Our power dynamic was nothing if not constantly fluctuating and complex.

Another member of Ritalin Cowboys was a woman named Lydia who played guitar along with Gideon. Lydia was, by far, the smartest person in the band as well as the most mature and what is conventionally considered normal, at least on the surface. She was gainfully employed, a relatively monogamous lesbian, had acceptable grooming standards, and was free from the psychotic breaks from reality that plagued the other members of the band. Lydia's stability was, however, always hanging by a tenuous thread. She was, after all, a key member of Ritalin Cowboys. The deck was stacked against her.

Lydia was a great guitar player, generally low-key, and incredibly intense. I liked her and trusted her the most of all the band members, if for no other reason than she was generally solid and did less coke than her cohorts. But as time wore on, the rigors of life in Ritalin Cowboys took their toll on her and this formerly even-keeled person began resembling the mental cases she spent so much of her time with. In a nutshell, Lydia took to having throw-down fights with her girlfriends outside of the various lesbian bars she, and consequently the rest of the band, frequented. Meow Mix is the primary watering hole–cum–boxing ring that comes to mind, and I recall fights that involved slapping, throwing random objects, and possibly trying to deposit whoever was her girlfriend at the time into a Dumpster. These precious moments loom large in my memory because, despite having attended all-girls school and camps, I had never seen anything as demented as Lydia's girl-on-girl fights. They came out of nowhere and evaporated just as quickly, ending in tears and hugs. I had never seen two women

fight like that over primarily romantic slights before, and
to this day it is one of the very few things that make me
think it's easier to be a relatively well-adjusted heterosex-
ual woman. We have our relationship drama, but in my
crowd it rarely ends with finding oneself in a Dumpster.

Ritalin Cowboys had Ira, Gideon's ever-present familiar, on bass. He radiated absolutely no sexual vibe at all,
which was a blessing, considering his general state of
hygiene. He did have a front-row seat to everyone else's
romantic and sexual debacles and for the most part removed himself entirely. If he did react, it was as a sympathetic uncle who patted shoulders and spirited himself
away as quickly as possible.

The only remaining member of Ritalin Cowboys to
catalog is the drummer. As with Love Craft, Ritalin Cowboys' drummer has faded into oblivion. I have no memory of who he was, probably because the poor thing was
blocked out by the massive coked-up egos lined up at the
front of the stage at every gig. The rub is that I bet no
one else who was in Ritalin Cowboys remembers who he
was either.

Although she wasn't a member of the band, there
was an unofficial sixth member. She was Morgan's best
friend, in her early twenties; carried about twenty-five
extra pounds on her that added to her sexually ambigu-
ous look; and was a lesbian who prided herself on special-
izing in getting straight girls to sleep with her. She was
totally butch as far as her body and clothing went. From
the neck down she was as diesel as they come, wearing
white ribbed tank tops, Levi's, a wallet with a chain attached to a belt loop, and black work boots or motorcycle

boots. From the neck up she was a glamour queen, re-splendent in a full face of Chanel makeup, elaborate hair-dos, and wildly expensive status sunglasses. She was a walking contradiction of types: butch, lipstick, diesel, femme, whatever you want to call it. Liesl was avowedly gay but was in a constant state of worshipping Morgan and wanting to sleep with him. Not a problem for any-one, except perhaps Morgan. But it was another drop in the bucket of oversexed line crossing that was part of our steady diet of weirdness.

In the midst of the formation of Throws Like a Girl and the ascendance of Ritalin Cowboys, I was still hold-ing down my nine-to-five job and trying to make a mark at Rook Publishing. As if I wasn't already living in bizzaro world, it was at around this time that my boss decided to have what appeared to be a nervous breakdown. He stopped coming to work with any regularity and when he was around was either totally ineffectual or explo-sively angry over obscure issues. He finally took an unof-ficial leave of absence, and as it was my job to try to bring in some money, I renewed my efforts to find business and even tried not to party too hard during the workweek so I would be able to focus and hit my productive stride.

As a direct result of this last decision, I quickly learned about what habitual drug users affectionately call "sui-cide Tuesday." If you're doing a significant amount of drugs, be it cocaine, ecstasy, or anything else that messes with your serotonin levels, and then stop altogether on Sunday, you think you're in the clear Sunday night and Monday. You feel fine and you're totally functional. Then Tuesday comes like the Black Plague. You hit bottom and you're reduced to a grouchy, weepy, angry, and often sick mess. A nice tidy little suicide in the comfort of your own home seems like a better option than venturing out into the bright, loud, and horrifyingly annoying world beyond your front door. But I did venture out and went to work in the throes of the effects of suicide Tuesday on several occasions.

One of those Tuesdays will live in infamy for the whole office. I stumbled into Rook and called the deli for my usual order: an iced coffee with milk, a toasted bagel, and olive cream cheese on the side. The cream cheese could not be spread on the bagel. Ever. If it was, the cheese would melt and the whole experience would be ruined for me. On that day, I called in the order and it took far too long to arrive. I called the deli again and demanded to know where my fucking food was. At that point I should have been aware of the fact that whatever came would most likely have someone's phlegm in it. The woman who answered the phone assured me that it was leaving that moment. The food arrived and the bagel had not been toasted. I went berserk, kept the delivery guy in my office, called the deli again, and explained in no uncertain terms that my fucking bagel wasn't fucking toasted, could they please get it the fuck right? My office door was open so the entire staff heard what was going on. The delivery guy left without payment and with a promise to bring back the correct order.

He returned ten minutes later and the entire office held its breath to hear the verdict. I opened the bag and the bagel was toasted. And covered in cream cheese.

That was it. I picked up the phone to make my last

call to the deli for several weeks to come and let loose a stream of invective that was so foul I have no idea what I said. My more civilized sensibilities have prevented me from retaining any of that rant.

On the third try, they got it right. I, on the other hand, was not right in any sense of the word. I ate the bagel, got through the day, and began reconsidering my recreational drug use. It was one thing to drag ass into the office. It was another thing entirely to publicly open a can of whoop-ass over breakfast preparations. After that incident, I scaled back on what I snorted, swallowed, and smoked. The result of which was that I functioned far more sanely at work (which was essential considering our boss was still AWOL) and I was infinitely more aware of just how much blow and everything else Ritalin Cowboys, its hangers-on, and most importantly Gideon were ingesting.

My scaling back not only led to better relations with my local deli but also brought my first true understanding of the toll that Sex, Drugs, and Rock 'n' Roll can take on a person. Or, more specifically, my cronies and me. I really had thrown myself headlong into the Lifestyle and craved all that it promised, but the glimpses I'd had so far of the resulting mayhem had indeed prompted me to take the first available exit off the highway to hell to assess where I was. I can't say that the time I spent gathering my wits at that rest stop ended with a decision to stay off the highway and, if not choose the straight and narrow, at least take the back roads. But the need to take a step back served as the first warning sign, of many to come, that the Lifestyle was not sustainable. In other words, it wasn't really a Lifestyle. It was a "part of your life"–style. If you couldn't wrap your head around that reality, Hendrix's astute commentary about the Sex, Drugs, and Rock 'n' Roll trilith would surely come home to roost for you. And no one, least of all me, wants to spend the rest of their life staring vacantly into the distance muttering, "Of all the things I lost, I miss my mind the most." I knew that for sure, even as I was terrorizing the innocent deli workers of New York City.

8

ERUPTION;
OR, THINGS GET WEIRD(ER)

When the endless fuck-a-thon/love-a-thon with Gideon got too intense or he was so busy with other women—who would mark their territory in his apartment by leaving behind more underwear, cosmetics, and suspiciously rumpled sheets—that I was driven to distraction, I steadied myself by turning to C.C. and the ongoing formation of our band. Throws Like a Girl had been steadily writing and playing songs, first at my apartment, then at C.C.'s law firm after hours, where we would regale the cleaning crew with our angsty rockabilly and bubblegum pop. The maintenance staff never commented on the strange performances they were subjected to, but C.C. and I thought we were coming along nicely. C.C. would play his guitar while still in full business attire, and I sang in what had become my uniform of leather pants, T-shirt, and some kind of high heels depending on what the weather allowed. If it wasn't leather pants, it was jeans or cords that were so tight and low-cut that sitting down wasn't an option. The advantage of the low-slung pants was that they showed off my newly acquired tattoo.

I had gotten my first tattoo in a fit of rebellion about six months before Gideon entered my life. It was a harbinger of what was to come, but there was no way I had the required perspective to understand what that little inkblot was insistently broadcasting to my deaf ears. In my family and general milieu it was considered beyond gauche to have a tattoo. This was before everyone and their mothers, brothers, sisters, and cousins started sporting ink as casually as a piece of jewelry or makeup. This was also long before tattoo artists became celebrities with their own TV shows, books, and cosmetics companies. Research shows that when I got my tattoo, about 15 percent of the American population had one, as opposed to the roughly 40 percent of the population just between the ages of twenty-six and forty who are tattooed today. The offering of these statistics is not an attempt to establish my cool factor or trend-spotting abilities, but rather to show that what I was choosing to do to myself was still considered to be at best out of the ordinary, at worst déclassé for young women of my ilk.

The only person with whom I could pursue that first attempt to break out of my shell was Alex. Not only because she was open to anything anyone wanted to do, but because she was not-so-secretly harboring a deep desire to get a tattoo as well. Having done close to zero investigation into who was considered capable of doing the job or what tattoo parlors were clean and civilized, Alex and I hooked up near NYU and walked into the first place we found, on MacDougal Street. I already knew what I wanted to carry around on my body forever but Alex had no clue and took a while to examine all the flash art that decorated the hole in the wall that we had wandered into. She settled on having a sun put on her shoulder, and I produced the artwork I wanted the tattoo guy to draw on my ass. I had chosen a little griffin-like creature from one of my favorite Edward Gorey books, *The Unstrung Harp; or, Mr. Earbrass Writes a Novel.* In the story, which details how nauseatingly difficult it is to discipline oneself to sit down and write a book, Mr. Earbrass takes a break from not writing to go to a local curiosity shop. In it, he lingers over my little creature, which has been stuffed and mounted under a glass dome. In the book, the creature is identified as a fantod, which is a Victorian term for being in a state of extreme nervousness or having the horrors. Being subject to high anxiety myself, I was instantly drawn to the concept of having a case of the fantods. What was probably even more notable, had I been clever enough to pay attention, was that I was drawn to the image of a creature trapped inside a bell jar until the end of time.

That first tattoo didn't hurt. It was just a black line drawing on a very fleshy behind. No big deal. The second tattoo Alex and I got about a year later was another story. To commemorate entering our thirties, we decided to get matching tattoos that would be cool but also spoke to us in some way. We made the decision to do this on a whim and showed up at the same tattoo parlor where we got our first tattoos with a T-shirt that had the Wonder Woman logo on it. We told the guy to give both of us that image on our lower backs, having no idea that within a year or two a tat in that spot would be forever known as a tramp stamp, or worse, a Jersey license plate.

Suffice it to say that the lower back is a horribly painful place to get a tattoo. Alex and I both nearly threw up or passed out during the ordeal, but we got through it. Afterward, we stood in the street and kibitzed for a while, but she had to get back home to deal with the kids and I was desperate to get home to lie down and recuperate. Which is exactly what I did for two days until the damn thing healed enough for me to put on clothing without screaming in pain. The end result of all of this craziness was a tattoo that was about twice the size of what I had originally intended to get. Six inches wide and almost three inches high, it was a masterpiece of silliness that most people couldn't identify. Alex and I thought everyone would know the Wonder Woman logo and recognize our pop culture pronouncement of female empowerment. Instead, I was asked on a regular basis if I really liked Van Halen or the World Wrestling Federation.

When I got my first tattoo I was in a panic that my parents not see it because I just didn't want to hear their exclamations of horror and reprobation. But I couldn't help myself and was compelled to show them what I had done. The decision was a mixture of desire to shock and get the business of them finding out when I was in a bathing suit at their pool during the summer over and done with. To my surprise, the people who had raised me in the preppiest way imaginable and who threw up at all things possibly perceived as tacky, trashy, or trendy were totally unfazed. My father's only comment was, "It's your body," and my mother actually examined the little griffin admiringly and floored me by saying, "You go, girl." I don't know which was more surprising, that she understood where I was coming from or that she knew and would use the phrase "You go, girl." Even more surprising was the revelation that I might not have had quite so much to rebel against in the parent department as I thought. When the second tattoo came around, they were equally unconcerned (still flooring me) but did comment on its rather alarming size.

Those tattoos were an important part of my process of breaking with everything that I had been taught to believe was right for me and what I had convinced myself was the right way to behave. So it was no surprise that once Throws Like a Girl was born and my rock-chick persona was forming, all clothing, like what I wore to C.C.'s office to practice, was chosen to display my declaration of war on my former conventional self.

C.C. and I grew closer as the weeks went by. Our conversation moved from chats about musical tastes to deeper discussions about our backgrounds, the life choices we'd made, and whatever issues we were grappling with at the moment. C.C. also had easy insight into my mental state thanks to my outpouring of lyrics about love, heartbreak, and rage, most of which were inspired by Gideon, whom C.C. regarded as a human wrecking ball but who captivated him equally. C.C. understood where I was coming from because he was also drawn to Gideon's charm and magnetism, probably not as much as I was, but it was damned close. Our mutual attraction to and reliance on Gideon led to our questionable but ultimately inevitable decision to ask him to join the band.

C.C. and I had been playing and writing together with only C.C.'s guitar to back us up and we had reached the point where we needed a drummer and bass player and possibly a second guitarist. We turned to Gideon for help, at first only asking for recommendations but then pressing him to step up to the plate himself. We wanted him to play guitar, but Gideon didn't want to; my guess was because he didn't want to play guitar for another band when he had already pledged allegiance to Ritalin Cowboys. He also wisely pointed out that we could live without a second guitar but definitely needed a drummer, a spot he was willing to fill. He had started out as a drummer, not a guitar player, and seemed excited to return to a lost part of his youth. We all agreed on the arrangement and booked a studio for the first time so we could get Gideon behind a drum kit, C.C. plugged in, and me behind a microphone.

To Gideon's infinite surprise, he didn't hate what we were doing. I don't think he was bowled over, but he didn't find us embarrassing or too tragically uncool to play with. Gideon was a born teacher, so the opportunity to instruct both of us on the basics of Rock 101 as well as play with us was too tempting for him to pass up. That first day in the studio went well. Gideon was rested and wasn't high, and any anxiety C.C. and I were experiencing at sharing our first stabs at bandhood went away when Gideon listened to our stuff and then seamlessly joined in with a very basic beat to guide us. That was when we knew for sure that what had been two novices screwing around was going to gel into a real band. C.C. and I were delighted. We stayed delighted through our first few practices with Gideon and were even more pleased when Gideon brought Ira in to play bass.

C.C. and I were less delighted when the two new members of Throws Like a Girl let down their guards and showed us what it was really like to be in a band. When C.C. and I were writing and playing we were polite and had a relatively cerebral approach to our creative output. Once the two maniacs joined us, we were just like every other band that came before us and all of those who came after us: we were in a soul-sucking bottomless pit that drew us further and further down into fighting, drug taking, romantic debacles, and constant threats by one person or another to quit. Gideon's teaching style became increasingly brutal as he got more comfortable with the songs, and he would torture C.C. about his guitar playing by lambasting him for having no rhythm and poor technique. He would then lay into me for not being ballsy enough as a singer and being off-key. He might have initially been right about my moxie quotient, but the accusations of being off-key were untrue and I knew that he was screaming about that just to be mean. That was a tip-off that he had gotten comfortable enough with the band to do blow before he came to practice and occasionally during. I retaliated by writing songs about him that were critical, questioned his intelligence, and basically called him an unredeemable shithead.

There was no doubt in C.C.'s mind or mine that Gideon was as violently nuts with us as he was because of the astounding amount of coke he was doing by that time. Ira was never in Gideon's line of fire, but even he would quietly acknowledge that his pal had gone totally off the reservation and that drugs were a key factor. Whenever C.C. or I would allude to it, Gideon left the room—frequently to do more drugs. For the most part Ira would remain silent during Gideon's diatribes, but as a bass player he couldn't quite keep himself from joining in when Gideon was roughing C.C. up for his guitar playing. C.C. grew to loathe Ira but would put up with it because he was so dead set on the band coming together that he wouldn't sacrifice having a bass player.

When it came to me, Ira's attitude was more embarrassing than if he had joined in with Gideon's taunts. Ira could see that his buddy would frequently have me on the verge of tears in his efforts to dominate and occasionally humiliate me during his more out-of-control drug-soaked days. Ira would shake his head in disgust, easily able to see our growing power struggle in action and displeased with his friend's behavior. Ira, no matter what he looked like, always acted like a gentleman with the women around him. During Gideon's episodes of unleashing on me, Ira would do the unthinkable and silently put a hand on my shoulder as a show of support and comfort. This was beyond horrible. His sympathy validated the fact that I was addicted to being intertwined with someone who had gone from being loving but challenging to a guy who could be so horrendous, and that my tears were not only pathetic but also appropriate.

The studio sessions from hell would generally end with Gideon inexplicably saying that it was a good rehearsal and everyone had done well. C.C. and I would be scratching our heads over Gideon's mood swings and staggering lack of self-knowledge but still allow him to lead us all to a vile bar on Eighth Avenue called Walter's for drinks.

While Throws Like a Girl continued to try to find its voice through the haze of cheap beer and blow that was our steady diet, Ritalin Cowboys used the same sustenance to build itself into a band that had a lengthy playlist (most of which sounded remarkably like the Foo Fighters), which it performed in bars across the city in a steady rotation. The members of Ritalin Cowboys possessed an undying faith that they were eventually going to get heard by the right people and "make it." If by "making it" they meant getting signed as a Foo Fighters cover band available for Bar Mitzvahs and weddings, they were on to something. If not, they were in for a world of disappointment, recriminations, and tears. Added to the challenge of their glaring unoriginality was the constant drug use by all band members except for Ira. This combo made Ritalin Cowboys rehearsals, performances, and social events even more explosive than what Throws Like a Girl had become accustomed to in our own little bubble of crazy. So Ritalin Cowboys was another unstable element in the alchemy of our lives in which Gideon would take refuge when cultivating Throws Like a Girl or our romantic relationship became too difficult for him to put up with.

Ritalin Cowboys was busily creating its reputation as the most coked-up and dysfunctional band performing in New York, and doing an excellent job at it. Throws Like a Girl, on the other hand, was just trying to get itself together enough to play out even once, much less cultivate a reputation, infamous or otherwise. We continued to practice, and C.C.'s sense of rhythm improved, even if the constant haranguing he was subjected to did

make the possibility of his having a stroke a serious reality. I finally stopped crying every time Gideon punctuated our ongoing love-fests by letting loose on me with
a bitchy tirade about my performance and channeled all
that rage into my singing. Miraculously, we started to get
the sound that we were all looking for. Ira, as always, remained unchanged. Gideon's drumming also got better,
but his improvement was sporadic, dictated primarily by
how much time he was spending with Ritalin Cowboys
and how much coke he was doing. On the days when he
would enter the rehearsal studio with his skin a remotely
normal color, cracking jokes and with a spring in his step,
practice went well. When he was ashen with purple and
gray bruises under his eyes, scowling sullenly, or raving
at us, we knew we were in for the worst Gideon had to
offer.

Eventually it was time to try adding another guitar to
the mix to support C.C. Throws Like a Girl spent hours
and hours in the studio, auditioning second guitarists. All
of them were desperate to be Eddie Van Halen and would
come in and play "Eruption" or something equally hackneyed. C.C., Gideon, Ira, and I would exchange glances
and then promptly boot the hapless guitarist from the
room.

One notable example of this exercise in futility was
the hubris-soaked and horribly obnoxious guitarist
whom C.C. met and invited to try out for us on a whim.
There was something almost riveting about how disrespectful that guy was to us, on top of being wildly critical
of the music. As the rudeness and hostility in the room
kept mounting, C.C. was mortified but wasn't up to

single-handedly kicking the guy out of the rehearsal studio. In a surprise move that showed complete solidarity, Ira, C.C., and I solved the problem by turning our backs to the guy and continuing to play while shutting him out. Gideon kept playing without making eye contact even though he was facing C.C.'s hideous acquaintance.

We never did add a new guitar player to the band, partly because of that day. In that moment that we all turned our backs on the outsider and focused on one another, we realized that all we needed to play the songs was each other. It was a beautiful moment. I had a flash of pride because of what I had created, or at least initiated. The band had come into being because of my first phone call to C.C., and I could see that I had been a vital part of creating a cohesive unit. A real band, warts and all. The best part was that I had broken into an arena that I had so badly wanted to be part of but didn't think I could properly join. In that moment I knew I had squarely landed in the life I was aiming for. And not just by joining it but by helping to create part of it.

Aside from dealing with weird guitarists, too many drugs, and interpersonal conflicts aplenty, we spent our time trying to perfect the twelve or so songs we had that were good enough to play and generally working on having a good time together. This proved to be a bit of a challenge, as perfecting the songs was impossible. Each of the guys suffered from his own peculiar brand of OCD, none of which ever allowed for a song to be declared good enough to present to the public. "Fallen," that raw, dirty song about my relationship with Gideon, was the only song that made the grade without difficulty.

With all other songs, we wound up practicing them over and over, listening for just the right moment when C.C.'s solo annoyed Gideon, Gideon's beat didn't match what was in C.C.'s head, or Ira's bass playing was too simple for either Gideon or C.C. to bear. And then the guys would jump all over each other, arguing about a single measure for so long they ate up all the rehearsal time we had paid for.

As for me, I just prayed that we could get through a practice and check at least one more song off our list and label it ready to perform. I also made sure to duck and cover as much as possible, never taking anyone's side but not remaining so neutral as to allow that to constitute a position unto itself. Once in a while we got close to creating a coherent set list, but then Gideon would come to rehearsal all coked up and tear everything we had done to date apart, insisting that we start again because there was no use doing what we were doing unless we were going to do it perfectly. It's no wonder that he drove the rest of us to drugs and drink so effectively.

Which is not to say that there weren't moments of extreme levity, intended or not, during and around band practice. In addition to the original songs C.C. and I had written, Gideon and I wanted to do a few cover tunes just for fun. The guys had agreed to learn "Needle in the Camel's Eye," a Brian Eno song that I loved, which had guitar parts that drove C.C. to distraction as he tried to master them. We kicked around a few other ideas, and one day, possibly under the influence of major narcotics, Gideon and I triumphantly announced the new song we wanted to cover to C.C.

"Dude! We've got it, it's perfect! Let's do 'Hold On Loosely'!"

C.C. looked like he had swallowed a bug. "Are you two talking about covering .38 Special?"

"Yeah, man! It'll be so cool!"

C.C. turned purple and started screaming his head off. "No way! That is, that's just, well . . . that is just disgusting! There is no *way* I'm playing that. If you two want to do that kind of shit, fine. But I'm going to have to quit the band."

Gideon and I were stunned. We had no idea that anyone could have such a violent reaction to a Top 40 hit, much less .38 Special. We cracked up, holding our sides and gasping for air. Normally, C.C. and I were a unified team in band practice as the founders and songwriters of Throws Like a Girl. This was a delicious moment of sharing a band moment with Gideon. Who later suggested covering a Stones tune, a concept that C.C. couldn't find any reason to complain about.

On later reflection, we should have made a serious ruckus about Gideon's song choice. On the surface, covering a Rolling Stones song seems easy, a no-brainer. Based on the blues, easy to simplify, usually crowd pleasers, Stones songs were totally acceptable to both C.C. and me. What we didn't know was that Gideon would pick the one song in the entire Stones catalog that, so it turned out, sucked.

Gideon's Stones tune was the lugubrious "No Expectations." We practiced it over and over with me singing the thing so slowly to stick to Gideon's tempo that it sounded exactly like a dirge. It was awful. It was, however, the way we settled the "Hold On Loosely" issue, so C.C. and I agreed to stick to our attempts to go with Gideon's suggestion and perfect the song. Gideon was an unholy taskmaster. The song was his choice and he wanted it to be the embodiment of all things rock that moved him and made him feel cool. And that would possibly justify the ongoing tightness of his pants and other questionable seventies-inspired sartorial choices. Gideon had us rehearsing endlessly and criticized every bit of C.C.'s and my performances. He wouldn't dream of listening to our suggestions that "No Expectations" might not be the best song for me to sing or us to play in front of other humans, as it might inspire them to slit their own throats. Gideon didn't care and booked us to play it and a few other tunes at 7A. Other than a handful of gigs at Freddy's, this was one of our few big nights out playing for the public. Oh, the humanity.

We started out playing "Needle in the Camel's Eye" as well as "Fallen" and then performed that infernal song. We did it with acoustic guitars, no drums, no bass, and just my voice. I will never forget delivering that performance and watching the faces of the horrified audience. All that C.C. would say about the gig after the fact was that considering that "No Expectations" was the name of the song we had decided to showcase, the audience should have been prepared for what we had to deliver.

Gideon never admitted that his choice had been lousy and that the performance blew. He did, however, elect to remain silent on the subject. A wise choice, considering that C.C. and I took about a week to recover from our dumbstruck horror. Who knows how long it took the audience to recover.

• • •

If Gideon had been all bad, all the time, there is no way that he and I would have stayed together as long as we did. It's true that he was still my passport to a world I hadn't yet fully experienced, nor was I willing to leave it, but his other saving grace was that he had a boundless capacity for romantic love that was unlike anything I had experienced before him. Gideon was a true love junky. He had the ability to be in love with love, which you see so frequently in girls and women but rather infrequently in men. Gideon loved to be touched, be cuddled, and have intimate moments and in-jokes with me. It was that collection of ineffable romantic qualities that Gideon could pull out of his back pocket at exactly the right moment that worked to counterbalance the constantly swaying scales of his personality.

On one side of the scale was the adorably cute love monkey who would feed me from his plate and insist that I sit on his lap while riding the 1 train, and on the other side was the sadistic, drug-addled relationship power broker who either drew strength from my suffering or wrecked me by not bothering to torture me at all. Gideon's romantic allure was as much an intoxicant as

the narcotic residue that had fallen between the cushions of his infamous love couch over the years. When he
was sober or close to it, he would wait for me outside his
apartment, running down the block with open arms to
greet me with a hug that lifted me off the ground so he
could carry me into his apartment. When we were out
with his friends at someone's gig or dancing at a bar, I
knew that if I glanced in his direction he would be riveted
by whatever I was doing. He'd have that wolfish look
about him that simultaneously broadcasted proprietary
instincts as well as his libidinous appetite.

Gideon's intense desire to look after me, even though
he could barely look after himself, was one of his finer
points. He grew alarmed at how thin I had become since
we first met and would order enormous dinners for me
when we went out (I usually paid for both of us but his
heart was in the right place). It was impossible for me
to eat more than a few bites while at the table, because
I was never truly able to banish Andrew from my consciousness entirely, so Gideon would make sure to have
my dinner packed up to go. He'd stash it in his fridge for
me to nosh on later. It was a good move, because I usually did get into those foil-wrapped packages at around
three in the morning when we had finished ravishing
each other and the endorphin rush of sex relaxed me
enough to chew and swallow the falafel or veggie burger
that was waiting for me.

Gideon told me, much later in our relationship, that
his guilt over his philandering and drug taking usually
kept him up too, or at the very least kept his sleep light,

and he would hear me rummaging around in his kitchen for my late-night snacks. I also later found out that his guilt forced him to conclude that while I might have been having a light nosh, it was also entirely possible that I was searching his kitchen drawers for lighter fluid and a match with which to incinerate him in his bed. The poor guy had to lay off the Farrah Fawcett movies. Setting him aflame for his misdeeds never occurred to me, but the idea that he was up nights sweating it out over whether or not we were going to wind up on the front page of the *Post* with a headline like TRAGIC LOVE AFFAIR HEATS UP later caused me a twinge of sadness. The reality was that I loved him too much to ever do damage to him, much less incinerate him. As much as Gideon tried to be sweet to me, I reciprocated the best I could. I always took him out to dinner, spent time with him if he was feeling needy even if it was precarious for me, and would lull him to sleep by speaking to him in French, which he curiously loved. I even took him on vacation to a beach resort when I felt he was spinning too far out of control and needed a break.

In spite of our tender feelings toward each other, Gideon never stopped flagrantly sexing it up with the other members of the motley crew that constituted his harem and coking himself up into a state of insouciant malice regarding me, specifically my unwillingness to succumb to his will completely and renounce any part of the life I had had prior to meeting him. Including Andrew. I had suffered through several indignities at Gideon's hands as a result of his aggravation and was so angry that I finally wanted to retaliate.

The opportunity to do so arose when, for the ump-
teenth time, Gideon badgered me about having anal sex
with him. I was not interested. Even if doing it had been
up my alley, I knew that I would never do it with Gideon
in a million years. It doesn't take a lot of thought to come
to the obvious conclusion that anal sex is rife with power
dynamics and the need to trust the person with whom
you're doing it. Gideon's behavior with other women certainly didn't inspire trust, and as we were already locked
in a power struggle I saw no need to act it out further on
my body. Not a fun night at home. I would say so repeat-
edly, and Gideon's persistence in the face of my protests
confirmed my feeling that he was becoming obsessed
with finding a new way to try to dominate me. I had to
find a way to communicate that while I was undeniably in
his thrall, this kind of sub/dom crap would not fly.

After one of his endless obnoxious demands to violate
my ass, I decided to shut the whole thing down by saying
I'd do it. Gideon couldn't believe his ears. He was so glee-
ful he was practically rubbing his hands together. I did,
however, say that there was one condition. That didn't
faze him.

"Okay, what is it?"

"If you want to do it to me, I've got to do it to you
first. Fair's fair."

That stopped him in his tracks. He hadn't seen that
coming. Gideon considered it and asked, "How exactly
do you propose to do that?"

"You know, the usual way. I'll get the necessary equipment, dildo, lube, what have you, and you'll just, you
know, go first."

I was trying to sound incredibly nonchalant while I was spinning my web. Gideon flew right into it.

"Okay, fine. If you really want to do that, I'll do it. But you're definitely doing it too, right?"

"Yup."

"You know you'll never get all that stuff. You won't go out and buy it."

"You're sounding like you don't want to do it now. Is that a challenge? Want to see me come home with everything needed for a night of Bend Over Boyfriend 101? No problem, baby."

"I'll believe it when I see it."

Several weeks passed before I went to a nonthreatening girl-friendly sex shop downtown and purchased everything I said I would. Just enough time had gone by for Gideon to back-burner the issue. It was a perfect time to spring my new loot on him. One evening while we were cuddled up on his couch, I announced that I had what we needed to get the ass show on the road. Gideon had a look of total disbelief glued to his face. Apparently, he really hadn't thought that I'd be up to the task. Surprise!

I poked him in the chest and said, "Are you ready? Want to go for it?"

Gideon looked like a trapped rabbit. He knew that this was the only way to get what he wanted, but he wasn't going to like one minute of it. Even so, he was hell-bent on his mission and finally relented. He responded with bravado, trying to cover up his apprehension and seemingly hoping that if he readily agreed I'd be the one to back out, too grossed out by the whole thing to really go through with it.

"You don't really have a dildo here."

"Oh yes I do. It's go time, baby. Now or never."

Gideon paused for another second and said, "Let me see it."

I crossed the room and picked up the tote bag I carried every day. Nothing scary looking yet. I put the bag on the couch and pulled a plastic bag out of it. When Gideon saw the outlines of my booty through the plastic, he blanched but remained resolute.

"Okay, let's do it."

Gideon was a champ. For someone who professed never to have done it before, there was no whining or carrying on. He took it like a man while behind him I was in a total state. Part of me was laughing hysterically because I knew that this person who had made me so angry with his needling desire to get the best of me was in the last situation on earth he wanted to be in. Another part of me was intrigued, a little grossed out, and a little turned on by both the act and the undeniable sense of power it gave me. And another part of me was having an out-of-body experience, looking at myself from a few feet away, not unlike the day I first met Gideon, and was thinking, *You are* not *doing this! Gross! Who* are *you? What the hell, Jessica, is this the new you?*

That night, it was.

I did get a little nervous at one point when Gideon had been silent a little too long while I had him on his knees. I asked, "Are you all right?"

"Mmm-hmmm."

"Do you want me to stop?"

He shook his head no.

I paused and asked what hadn't occurred to me until that moment.

"Do you *like* it?"

And in the teeniest voice imaginable, Gideon replied, "I don't know."

Well, at least he was honest. I had expected an indignant "*No!*" Kudos to Gideon for considering the question seriously while in the midst of his own personal purgatory, if not hell.

That was all I needed to hear. The session was over.

Not a week had gone by after the jolly rodgering, and Gideon was ready to claim his prize. We had been sweetly canoodling in his bed, laughing, kissing, and lovingly teasing each other as we did whenever we were feeling particularly connected. Gideon chose that moment to say, "Your turn."

"My turn what?"

"You know. Come on, honey, don't pretend you don't know what I'm talking about. The time has come for you to give up the ass. Get that tush over here."

"No." I remained resolutely lying on my back, no ingress on offer. I was practically hugging the side of the bed to anchor myself.

Gideon's face flashed confusion, disbelief, anger, confusion again, and finally shock at me. "Oh my God. You are not going to back out of this. You promised. You promised!"

I tried to remain nonchalant while keeping my back

glued to the mattress, edging away in case I'd have to make a run for it. "Well, I reconsidered. And I don't think it's for me."

"I let you stick that fucking thing up my ass and now that it's your turn it's not for you? That is bullshit!"

"Yeah. I don't think I'm going to like it."

"You told me you've done it before! You can't say you're not going to like it *now*! That is a total lie. You're a liar. You fucking suck."

Gideon pouted and threw himself back down on the bed. We lay there in silence, him fuming and me holding my breath waiting to hear what he would come up with next.

"Okay, how about just the tip?"

"Gideon! I'm not bargaining! Not going to happen!"

My changeup of the balance of power for the time being was a success. It turned the tables on Gideon and let him know without a shadow of a doubt that while I put up with a lot of his bad behavior just to be with him, there were limits to what I could take. Mess with the bull, get the horns. I'm not proud of my Br'er Rabbit moment, but under the circumstances and in light of my desire to stay with him, I felt a lesson had to be taught.

Even though I had had that victory, it had a whiff of the pyrrhic about it. Gideon had gotten my message loud and clear but dug in his heels and didn't change his behavior. I vacillated between harboring an overwhelming need to scream at him while shaking him until his teeth rattled for his growing dedication to drugs and flaunted sex, and still being physically drawn to him. Sometimes I even slipped back into adoring him. Gideon was like the little girl with the little curl right in the middle of her forehead. When he was good he was very good, and when he was bad he was horrid. The way in which he was bad was consistent, but the sting never got old. But the ways in which he was good were unpredictable and occasionally so arrestingly sweet as to wipe all the emotional gunk he spattered on me from my mind.

Gideon would disarm me by stopping band practice to get out from behind the drum kit, walk over to me, and kiss me passionately when I sang something the way he thought it should be done. Those open displays of affection wrecked me. He took a tour of my high school, which I held very dear, just so he could get a glimpse into a part of my past that he never would have understood otherwise. But the most killing sign of his love for me and dedication to being with me was his obvious pride when we would go out with Ritalin Cowboys or any other cronies of his. Gideon would wrap his arm around my waist and announce to anyone who was within earshot that I was with him. He loved having me greet his friends warmly and with all the good grace that had been drummed into me by my parents and high school–cum–finishing school. Gideon wanted to show that he could hook a bigger and better fish than anyone else, even if that fish came with serious complications.

My complications at home weren't getting any easier to manage as my relationship with Gideon became more enmeshed and surreal. Even during crazy episodes like the Bend Over Boyfriend debacle or the obsessive songwriting or the sex that shockingly turned into lovemaking, Andrew wasn't far from my thoughts. He was a specter who drifted in and out of my consciousness with the same ineffectual wispiness with which he drifted in and out of our apartment and our life. I was staying at Gideon's overnight with great regularity, and I'd stopped going to movies with Andrew or doing anything fun on the weekends because all my time was spent in rehearsal studios or Gideon's apartment. On the weekends I'd wake up so late and hungover from the partying we were doing that there wasn't any time to make plans with Andrew, much less follow through on them.

And throughout all of this outrageous behavior, Andrew still said nothing about the root of the mayhem I was bringing into our apartment and our marriage. He would comment on my exhaustion, inquire into when the band would finally perform, and make occasional suggestions about things we might do together, but he never said anything along the lines of, "You are obviously partying too hard and sleeping elsewhere, which usually means someone else's bed. What the fuck?" I never got a hint of "What the fuck?" from Andrew, which mystified not only me, but Gideon as well. He couldn't understand why Andrew wasn't staking his claim. Gideon would announce that if I were his wife he would lock down my behavior in seconds flat. While I doubted he could, he still had a good point.

Although they didn't seem related at all on the surface, my activities with Gideon were nearly identical to those with Andrew. I was pushing the boundaries of what I had heretofore considered acceptable with both of them.

With Gideon I was out on a limb in the most visible way, engaging in illicit and licentious behavior that not only violated codes I had once held dear but codes that were considered the societal norm. With Andrew, I was pushing the boundaries of what he could stand in a relationship in order to see what it would take for him to stand up and fight for me. I was also exploring and pushing the boundaries of what it meant to me to be a wife. Was I still a wife if I was in love with and sleeping with someone else? Was I still a wife if I was lying to my husband? Without any answers to those questions, I lived our life together on a day-to-day basis, hoping for the best and praying that nothing too revealing would raise its head, forcing us to confront the mess that dare not speak its name. As for Andrew, he definitely stayed mum, and while I could guess what his reasons might be, I definitely didn't have an answer.

In keeping with things that dare not speak their name, there was another boundary that I tried to push, but it was one of the few areas of rebellion in which I failed miserably. It had come to my attention that Liesl, hanger-on of Ritalin Cowboys and best friend of Morgan, had a crush on me. Gideon had told me about her affections but I didn't believe him. There was no way that she could have a thing for me. Liesl prided herself on being able to get straight girls to have sex with her but she knew that I was besotted with Gideon; I couldn't fathom how she could get it into her head that I would be a reasonable target for her affections and advances. What I hadn't taken into account was that she was roughly twenty-two years old and had enough bravado to believe she had the power to achieve anything she set her mind to. Liesl was a living embodiment of Nietzsche's will to power. She would shower me with gifts (the most effective ones were Edward Gorey books signed by the man himself) and spend hours and hours talking to me. She was funny and smart and constantly making fun of me for embodying so many clichéd Jewish yenta proclivities and would have me on the floor every time she teased me. Her jibes were situational so I can't recall any of her best bons mots, but she would very likely come up with something like:

"Growing up, my house smelled like bread baking. My mother baked all the time. What did your house smell like?"

I'd absentmindedly tell her the truth and say something like, "Cigarettes and mothballs."

Without missing a beat, Liesl's answer would be, "So you're Jewish?"

And I'd be on the floor, laughing my head off at this girl of nearly indeterminate gender who had the face of an angel, the body of a teamster, and the sense of humor of a regular on Grossinger's main stage.

Even with her relatively effective wooing, I naively managed to miss where she was going with her efforts. I thought her woo was all about girly friendship like the kind I had enjoyed in high school. Liesl must have been dying, because my obliviousness finally forced her hand and things came to a head one night outside of Meow Mix. Ritalin Cowboys was playing the lesbian bar because the band members were tight with the bartenders, so Liesl and her posse were there in full force. The packed bar was deafeningly loud and so hot that everyone had started peeling off whatever layers they could before they got down to underwear. Rather than get naked, I stepped outside with Liesl, Lydia, Morgan, and a few others whose faces I recall and whose names are long gone. Liesl grabbed me by the shoulders and from seven inches above me loudly announced that she was going to kiss me, and then I'd see that I could get into kissing a girl just as much as a boy. I rolled my eyes and laughed at her.

In the chaos that was my life, there were only a few things I was still sure of. One of them was that I had no penchant for pussy. But in Liesl's mind it was a misguided conclusion that was begging to be rectified. I shrugged my shoulders and told her to give it her best shot. In a flash, Liesl picked me up, plonked me on top of a mailbox that was conveniently waiting on the corner for this moment, and smoothly stepped forward to press herself into the mailbox while grabbing the back of my neck to steady me as she went in for the kill. The kiss was nice. Not too wet, not too tonguey, soft lips, fine breath, everything one would hope for with a first kiss. Except for the sad fact that I was mentally going through the contents of my closet while Liesl was giving it her best shot; I wondered if I needed to buy new boots for the fall and if Barneys was having any sales yet. Even though I was cataloging my wardrobe I still kissed Liesl back, trying to be a sport and take her challenge seriously. I pushed my shoe fetish to the side, wrapped my arms around her neck, and tried to pull her in even tighter.

That must have been the last straw for my poor friend. She broke out of my grip and stopped kissing me so suddenly it took a second to register that I wasn't still being kissed. Sort of like when you're on an amusement park ride that makes you so dizzy you have no idea if the ride is still going on or if your internal gyroscope is so fucked you haven't realized yet that it's long over.

"Jones. That was the worst kiss ever. You weren't kidding."

This entire performance and exchange had been witnessed by our crowd, and, unbeknownst to me, Gideon had come outside just in time to see the tail end of the kiss. Everyone else was hooting and having fun with the spectacle and Gideon laughed along. At the end of the night, when Liesl let me go and Gideon and I were in a cab on the way back to his place, his only comment was, "You didn't have to kiss her back like *that*."

Gideon's insecurity at that kiss, or any contact I might have with anybody other than him, became just as oppressive as his constant drug use, crankiness, bossiness in the rehearsal studio, and the newest addition to his repertoire: relentlessly demanding that I end my marriage so I could be with him properly. He swore up and down that if I divorced Andrew he would be the model of fidelity and the intensity of his love for me would never fade. This would have been intoxicating if he didn't keep insisting that I throw my wedding ring in the East River as a symbol of my intent to be his and his alone. That was never going to happen. My attachment to Andrew, or at least our history, whether it was being expressed in a sane way at the time or not, would never allow me to throw away one of the most important reminders of our relationship.

Gideon had another kind of insecurity that I had no

knowledge of until one special night when a window into his psyche opened and a gale-force level of crazy blew into the room.

I was either claiming a late band practice or some other arrangement had been made with Andrew, but I was sleeping over at Gideon's, as I had been for some time. Normally, when a man and woman spoon in bed the guy is on the outside because he's bigger and it's easier to wrap a big person around a smaller person. Not a complicated concept to grasp. With Gideon, the normal rules of spooning did not apply. He always wanted to be the inside spoon even though he was about a foot taller than me. I deduced, as anyone would, that he wanted to be cuddled because it is very nice and cozy. I also deduced that he orchestrated this arrangement so he could have things his way, because once he was asleep he was like a dead man and there was no switching things up. That night, we went to bed and had coke-free sex that was very nice, sweet, and loving, and everything seemed normal. Which was not normal. But I wasn't going to second-guess an evening of good fortune. We spooned for a little while in the customary Gideon way, and then I got up to get something to eat. I finished eating my leftovers and got back in bed, settling in to lie on my back. Gideon wasn't fully asleep and could tell that I wasn't cuddled up next to him. He grabbed my arm, pulling me over onto my side with my left arm awkwardly hovering above him, and in a complaining, whiny voice instructed me to "hold the baby."

I lay there in the dark with my eyes popping out of

my head and mouth open, dying for someone else to be in the room to confirm what I had just heard. Hold the baby? What the fuck was that? Was I supposed to be Mommy? Was Gideon even aware he had said it? Was he the baby? Was it a joke? I lay there in a rigor, too disturbed by this new nugget of dementia to settle down to sleep holding him and too curious about where he was going with this request to let it go. I figured I had to play along a little to get to the bottom of whatever the hell was happening.

"You want me to hold the baby, honey?"

"Yes." This was delivered in a pouty voice. Gagness.

He pulled me closer to him, tucking my arm around his body and pressing his back into my stomach until we were wrapped together in a vise grip. It was abundantly clear to me that Gideon was the baby in this scenario, I was the caretaker (God forbid, I might actually be the mother), and in his half-waking haze Gideon had just revealed what was most certainly the source of his penchant for blow, women, and adulation from any audience who would watch him play. Gideon, like most attention-seeking, self-medicating narcissists (my diagnosis came from the DSM-IV, which I did actually consult), wanted the love he hadn't gotten enough of as a child and was spending his life trying to find it using anything or anyone who could give it to him. Hold the baby, indeed.

It was this openly stated declaration of codependence from Gideon that made me take a hard look at where I was in my life, my relationship, and what I was doing. Was I with Gideon because he was the One? Was I with him because Andrew had driven me away with his particular brand of dispassion and I had simply thrown myself at the first person who made me want to jump his bones? Was I with Gideon merely because I had never taken a walk on the wild side and needed to now with a vengeance? Was it that I needed to grow and there was no way to do it in a relationship that had started when I was eighteen and hadn't substantively altered its dynamic since? They were good questions. And I was horrified that no matter how hard I tried or what I did, I still wasn't able to answer these basic questions that had been chasing me for so long. Any answers I came up with were about as deep as the offerings of a Magic 8 Ball. "Should I return to the life I had before?" "Ask again later." "Is Gideon really my one true love?" "Cannot predict now." "Am I still totally confounded and royally fucked?" "It is certain." The thing was that before the "hold the baby" incident, I still felt like I was on a ride worth experiencing. After our codependence became so clear to me, Gideon was just a little less sexy, and my need to know where I was headed seemed much more crucial.

I knew that there was no way on earth to get answers without talking to Andrew, the essential task that I now dimly knew I should have done earlier, before things had reached this horrible point and I became unhinged. I prayed that Andrew would be willing to finally talk about the elephant in the room, but there was no avoiding that he'd be upset and I still couldn't bear to see him in that state. Which accounts for why I had been playing around like such a libertine and then hiding out at

Gideon's underground lair, ensuring that I wouldn't have to face the music, much less Andrew's tear-stained face. The fact is that I was terrified of hurting Andrew but also of being wounded by whatever his reaction would be, be that tears, screaming, instant rejection, whatever. It's not quite fair to fear someone's rejection when you're in the midst of rejecting that very person yourself, but that's how I felt. Like so much of this increasingly mad situation, every emotion I had was circular like that. Both my emotional life and the things I chose to do wound up making me feel like I was a snake biting its own tail.

In a surprising show of insight, Gideon finally forcibly ejected me from his apartment so I could go home to sort things out. He couldn't take the ambiguity of the situation anymore and wanted me to be with him or to call the whole thing off. It sounds more thought-out than it was. He basically just freaked out one day when I couldn't tell him what I planned to do, and ordered me to stop avoiding making decisions and hiding out at his place and deal with my life. My life with Gideon had been effectively suspended and my life with Andrew was about to be placed center stage. Panic doesn't even begin to describe how I felt. I had been rejected by my lifeline to love, sex, and the magic of a crazy louche life. I had to go back to Andrew and deal with our horror show if there was any chance of getting back to Gideon. If that was what I was going to do after Andrew and I spoke. I left Gideon's, got on the bus, and was on my way back to the land of functional people to deal with what was really going on with someone who could form coherent sentences, didn't refer to himself as "the baby," and had a legitimate beef with me.

While riding the subway, I mentally consulted my Magic 8 Ball about how this was all going to turn out. The answer that came to me was predictably disheartening. "Outlook not so good."

9

KLONOPIN LUNCH

Being cut off from Gideon was hell on earth. I immediately turned to C.C. for support and guidance. He asked me for a full status report; he needed to know exactly how I was feeling. I mustered up something along the lines of, "It's like the heartbreak of psoriasis, only mentally." C.C. understood completely. His remedy was a fistful of orange painkillers he had filched from his grandmother's medicine cabinet and listening to Buddy Holly until I was singing "Peggy Sue" in my sleep.

We also spent some time writing new songs and recording them using the setup that C.C. had put together on his computer. We made more progress working that way than we did in the studio, particularly because Gideon's drumming and attendance had become increasingly spotty. I hadn't given Gideon the answer he wanted (agreement that I would throw my ring into the river and divorce my husband immediately), so he spent his time giving me a full-on seventh-grade cold shoulder. I knew that it was just more impulsive and childish behavior from him, but it still hurt. Horribly.

Poor C.C.; during every rehearsal and every songwriting session all I could talk about was how much I missed Gideon. I talked about it nonstop. C.C. was a champ. He tolerated it all, probably hoping for some good lyrics to come out of the mess (they did), and managed not to throw me out the window of his loft when I started crying about how Gideon smelled like sugar cookies and I couldn't bear not smelling him. I would apologize for my histrionics over and over again, and C.C. would always brush off my embarrassment at being such a nut by saying something like, "You have a right to be crazy. You live in New York. That's why you stay. That's why we all stay." He would listen to more of my boo-hooing; silently hand me an orange pill, a white pill, or a joint; or just hold my hand and wait for me to calm down.

Throws Like a Girl forged ahead, with or without Gideon and Ira's participation. If Gideon didn't show up, neither did Ira, but he annoyed C.C. so deeply his absence was a blessing. C.C. and I kept going with the band because when we were together we had fun. It was as simple as that. We enjoyed each other's company and each of us always understood where the other was coming from. It was also a relief for me to hang out with C.C. because even though he knew everything that was going on between Gideon and me, he was nevertheless an oasis of nonjudgmental friendship. It was in that environment that Throws Like a Girl began to blossom. C.C. and I were more relaxed when it was just the two of us and we were in a craze of songwriting. C.C. was always happy just to play guitar and compose, but for me the songwriting was a catharsis. Everything that was bothering me, confusing me, and turning me on went into my lyrics and each song was like a teeny tiny exorcism. Sometimes the little demons would come back, but the songs were an excellent way to keep shooing them away.

Even though he was squarely behind me with my songwriting efforts and the results of my little exorcisms, C.C. finally admitted that he was more than just marginally worried about me. He delicately pointed out that it was a little alarming that every song I wrote was so very dark. C.C. expressed his concern in the normal way that people do, trying to have a coherent conversation, but didn't get the response from me that he was looking for. So my friend tried another approach. He tried to jolt me out of the downward spiral he suspected me of being caught in through the music.

C.C. challenged me to write a happy song, knowing I'd rise to the bait if he said I couldn't do it. I wrote that song just to show C.C. that I could do anything I was asked to, and better than expected. It was also a great assignment and I knew it. C.C. was a terrific amateur psychologist because that song told him everything he needed to know about my mental state and general well-being. Like all the other lyrics I wrote, it said what I was feeling but hadn't realized until the song came out.

I was on a plane on my way to visit relatives in Florida and had forgotten to bring a book with me when inspiration hit. I asked the flight attendant for a few cocktail napkins and wrote the whole thing in one try. I brought it back to C.C. after I returned from Florida to see what he thought. Being C.C., he loved that the song was on cocktail napkins, showing that I had written when the time was right, not because I was dutifully fulfilling an assignment. He read the napkins carefully and smiled. We set it to a boppy ska riff and my dear, loyal friend knew that I was going to be all right no matter how things looked at that moment when he heard me sing what we'd always call "The Happy Song." The opening lyrics said it all:

> *Breaking through the haze, breaking through*
> * the haze of a polluted day*
> *breathing in deep, breathing in deep, like a girl*
> * set free*
> *looks like things have changed, changed for the*
> * better, looks like things have changed.*
> *But they haven't. The only thing that's changed*
> * is me.*

After Gideon kicked me out, I went back to living at the loft full-time with Andrew. We had not yet discussed anything that needed to be dragged out into the light, and I tried to keep it together enough to go to work and speak in full sentences. Andrew and I were polite with each other, occasionally even loving, and slept in the same bed, as we always did when I wasn't at Gideon's. I was living in bizarro world and so was Andrew, but it was easier than having the Talk, so we carried on. It was hard not to be weepy about Gideon while at home, and when I did mope and cry Andrew didn't ask much about it. Being one of the smartest people I know, there's no way Andrew couldn't figure out that my full-time return to the loft must have been the result of some kind of tiff with Gideon. But he didn't press me on what was going on. I guessed that he was using the time to gather his own senses too and figure out what he wanted out of our sudden reunion.

We tiptoed on eggshells while we tried to get our bearings. Even so, the signs of imminent doom were always around us. During my time back at the loft, my engagement ring, which I hadn't taken off since the day it was put on my finger, broke. One prong came off and the center diamond was in constant peril of tumbling out of the setting. Rather than fix the ring, I put it in a drawer and didn't mention it again. I also stopped wearing my wedding ring on a regular basis. I wasn't going to chuck it into the East River, but I didn't feel right wearing it. I knew that I lied to Andrew every day, but those lies felt ephemeral because they were just words or the absence of words. But wearing that ring was a tangible lie. Wearing it made me feel like I was wearing a sandwich board that had LIAR written on one side and CHEATING FRAUD on the other. I claimed that my weight loss had made the ring too loose to wear safely. Andrew didn't comment. His only comment was a silent protest of keeping his ring firmly on his left hand.

Both Andrew and Gideon, and my efforts to deal with them, were overwhelming reminders of the crap my life had become. Or, more accurately, the crap I had made of my life. I couldn't bring myself to commit to Gideon because he was such an obvious loose cannon and I had always valued security in my relationships. There was no way that he could give me that. I was addicted to him but seriously doubted that he could go the distance with me, and I wasn't ready to take a flying leap into his arms only to have him catch me, then drop me on my head. I couldn't recommit to the life I had led prior to that first fated guitar lesson because now that I had rebelled I saw that there were so many more options for me than the ones I had chosen before meeting Gideon. Andrew was tied to all of those old decisions, so he was also a dubious choice. I had acquired a coterie of "friends" through Gideon who constituted the majority of the people I hung out with because many of my old friends were a little too thrown by the new me to deal with what I brought to the table. But these new people were not exactly what I would have previously referred to as "people." I would not-so-infrequently catch them eyeing each other if I used a word that exceeded two syllables. That was a quick lesson in "better to be alone than in heavily drugged and volatile company." As for the heavy snowstorm of drugs that blew around me, I felt like that woman in the famous Dorothea Lange photograph "Woman of the High Plains" who is staring out into the distance in the dust bowl of the Texas panhandle, watching her farm blow away. But instead of dry dirt and debris swirling up into my face to blind me, I had a flurry of cocaine and its supplicants to contend with.

Every day at Rook was an exercise in self-control. Not only was it enormously difficult to concentrate on whether or not it was a good idea to solicit American

Airlines as a potential client for a custom-published magazine, but Rook was a mere eight blocks from where
Gideon worked. I had definitely not decided if I should
stay or I should go, and Gideon was still too wounded,
angry, pissed off, or high to contact me. Whatever the
reason was, he remained incommunicado. I missed him
so terribly I was willing to take him any way he was at
that moment; coked up asshole or weepy "hold the baby"
boy, both versions were fine with me. I tried sticking to
the program of making a best effort to decide what my
fate should be, but just as Gideon was increasingly obviously addicted to blow, I was hooked on him. Over the
course of the next week or so, my lunchtime walks had
me edging closer and closer to Gideon's workplace in the
hope of running into him and pretending that I was only
there to get a slice at the pizza place on his corner.

My strategy for getting to Gideon was totally silly. It
was essentially to behave like a particularly bold pigeon
(the actual metaphor that I used at the time) desperate to get at a slightly chewed bit of hot dog that had
been tossed into the street but that seemed so elusive
as cars whizzed past and over it. I was willing to take a
flying leap (or flap) to get at what I wanted (just to be
clear, Gideon was the hot dog in this situation, which
as a vegan would have disturbed him greatly, but the
other obvious association would have pleased him, so
hot dog he was) but had no assurance that if I went
for it I wouldn't be flattened by a fast-moving vehi-
cle. I decided that I was willing to risk the flattening if
there was a chance that I could take a peck at the tasty

snack that was lounging there in the gutter, taunting and tantalizing me.

I finally stopped hovering around Joe's Pizza and made it down the street to Gideon's workplace. The bell jingled as I entered the guitar shop and all eyes were on me, including Gideon's, as I perspired my way over to him. It was like high noon at the O.K. Corral.

"Hey, Gideon."

"Hello. What can I help you with?"

Oh Jesus. Was he really going to treat me like a customer? This was too stupid to be believed.

"I'd like twenty guitar picks and to speak to you. Outside."

"I'm sorry. I'm not on my break right now." He counted out twenty picks, put them in a bag, and handed them to me. My eyes welled up. I leaned in to speak to him and caught a whiff of sugar cookie. That was it. The pigeon was flattened. Oh help.

"Please. Come. Outside. Now. Or I will cry in the store. Loudly."

Gideon knew this wasn't an idle threat and told the guy behind the register that he'd just be a minute. We left the store and stood on the sidewalk facing each other, saying nothing. I broke first.

"Oh come on. Please. You can't expect me to just change everything in my life all at once for you while you're fucking everyone else in Manhattan and being mean to me! I want to be with you. You know I want to be with you. Meet me halfway! Do something to show me that you really want to put me first!"

"I told you what I want you to do. Throw the ring in

the river with me. If you do that, we can talk." He was aggressive, dismissive, and already looking inside the store to see what was going on in his absence.

"If I do that *we can talk*? That isn't fair. That just isn't fair. You want me to reassure you completely and you're barely giving me a thread to hang on to."

"Those are my conditions. I'm getting sick of this anyway." Gideon was twitchy and gray, nervously smoking a cigarette and darting his eyes up and down the block. It dawned on me that he was tweaking. Gideon had just taken a load of coke or speed or whatever, and his behavior was in some way affected by what he'd snorted, most likely in the bathroom of the store moments before my arrival. Great.

"You're getting sick of me? Fine, I'm getting sick of you. I'm sick of you being so fucking high all the time. You think I don't know what's going on here?" I was shrill and hysterical. What was I doing? Why was I fighting to be with this guy? He was a mess and nasty. Even so, standing next to him I still wanted to pounce on him. I was the bigger mess of the two of us. He at least had the excuse of being fucked-up on drugs. I was just mental. I wasn't willing to say die, even though I was fighting for a husk of a man who cared more about his next score than me or anyone else. It was in that moment that I realized he was an addict. And I wanted him all the more because now I felt sorry for him. I could save him and make him the most loving, exciting, sexy, but still stable version of himself and be happy with him forever.

Gideon flicked his cigarette into the street. "Why don't you just get out of here? I'm sick of you, I'm sick of this shit, I'm sick of you being around but not being around. I'm sick of your little band. It's all shit. Just walk back to your fancy office and go where you belong."

I stood stock still during this invective of bile, not knowing how to respond or what to do. I was frozen, not aware that I was holding my breath until Gideon went back into the store, leaving me on the sidewalk for his coworkers to gawk at through the front window. I hadn't seen this coming. I knew he might not be interested in talking to me, but the intensity of the venom he had spewed at me was not anything I had expected. I kept holding my breath until I was out of eye- and earshot of the store and finally let out a deep shuddering sigh, followed by an intake of breath that was equally shaky and terminated in a sob so loud I shocked myself. The tears came next, then the hysteria. And so it came to be that I was aimlessly walking around Chelsea and then the Village, sobbing and blindly searching for somewhere to go where nobody would wonder why a sobbing, snotty mess of a woman was in their establishment and how to get her the hell out.

A moment of clarity descended on me and I fished my cell phone out of my bag to call Edward, who lived in the area. He was perfect. I have no memory of why I knew he would be at home at that time of day but I was sure of it, so I rang him. When he answered, I was sobbing so uncontrollably he couldn't make any sense of what I was saying. Eventually I got to the crazy hiccupping stage of crying and managed to stutter out that Gideon had been horrible to me and that I didn't know what to do and that I loved him and that I couldn't live without him but I couldn't just leave Andrew and that I was freaking out and I was alone in the street and I couldn't go back to my office in this condition. That was delivered all in one breath. Edward remained silent throughout my rambling and said the only reasonable thing possible under the circumstances.

"Come over, I'll make you lunch."

It *was* lunchtime. I had left the office to go to lunch, even if my lunch was supposed to be spent talking to Gideon. This was a good idea. Edward would make it all better.

I arrived at Edward's apartment building, entered the vestibule, rang the doorbell, and was immediately buzzed through the second set of doors and up to the second floor. He was waiting for me in the open doorway to his apartment, smiling. I tearily asked him, "Are you sitting down for this one?"

With his usual pitch-perfect timing, Edward replied, "Actually, I've been lying down. I've been lying down for the past fourteen years because I never know what's going to come out of your mouth. Come in."

But when he saw the tragic expression on my face he switched from arch world-weariness to a sympathetic frowny expression with his arms outstretched. When we were in college, if I was indulging in a particularly gigantic pity party, Edward would put me on his lap and say something along the lines of, "Woozah, woozah, woozah, you are going to be just fine. You are so strong. You are so brave. If I were you, I would be nothing but a quivering lump of marmalade." Embarrassingly, it always helped. Edward folded me in his arms and delivered this tried-and-true speech. I knew what he was saying was absolutely untrue and if he had been in my shoes none of this would have happened in the first place, but I was so glad to be on the receiving end of his show of love that I wasn't going to quibble.

I snuffled into his shirt and tried to explain what had happened. We stayed in the hallway while I told him about Gideon wanting me to pledge allegiance to the flag of his crazy, that I felt horrible about Andrew, that Gideon was clearly so far into drugs that he couldn't be counted on to act like a normal person at any given moment, and that despite everything I knew to be good and right, I still loved him. So there was no doubt that I was crazy too. I also wept into Edward's sleeve that I couldn't bring myself to live without Gideon, nor could I imagine life without Andrew, so I was stuck between two men with no idea about what to do.

I let Edward lead me into the dining room and started to laugh when I saw what he had done to prepare for our lunch. He is truly high WASP, so I was expecting a sliver of ham and a few peas if I was lucky; maybe he'd whip up some chipped beef on toast if he really wanted to kick it old-school. I wasn't wrong about the food. It was the rest of the setup that was so brilliant.

One of Edward's best qualities was that he always had a flair for the dramatic and the ridiculous. Any outfit he assembled for himself was always just a little over the top, not so much as to be insane, but just enough to be noticeable and puckish. He had a perfectly put-together living room filled with furniture that had been handed down through his family, but his throw pillows had dogs on them because his partner was allergic to them and this was Edward's silent protest that a dog should be a part of their life. On this particular occasion, Edward's unerring dramatic touch was put to use to such perfect effect that I will never forget it. That lunch cut right to the chase.

His gorgeous dining table, polished to a mirrored shine, had two place settings that were so elaborate Edward would not have been caught out had the queen mum herself decided to make a surprise appearance. He had laid out every silver utensil—forks (from appetizer to fish to dinner and beyond), knives, and spoons—that the most formal dinner party could ever call for. A full complement of the finest china had been pulled out of the sideboard for the occasion as well. I remember a soup plate stacked on top of a dinner plate, with a lunch plate and a butter plate off to the side. I'm sure I have some of it wrong, but I know Edward so I know it was *perfect*. The crystal was out too, all lined up: water goblet, white wine glass, red wine glass, and so on. Edward was going to make me feel better and there was no way that could happen if we were eating off of Chinet.

The water goblet was filled, and the white wine glass held a generous pour of chilled Chablis. All the other glasses were empty. The soup plate held a perfect portion of warmed-up right-out-of-the-can Campbell's tomato soup, and on the lunch plate was a classic white bread and

Kraft American cheese grilled cheese sandwich. On the butter plate, instead of a roll and pat of butter, Edward had supplied the one and only thing that ensured that the day could and would get better. This was the kicker, the ace up his sleeve. Along with all the comfort food he had thoughtfully prepared, he had also provided a cheerful little blue pill. It was a Klonopin, and it held all the magic of Willy Wonka's everlasting gobstopper or Neo's red pill that would free him from the tyranny of the Matrix. That Klonopin would take me from crazy, sobbing love slave to calm, introspective person who could listen to what Edward had to say.

Edward chatted away about nothing terribly memorable while I ate the school cafeteria food, and then I downed the Klonopin with the Chablis. Within no more than ten minutes, my tears had dried and I was as calm and cool as if I had just spent a month at the Esalen Institute. I was ready for whatever Edward had to say.

What Edward told me that day was neither new nor surprising. What was surprising was that I was ready and able to hear him. Maybe it was the Klonopin lunch he had brilliantly concocted that allowed for the breakthrough. Maybe it was just the luxury of being in a beautiful and quiet place. Whatever it was, Edward made a difference. He asked me to tell him, calmly this time, what was wrong. I did.

Edward listened again, thoughtfully chewing the crusts of his grilled cheese. He drained both his water glass and wineglass while I rambled on about love and how I needed it and needed to live a new life but I knew that the life I was leading couldn't possibly be the one I would wind up with. I told him that I loved Gideon so much that it made me feel physically ill (Edward might have chimed in that it made him slightly ill too; if he didn't, he should have) and that the sex had been life-changing. Sex with Gideon made me understand what I had been missing and that I couldn't ever go back to living without that kind of ardor. Again, Edward listened patiently without editorializing. He asked me what had me in its grip with this Gideon guy beyond the sex, and I explained the band and the rush of singing again and playing guitar and how powerful I felt doing it. I described the connectedness that Throws Like a Girl experienced when we were playing well and "in the pocket," as the guys would say, and how singing while Gideon played drums was such a high.

This monologue took about half an hour to breathlessly get through, during which Edward said nothing. I waited for his words to come. I desperately wanted him to be my guru. He was my best buddy, with the most brilliant and incisive brain on earth. He would know how to cut through everything that was plaguing me and set me on the path to wellness. He knew enough to dose me with comfort food and Klonopin; how wrong could he possibly be?

"So let me get this straight. You love him. You're insanely crazy about him even though he's insanely crazy."

"Yes."

And then Edward delivered his verdict with a wave of his hand as he got up to clear the table.

"Oh please. He's nothing that a dildo and a drum machine can't replace."

With that, Edward swept into the kitchen. I was left staring down at the monogrammed linen napkin that I had twisted into a knot with white-knuckled hands, not sure if the twisting was justified anger at his harsh words or pure fear at the knowledge that he was right.

10

UNCOMFORTABLY DUMB

Even though I had not thrown my wedding ring away, Gideon had eventually caved and started e-mailing me regularly, sending romantic notes and asking me to spend time with him again. I was loath to do it, not interested in sustaining another messy heartbreak. Life with Andrew was stiff and uncomfortable with the elephant still taking up residence in the room. But it was stable and therefore restful. I needed a rest after everything Gideon and I had gone through. Even so, the lure of being romanced by Gideon and playing with all the members of Throws Like a Girl again sucked me back into his world. It was too enticing when stacked up against the steady grind of staying at home, going to work, and not much more.

I had my first inkling that Edward might have been on to something a few weeks or so after our lunch, when I found myself in a most unusual and uncomfortable situation, thanks to Gideon and his tribe. My tour guide had taken me to odd places before, both physically and mentally, but this place transcended "odd" and landed me squarely in "weird and creepy." Gideon's status as gateway to a groovier existence was becoming seriously questionable.

I was in the back room of the infamous Cock in the East Village, gay bar to some, sex emporium to others, drug den to many, sitting in a bathroom stall surrounded by Gideon, Morgan, and God knows who else from Ritalin Cowboys or otherwise. To my left was a hole in the wall that separated the two stalls, which might have been either the result of shoddy carpentry or a thoughtfully provided glory hole. I suspected the latter but hoped for the former. We were crammed in there with a bag of blow that someone had procured and as the only woman in the stall, which was clearly a novelty at the Cock, I was offered first go at the bag. Always careful not to get too high, or risk rudeness by piggishly taking more than I was really being offered, I dipped the tip of my house key into the little plastic bag and came out with the perfect amount for a bump. Sniff, sniff, straight up it went.

I sat there and listened to the guys talk as they snorted their way through the bag. As usual, there was a lot of discussion about how cool everyone was, and how what they were planning to do was genius, and how it was going to make them millionaires, or famous, or infamous, or get them laid. The conversation rarely changed. I wandered out of there to get a drink and a break from the moronic conversation. By the time I had gotten my drink, the guys were at the bar too and Morgan had started making out with someone, and Gideon (whose skin tone was now a permanent cement gray) was talking to C.C., who was nodding so emphatically it seemed possible that his head might launch off his neck.

Several beers later, I was talking to C.C. and realized
the others were gone. I was ready to leave and wanted to
collect Gideon. He was nowhere to be seen in the crush
of sweaty men who were getting increasingly drunk and
agitated as they pounded beers, did shots, and popped amyl
nitrite (who still did that?) on the Cock's makeshift dance
floor. I had an idea that Gideon might have gone back to
glory hole central to do more coke, so I shoved my way
back there to see what was what. What I saw was his legs
and those of another guy in a stall, facing each other. I had
no clue if they were talking, doing drugs, making out, making out so Gideon could get drugs—the possibilities were
endless. The point was that, in a flash, I knew that any of
these choices were legitimately in the running. I had to get
out of there. I felt sick and out of my element in a gross and
horrible way, like I had a film of sweaty filth on me.

I pounded on the bathroom stall door and told Gideon
I was leaving. He made some noises about how he would
be right there. It didn't matter to me at that point. I was
too freaked-out and upset by my realization of how far
he might be willing to go to get off with drugs or other
people, and I walked out into the night. I remember it
being cold, but it might just have been the contrast between the oppressive body heat generated at the Cock
and the normal outside temperature that struck me. Either way, I was shivering and wanted to go home. Shockingly, that wasn't the last straw.

Of course I knew that there was a seedy side to what
we were doing; it was what drew me into Gideon's world
in the first place. It was just that I didn't realize how seedy
it could get. My naïveté was beginning to show, not just

to the people around me, who no doubt were aware of it all along, but to me as well. My status as a tourist was more and more evident every day. One night we went to Niagara, a bar on Avenue A and Seventh Street, which I liked because it was more of a hipster bar and dance place than the average dive bar or junky bar that Gideon and Ritalin Cowboys normally gravitated toward. There was a bar upstairs, but another one downstairs in the basement that also had a kitchen of sorts, a dance floor, and what passed for a DJ booth.

I loved going to Niagara because it was one of the few places left in the city where you could dance. I was a teenager and in college during the heyday of giant dance clubs and missed going to the Limelight, the Palladium, the Underground—anyplace where you could drink and dance like a lunatic all night. Those giant clubs had all disappeared and in their places were clubs and lounges with the occasional dance floor awkwardly occupied by a few people attempting to dance. Niagara was different. The dance floor was tiny but it was always packed, and no one cared if they were dancing with the person they came with or someone new who looked interesting or like they could move.

The DJ, Mitchell Q, was a gender-bending androgynous boy who had David Bowie pretensions but looked more like Rufus Wainwright in drag. Mitchell Q had a deep love of hairspray, pancake makeup, severely arched eyebrows, and very glossy lips, which made him a little alarming to look at in the wrong light. But he loved Morgan and the other members of Ritalin Cowboys, and they loved him. C.C. got in on the act too because he was such a music fan and would quiz Mitchell Q about every song he played and why he liked it. Mitchell flirted relentlessly with all of them, which wasn't a problem for me because it kept all those crazies busy while I was shaking it to an old Deee-Lite tune with some nice boy from the boogie-down Bronx.

Little did I know that even more transgressive behavior than what went on at the Cock was going on at Niagara. One evening, which really was the final straw for me, ended with my witnessing a cavalcade of weird licentiousness, with Mitchell Q in a back room on his knees in front of Morgan. Or I think it was Morgan. Could have been someone else. In my shocked and slightly inebriated state, that's how it registered. Even more surprising was that C.C.—and it was C.C. for sure—was participating in the melee by letting Mitchell Q lick his boots, and seemed delighted by it. To my utter shock, Mitchell was simultaneously fondling Gideon's leg. My worst fear was that Gideon was allowing it, and anything else Mitchell wanted to do, because he was reputed to always be holding some blow. And if there was blow to be had, Gideon would likely get it by any means necessary. I never saw the whole scene for myself; my vision was impaired by shock, the crowd of bodies, and my own inebriation. But I saw enough. I tried to push my way into the boys' playroom to gain some semblance of clarity. But, thank God for small favors, I was kept from seeing the whole shebang by some kind soul, probably Liesl, who physically held me back from witnessing what would probably not only drive me over the edge but also make me cause a scene. I did freak out to Liesl, but even more important, I was furious.

This was beyond the pale. Drugs, sex, attempts at rock 'n' roll—all good. But a flagrantly cheating boyfriend who was consorting with the DJ, possibly for blow, and in front of me was where I drew the line. I finally found my boundary. The cumulative effect of all of Gideon's tacky, insolent, and careless behavior came home to roost. The line in the sand wasn't drawn by public sex, drugs, cruelty, fighting, infidelity, or any of the other usual suspects. For me, it boiled down to a display of a level of wild disrespect that was not only seedy but a cliché. I knew that what I felt or didn't feel, needed or didn't need, had nothing to do with Gideon's behavior. What he did was based solely on his need to get what he wanted when he wanted it, and there was no room in his head or heart to consider anyone else for even a second. And that was that. Good-bye.

I left Niagara and went back to Williamsburg. I didn't say a word to Gideon. I just took off and in my fury and hurt knew that it was time for a reckoning. I had to address what was going on with both Gideon and Andrew, but I was going to start with the saner of the two. I got into a cab, which is no mean feat on the corner of Avenue A and Seventh Street. I found out soon after that cabbies hated to pick people up at that spot because it was notorious for supplying a steady stream of patrons who were on too many drugs, most frequently cocaine, to be either safe or sure to pay. I must have looked reasonable enough because one cab stopped, turned its "Off Duty" light off, and let me in. We sped over the Williamsburg Bridge and within what seemed like seconds I was back home.

Home. It's a tricky word. Home is where your stuff is, home is where the heart is, home is the roof over your head that keeps you and the people you love physically safe; home can be a lot of things. At that point, I didn't have a clear idea of where or what my home was, but the loft in Williamsburg was where most of my stuff was and where at least part of my heart was, so it was the best I could do. Andrew was there when I got back, sleeping, and I silently stripped off my clothes and peeled out my contact lenses before slipping into the bed next to him. I felt nothing for Andrew physically, but there was a sense of relief that overwhelmed me. If nothing else, Andrew was familiar.

I had thrown myself violently into a life of the unfamiliar in order to figure out who I was and had forgotten the allure of the familiar. I had forgotten that sometimes what's familiar is what makes you feel safe, no matter if it's what you ultimately want or not. And if there's anything I wasn't feeling during my time with Gideon, Ritalin Cowboys, the partying, even the emotional exercise of writing and playing with C.C., it was safe. I liked and desperately needed that lack of safety, but a steady diet of it was wearing me down. It was doing more than wearing me down; it was wearing me out so thoroughly that I was a wisp of what I once was both physically and emotionally. In retrospect, I see that being worn out was the most essential part of the process I had thrown myself headlong into. What I was doing to myself was perfectly mimicking what an addict goes through when he or she hits rock bottom. That person needs to self-destruct in order to have a clean slate from which to start again.

The night that I left the den of vice that I saw Niagara to truly be, I slept soundly without waking up in the middle of the night. I just slept, which was a novelty. I awoke slightly more rested than usual to the sounds of Andrew puttering around, getting ready to go to work. When he saw that I was up he greeted me kindly but tentatively, asking when I had gotten in. I told him in as breezy a manner as I could muster that it had been some time in the early morning hours and that I had tried not to disturb him. He nodded and asked if I'd be home that night. He didn't ask what I had done the night before. His question was heartbreaking. It showed that he had come to accept the unacceptable, which was a terrible thing for him to do to himself, but an even worse thing for me to set in front of him. It revealed so succinctly the chasm that existed between us that we couldn't bring ourselves to address. I said I would definitely be home and that I'd see him after work. He nodded, gave a little wave, and left.

That evening, I sat by myself in my giant white living room with the minutes ticking away. I thought about my growing indifference to getting on the L train and hauling my tired ass into Rook. The mixture of missing Gideon, feeling as guilty as ever about Andrew and the wreck of my marriage, uncertainty about how long my ambivalence was going to be tolerated at work, and being unsure how much longer I could keep up the charade that I wasn't leading two completely separate lives gripped me with terror. One of my usual waves of nausea overcame me and I had to put my head between my knees to try to breathe my way through my shame and desperation. Staring at the floor, inspecting the slightly dirty green Ikea rug that delineated the living room area, I knew what I had to do. It was awful. So awful that I wasn't really able to imagine how I would do it or how it would play out. But I knew what my next move would be. Although my life had become a hell of other people, not to mention of my own creation, I knew that despite Sartre's warning, I did have an exit. I was going to have to talk to Andrew. He deserved to finally be dealt with in an honest and straightforward way. I had only just begun to understand a modicum of what I was doing, but if anyone was going to be the first to hear what I was thinking and feeling, it would be him. Not only because he deserved my honesty and the ability to retain some of his dignity, but also because I knew that sharing what was really happening with Andrew would yield some insight from him. And while it was selfish, I wanted that insight. I needed it.

The next day, I went back to Rook and spent yet another day trying to interest companies that were already working with other publishers on custom-published magazines to jump ship and give us a try. Not the most inspiring endeavor, to be sure. After the usual eight hours, I made my way back home and waited for Andrew to return. The horror of the task before me was so grotesque that the only thing I could do was to sit on the edge of the bed and hold my throbbing head in my hands until he arrived home. Well, that and pour myself a glass of wine. And then another two. I moved to the couch to lie down. The wine had not done my headache a bit of good.

Andrew finally did return home and was surprised to see me sitting there. Who could blame him? My whereabouts had become so spotty that there was no way to tell if I was going to follow through on a promise to be home, call from a late-night band practice, or not call at all and simply not show up. He greeted me warmly but warily as he moved to the bedroom alcove to change out of his work clothes and into jeans and a T-shirt. I asked him to join me on the couch, which he did, and then started one of the worst conversations I've ever had in my life.

"Honey, things have been weird lately, right?"

Andrew looked ill. He was obviously horribly uncomfortable but had the stones to turn to me and look me full in the face.

"Yeah, things have been weird. Obviously. Look at you. I've been worried about you. But yeah, things are definitely fucked-up. By the way, are you drunk?"

"Not exactly, but almost an entire bottle of wine went into the decision to have this conversation so you'll have to cut me a tiny bit of slack. Or not. Your choice."

"Okay, what is it?"

Andrew looked like he already knew, which was not a surprise. He's one of the smartest people I've ever met.

"Honey, I'm really, really unhappy." And then came the tears. I didn't mean to cry; I tried not to—I was terrified of looking like I was trying to emotionally manipulate him. Andrew calmly reached out to comfort me a little by stroking my arm. That was, of course, even more horrifying.

"I know. I know you're miserable. You look like hell, you're acting totally bizarrely, you're never here, I hate it. But I figure you're going through something and I thought I'd just give you some space."

Andrew's impulse to be kind to me and give me space in the midst of that was mind-blowing under the circumstances. Not many people would have that reaction. I'd always known that Andrew was unique, but finally hearing his reason for staying silent all this time stunned me with its compassion and sweetness. It was gracious of him to support me quietly and without heavy-handed direction, but I couldn't get away from the fact that I thought it was totally nuts that he never stood up and said, "What the fuck?!?!" And even in this moment he wasn't saying it. He was reacting to my raising the subject and had merely agreed that things were screwed up. He hadn't made any move to question me, lambaste me, or even fight for me in the event that he had put two and two together and knew that I was screwing around. It seemed like all this time, while I was acting out and running around to find myself, he was sitting at home just waiting for my other motorcycle boot to drop. Well, here it came.

"Andrew, that's exactly what I need. I need space." I was crying harder now, the product of total fear of telling the truth, fear of losing Andrew the second I told him the truth, and the anxiety brought on by knowing that even as I was about to spill the beans I wasn't going to give Andrew the whole story. Which guaranteed that we wouldn't come to a real conclusion about what was

going on and that this exercise was really about bargaining for time and freedom.

"I don't know what's going on with me. I've been miserable for such a long time; you know that. I'm always
screaming at you and carrying on, or running off with
the guys in the band to do stuff that our friends don't
do. I'm totally confused, I feel sick every day, I can barely
keep it together at work, and I feel like the pressure of
keeping us together as a cohesive couple is too much
for me. And I'm obviously failing at it." I was sitting all
curled up in a ball on one end of the couch with Andrew
at the other. He was still calm. It was possible that he had
either suffered a quiet rage of such magnitude that he
had had a stroke and was actually dead, or the shock of
hearing all those words at once had made him go cata-
tonic. Either one would have been a reasonable response.

"So what you're saying is that you need space. Does
that mean space from me?"

"Yes. Space from you, but not because of you in particular. I just need space to think."

"And you can't think at home." I had no idea if this was
a question or a statement. I went with question.

"No, well, yes. I can think here. I just can't think if I'm
not by myself."

"Are you saying that you want me to leave?"

I started sobbing again. "I don't *want* you to leave. This
is your home too. I just want to be alone." I was now officially totally unhelpful. "I need space and this is where
I live. But you live here too and I don't want to kick you
out of your home. So I don't know what to say."

Andrew was finally getting a little red-eyed and weepy. He pulled me to him and we clung to each other. We hung on to each other like characters in a B movie, those classic figures standing on a platform at a train station, clinging to a friend or lover who they know they'll never see again. Of course we were going to see each other again, but after this conversation, it would never be in the same way.

I have to admit that I was a total wimp and didn't tell Andrew about Gideon at this point, though it must have been painfully obvious to Andrew. I focused on the fact that I needed to figure myself out (which was true) and that I needed to do it alone (also true) but never mentioned the role that Gideon and his love den played in it (giant lie of omission). Gideon, whom I predictably and embarrassingly missed, even after I had sworn off him at Niagara. Like any junky, I knew my drug was bad for me but I still wanted my fix. Despite all my moments of sanity and clarity, for the second time, I eventually found my way back to him. It's ridiculous to think of it now, and there's no way to justify it. I just couldn't breathe without him around, much as I couldn't breathe when Andrew *was* around. Sick, sad, but true.

Andrew's and my attempts to figure out the puzzle of how to "give me space" included everything from living under the same roof but sleeping apart and keeping separate schedules to my moving in with my parents (not if it was the only bomb shelter on earth and a nuclear warhead was headed straight for New York City). Finally, we settled on the obvious. At least to us. We would share the apartment. I would have it half the time and continue my habit of sleeping at my conspicuously undisclosed locations the other half, and Andrew would be in the apartment half the time, couch surfing with friends the other half. I look back on it now and there was such a sweetness and innocence to what we were doing. We genuinely thought the separation might be temporary and provide a doorway to a new life. After all, we weren't separating completely, only halfway. There was hope, right?

I gave Andrew the first crack at having the apartment on his own because I had made other plans anyway. They were insane plans, but plans nonetheless. I decided it would be a great idea to go on vacation with Gideon to a tropical location to relax and get away from all the partying and chaos that defined our lives. I was secretly hoping that it would jump-start a healthier lifestyle for Gideon and get him to reconsider the drugs, how he treated me, his wretched temper, basically everything. In essence, I thought that going to Club Med or its equivalent would achieve the same results as going to rehab. So off we went on our vacation to see what it would be like to be together without all the mania of our what I hesitate to call "normal" life.

The trip can be summed up like this: Gideon spent most of his time getting drunk and asking me to pay for his drinks. I joined him occasionally but was put off the whole endeavor the night Gideon got so wasted he decided to lie down in the road, ignoring the protests of the resort security team, and laugh his head off while I tried to get him back to our room. We did have a lovely time at the pool when he was sober. We had fun riding a scooter around the island. We had great sex every day and night, provided Gideon hadn't passed out from an unfortunate mixture of beer, rum, and sun. I devoured a beach read cover to cover and was charmed by the main character but was particularly taken with the dog in the book. I'd always wanted a dog but Andrew was allergic to them. I spent a lot of time thinking about the dog and how nice it would be to have something sweet and cuddly to hold on to. But my thought process was frequently interrupted by Gideon's drinking and its results. It would have been easier for him to have just hooked up an IV to his arm with a bottle of Red Stripe attached.

My ego and mental state sustained another one of Gideon's perfectly aimed direct hits during one of our evenings out and about on the grounds of the resort. We chose a bar, settled down on our bar stools, and because Gideon was already half in the bag from the minibar, launched into a discussion about our relationship. This is a terrible idea, even if you're a normal and healthy couple, because if things go haywire, you're stuck on an island with someone you're momentarily loathing and you don't have an alternate place to sleep. In our case it was a psychotic move. I can't remember who started the discussion, but it was generally about the usual gripes: I wasn't able to give Gideon what he really wanted because I was still married, Gideon wasn't being nice enough to me and I thought he spoke to me in a disrespectful manner, I was a pain in the ass because I didn't want to party as much as I used to, he was rarely sober and as a result was increasingly capricious and volatile. What I do remember is who ended the discussion. It was Gideon. In one sentence he ended the conversation and made me happier than a red-neck at a monster truck rally that we were going home the next day. He told me, "None of this matters anyway because I don't really love you the most. I love Rachel more and always have."

Because I was raised to be a lady, I didn't stab him in the eye with a swizzle stick and leave him for dead on that unknown island. I didn't speak to him for the rest of the night and did so only minimally on the way back to New York. Once we were back in the city, we were on the outs again. He had wounded me sufficiently on our vacation that I couldn't bear to speak to him. I distracted myself by throwing myself into the task of getting a dog. I had arrived at the loft the day of my return from vacation to find a sweet note from Andrew saying that he hoped I had had a good time, which only made the place feel that much more empty. My conviction that I should get a puppy was cemented then and there.

I decided to get a Brussels Griffon, a scruffy and ador-able breed, and I found a breeder who had one male left. The breeder told me the dog was the runt of the litter and he'd be ready to be flown to me from Arizona in two weeks if that was okay. I said that it was. Two weeks later, I picked the critter up at the American Airlines cargo hold. I was handed a plastic pet carrier with a gate in the front. I peered in and saw nothing. I opened the gate and way in the back of the carrier was a tiny beast that resembled a profoundly anxious-looking grumpy monkey. Ah, a kindred spirit. Oscar, the true love of my life, had arrived.

. . .

As predicted, Gideon was going nuts from the silent treat-
ment to which I was subjecting his jive ass. He called and
e-mailed but I just couldn't bring myself to talk to him.
I missed him but he had been such an ass while we were
on Fantasy Island that I would perish if I was exposed
to any more of the kind of pain that he was so expert at
dishing out. There was no doubt that the second he had
me back it would be business as usual, because the unstable power dynamic that plagued our relationship would
flip back in his favor. I might have been in a state of flux,
still unsure about what I really wanted to be when I grew
up and desperately in love with a nutcase who had a flair
for mind games, but I still had my pride. Or at least a little teeny tiny shred of pride. More like a pridelette. Or a
prideling. Whatever it was, it kept me from running back
to Gideon's arms.

Or at least from running back to his arms right away.
I managed to stay away from Gideon for roughly one
week. Apparently I had absolutely no pride and was officially the biggest failure on the planet. Gideon was so
persistent in his efforts to get my attention that my ego
was stroked to a high gloss. The physical craving I had
felt for him from the very first day we met was as potent
as ever and didn't help the situation one bit. So I went
back to him, taking Oscar with me (I also had to give
Andrew the apartment back, which was a shit reason to
go back to Gideon but it was just another shit reason on
an ever-growing pile of mental manure), in a maelstrom

of shame, relief, desire, and egotism. It was quite a mix. I will never forget how right I thought my decision was the moment I got out of the cab to meet him.

The taxi stopped at the corner and I could see Gideon standing, waiting for me, in the middle of the block. The second my feet hit the sidewalk, Gideon started walking toward me, then jogging, and I picked up the pace too, Oscar running alongside me like a guinea pig on speed. Gideon and I ran toward each other with arms outstretched, like the hero and heroine in the gratifying reunion scene of a saccharine, made-for-TV Lifetime movie of the week. We had missed each other so violently that a violent collision was the only thing we could do to express how we felt. So we crashed into each other like the skinniest sumo wrestlers on earth, Gideon lifted me off the ground, and we descended to his apartment to find each other again. And we did find each other, talking, petting each other, laughing, making love over and over again, and whispering how we loved each other. We stayed in that bed for what seemed like forever.

The new addition of Oscar to the mix only made things seem more like we had a safe and cozy home. Gideon fell in love with Oscar so completely that it was like he had given birth to the little thing himself. And so, for a while, things were in balance. But the conditions of our balance were so precarious that one inevitable wrong move would have everything crashing down in seconds. We were the king and queen of emotional Jenga, and while we were reunited and it felt so good, it was only a matter of time before one of us pulled out the wrong block and sent our harmonious life crashing to the ground.

One of the first blocks to get pulled out of our carefully constructed Jenga tower was the direction in which the band was going. To be more precise, it was the direction in which the band was not going. Gideon had derailed things so badly with his outrageous coke hoovering that C.C. was always wary around him in the studio. To add to the tension in the room, Gideon and I were pushing the others to continue to play out and to do it with some frequency. They insisted that we were not ready. I thought we could just do a little set before a Ritalin Cowboys gig, but Gideon didn't like the idea of mixing the agendas of the two bands. We could play open-mic nights or find another friend's band to open for; Ritalin Cowboys was off-limits. None of that really mattered because C.C. never felt like our songs were polished enough to take to the public. Ira seconded that emotion and continued to ride C.C. about his playing, only making him more nervous about performing. The icing on the cake was that Gideon's behavior had returned to full-on nasty since he had me back, in what he assumed was his control, and access to a steady stream of drugs thanks to the members of Ritalin Cowboys and other hangers-on. He was not a joy to be with and would leave rehearsals abruptly, yelling at all of us. Or just not show up at all. Or he'd play sullenly and poorly to piss us off.

But the point of a band is to play, and not just for yourselves. So our motley crew of neurotics and drug addicts did play out. We never opened for Ritalin Cowboys or any of the other bands that we were friendly with. But we played a few open-mic nights, we played at Freddy's (the very first place I saw Gideon play), and we played at a party. It wasn't a lot, but we did play for other people, which had been my goal from the start. The mission that Brynnie had set before me and I had accepted, while she had recused herself from the insanity she saw blooming around me once I formed the band, had finally been accomplished. I never invited anyone from my other life to see us play. I definitely didn't want Andrew to come because it would put everything that I had been shoddily hiding from him on full display. So the few times we played, we played for strangers, which is always easier because you don't have to be yourself for them. You can be anybody when you perform for an unknown crowd of, let's be honest, eight people or so. That's what was so great about it for me. I had become someone who was less fearful, no longer so sure about what was "right" and what was "wrong" and didn't really care about it anyway, and I had finally experienced passion, sex, love, and power in a way that I wanted so badly but hadn't known if it even existed. Now I knew. I knew that it all existed and that with this dangerous person, who may or may not have been replaceable with a dildo and a drum machine, I had reached my goal.

To be a little more precise, I had reached one of my goals, in no small part thanks to Gideon, which explains so much about why I loved him dearly in spite of the many things that were wrong with our relationship. During my time with him I had developed an astoundingly huge amount of insight into who and what my authentic self was. She was more aware of how judgmental she was, more tattooed, more experimental, less likely to say no to just about anything, and definitely did not think that the sun rose and set out of Martha Stewart's ass. All of that was essential, but it wasn't the whole picture.

There were also the issues of responsibility and loyalty to address. Those virtues had gone out the window when the other stuff was getting nailed down. The part of me that stood outside of myself, watching me figure out who I was without adhering to all the rules and regulations my family, my schools, my friends, and I had suggested I subscribe to, was starting to get a little stirred up. She was not impressed by my cavalier attitude toward my family, my husband, and my friends, to whom I barely paid a lick of attention during this whole period of self-exploration. Not to mention my feelings of guilt. But that part of myself that stood outside was happy about that crippling guilt. It meant that there was still hope for me. I wasn't really lost to a life of physical indulgence and personal indifference. That life was, not unlike every single aspect of my relationship with Gideon, an extreme to which my pendulum had to swing in order to eventually find its center. The guilt was the other extreme to which the pendulum could and would swing, reminding me that I still had to address the hardest question of all: now that I knew more about who I was, what would I do with that knowledge?

Two of the most bizarre things about the two years and a little bit that I spent running around finding myself under bar stools and tangled in questionably clean bedsheets were that I managed to hold on to a well-paying job and that my husband never, ever once confronted me about any of my odd, blatantly nonmarital behavior. Most people who go to work in what they wore the night before with crazy hair and sunglasses that don't ever come off tend to lose their job after about two weeks. Not so for me. I stayed gainfully employed. Most people who treat their marriage like an option (hmmm, should I go for the turkey sandwich or marriage today?) get dumped. At the very least, they get challenged. Not so with me, but Fortuna did spin her wheel and make decisions for me when my guard was down.

Andrew and I kept up our system of sharing the apartment in our quasi-acknowledged separation for a surprisingly long time. We kept dancing around each other, with him never asking questions and seemingly accepting whatever strange process I was going through, and me doing whatever I wanted to but never mentioning what I was doing because if I did it would upset Andrew. We never acknowledged the elephant in the room. And when the elephant invited its friends over to have a party, we politely allowed them their fun and cleaned up the balloons and cocktail glasses when they left. It was loony, but we were absolutely not going to mess with the status quo, because we knew how to handle our elephant-filled apartment but we had no idea what would happen if we anted up and declared the party over. We spent every day choosing the devil we knew over the devil we didn't. Until Andrew pulled a move that surprised both of us because neither one of us saw it coming.

On one particular rainy night, I had the apartment. It was my week or ten days or whatever amount of time we had agreed on, and I had Gideon at the loft with me. He didn't come to the loft often because seeing the reality of Andrew's presence made him uncomfortable. Which was one of the most normal human emotions he exhibited while we were together, so I liked it. Which might also be why I asked him to come over whenever I could. We were there at my place on my night, with little Oscar scampering around, and we started making out on the couch. We never became one of those couples who lose track of the importance and sheer excellence of making out, so that's what we were doing. And while it was great, it didn't last long.

Within ten minutes or so we had segued into ripping off clothes and some pretty frantic, loud, lights-on love-making. Okay, let's be honest, it was more like some relatively hard-core porny action. If you haven't guessed what happened next, you haven't been paying attention. In midstroke and midscream, the front door opened. The front door was about three yards from the couch. The couch on which the totally porny action was taking place. And in walked Andrew.

There was no way to cover ourselves up, no way to shield Andrew from what was going on, no way to keep him from having the image that we presented burned into his retinas forever. He took one look at us, his jaw dropped, and he hurried out of the apartment and into the street. I could hear the steel door slam, and the noise it made coincided with the precise moment that my heart stopped. It had to have stopped beating, because I knew I wasn't breathing and I felt like I had no pulse, no blood in my body; I had to be dead because I was truly and totally numbly blank. Gideon was horrified. He was babbling something unintelligible behind me, but I heard him as though he was yelling down a long hallway, his voice a diminished echo that meant nothing. And then, in no more than a nanosecond, all the blood rushed back into my body, my heart started racing, and I was breathing deeply so I wouldn't pass out.

I had to go after Andrew. I couldn't let him see that and just leave. It was hideous. It was too disgusting to even think about. I didn't know what I could possibly say or do, but I had to get to him. Gideon and his well-being were of no importance in that moment.

I grabbed the first thing I saw and put it on. It was my trench coat, and I stepped into a pair of heels that had been kicked off right near the door. In this getup, part flasher, part Gena Rowlands in any Cassavetes movie you can name, I ran into the street. Andrew was right in front of the building, holding his head and pacing back and forth. He wasn't exactly crying; he was making a noise that you hear people describe as an animalistic keening, but you don't know what it is until you hear it.

I grabbed Andrew's shoulders and tried to tell him it was okay, it didn't mean anything, he was going to be all right; I said anything I could think of that might calm him down. None of it worked. We stood in the rain, in a moment that was so ridiculously cinematic that it actually occurred to me at the time that between the setting and how surreal everything felt, it was like we were in a movie of our lives. I always thought about how shallow it was to have that observation at that precise juncture, but I think my mind would have wandered anywhere rather than be where we really were in those mind-bending five minutes on North Eighth Street. So I kept repeating nonsense and Andrew keened. And then he spoke.

"I knew this would never work out. I knew that I could never make a marriage work."

At the time, I was horrified. I was saddened that he hadn't had the confidence about our relationship that I thought had at least existed at some point. I was also enraged, thinking that if Andrew hadn't thought that he could make a marriage work, he shouldn't have married me and we wouldn't have been in this fine mess. It's so very easy to lay blame when you're naked in a trench coat and pumps in a rainstorm. Cold, wet, caught at being a giant ho . . . it was all so unbearable. Andrew's look of total despair was heartbreaking. He left then, walking down the street as quickly as he could, and I stood there watching him go, wondering what the hell I should do next. My husband had just caught me in flagrante delicto with my guitar teacher/bandmate, and said guitar teacher/bandmate was in my apartment, probably having a heart attack.

I walked back inside and found Gideon sitting at the dining table with his pants on. My brain was so fried from the whole experience that I was actually confused by the appearance of the pants. And finally, out of my mouth fell a turd of such unparalleled turdiness that even Gideon, who had done it all and seen it all, was shocked.

"Why are you wearing your pants? Take them off, let's do it again."

Gideon looked at me like I had three heads.

"Are you insane? Do you know what just happened?

How could you want to do anything right now? You're a monster! There's something wrong with you! This is the worst thing that could happen. I knew it would happen. It happened. Oh my God." He started clutching his chest.

If only he had a string of pearls on he could have clutched them too. Gideon had a flair for the dramatic. But he was right. My reaction was monstrous, but it was also the reaction of someone in shock. I thought that going back to having sex would be what Gideon wanted, so I suggested it. He didn't want to; he wanted to clutch his pearls and have the vapors. So that's what we did. We talked about what had just happened, Gideon self-flagellated for the first and last time that I ever saw, and I just sat in my big white apartment with a big white blank space where my brain should have been. For all the drama and craziness that had transpired in no more than a total of twenty minutes, only one truly important thing had happened. The elephant had stampeded out of the room and my marriage was finally over.

11

WELCOME, MAY I TAKE YOUR BAGGAGE?

Generally, things were taking a turn for the worse. Which makes sense, because you can only dance on the head of a pin for so long before you fall off or impale yourself. I had enjoyed my salad days of Sex, Drugs, and Rock 'n' Roll (remember, it was the lifestyle I chose, not the list) and had kept things together pretty well considering that nearly every choice I made was antithetical to everything I would normally have instinctively chosen to do. But my instincts had changed, so they landed me in strange places with strange people, doing strange things. Which was okay, but I could feel the pendulum starting its giant swing back toward its starting point. Things had to normalize a little bit or something really horrific would happen. The bad things I was starting to think about were the three big D's that had habitually haunted my neurotic brain for years but I'd lost track of while I was on my journey of self-discovery. No "eat, pray, love" program for me. I had proven myself to be much more of a "snort, kvetch, schtup" kind of girl. Nonetheless, my journey was changing course and the three D's of my nightmares came back to remind me that no one can play around forever because if you do, you'll wind up dealing with destitution, depression, and death.

Death was the first issue that raised its skull of a head. All throughout my romp through Gideon's world, I had enjoyed the fast pace, the risk taking, and definitely the drugs. But I wasn't wired for addiction. The person who was staring death in the face was Gideon. He had gotten to the point in his drug taking where he had passed permanent midnight a long time ago and was now stuck someplace around permanent three in the morning. Gideon's beautiful face, which had once been distinctive for its elegant pallor, now looked like the gray, crepey flesh of a corpse. He had gone from slim to gaunt and had the personality of a murderous and sullen teenager. I was no longer scared that he'd behave in some obnoxious way that would hurt me, I was scared that I would wake up one morning next to a dead body. I told him that he was in trouble several times, explaining how sick he looked and that he had to do something about it. Gideon brushed me off and said he could look after himself. He couldn't. He was so far past being able to look after himself that I knew in my bones that if something wasn't done for him soon he would at the very least wind up in the hospital.

I contacted everyone I thought was a friend of his, including the members of Ritalin Cowboys. I was frantic. I told them all that I thought Gideon was in serious trouble and that his drug use was actually killing him before our eyes and we were doing nothing about it. We had to do something. No one would help him. When I furiously

asked why, they all came up with the same answer: "Well,
I do drugs and if I try to do some kind of intervention
on Gideon then I'm a hypocrite." No, assholes, if you do
drugs and do an intervention you're helping your friend
and you might be able to turn your own shit around too.
I tried to explain that sentiment in a more palatable way,
but those fair-weather friends would have none of it. But
then one person came forward. Lydia said she'd help.
And she did. I went online and figured out which rehab
programs were in the city and which were the best for
cocaine addiction. Lydia went with me for moral support
when I checked them out. She didn't think that an intervention was a good idea because she didn't believe they
worked, and she told me she wouldn't participate if it
came to that, but she helped me out personally, for which
I'll always be grateful.

I spent a long time trying to figure out what to do
about Gideon. I had to ask myself if Gideon, no matter
how much I loved him, was the guy I was meant to be
with. I struggled with that for a long time. The answer I
invariably came back around to was that while I wanted
to help this person I had such deep feeling for to get
clean, I couldn't be with an addict. It tore me apart, but
he didn't seem to want any help with his problem and
rejected every attempt I made to bring up the subject. He
was making the decision for me, much the way Andrew
did when he walked in on the at-home version of *Deep
Throat* going on in his living room.

Gideon and I frequently had lunch at a cheap little Italian place in the neighborhood where we both
worked. We agreed to meet there and I was devastated

before either of us arrived or ordered. We both looked like death but for entirely different reasons. As we were picking at our pasta, I started crying and told Gideon that we couldn't be together anymore. I loved him and wanted to be with him, but with his refusal to do anything about his drug addiction I couldn't stay with him. I told him what a pity it was since I was really separated now and on my way to a divorce. I'd be free, but he was too much of a mess to deal with. So I sat there crying, so sad that we were through. But I forgot who I was dealing with. Even with one foot in the grave, Gideon knew how to play this scene. He looked me straight in the eye with a tragic expression of overwhelming fatigue and desperation and said, "Okay, take me to rehab."

The rest of that day was a blur. I took Gideon back to the store where he worked and left him in the street while I tearfully told his boss what was going on and that Gideon wouldn't be back for the rest of the day. And that he might not be back the day after that. His boss not only said it wasn't a problem but offered any help he could supply. I thanked him and went back outside to collect Gideon. Next stop was my office. I went into my boss's office to tell him what I was doing and that I needed a private place for Gideon to hang out in while I went to my own office to make phone calls to get Gideon into the rehab center I had chosen for him in case he ever made the right decision. My boss had already started laying people off so there was an empty office for Gideon. I installed him in it and went to my desk to get someone at the hospital with the best rehab program on the phone.

I got someone, but he said that it was too late in the day and that we'd have to wait until tomorrow. In that moment I turned into my mother. Every molecule in my body that she had contributed sprang to life and I channeled her like I was one of the Fox sisters.

"You listen to me. I don't care if you have a protocol. I don't care if you have some system that you're supposed to follow with time frames for accepting people into your program. Your job is to help people, and I've got someone sitting in my office who needs more help than you can possibly know. If you don't let him come to the hospital right now, immediately, he won't ever come and he will die. Do you want that on your head? Do you want to remember this conversation someday and wonder if this guy died? I don't think you do. Even if you can't officially admit him, let me bring him in so there's some action today that can be continued in the normal way that makes you happy tomorrow. If not, he's lost. Get it? He'll be lost. So what's it going to be? Are you going to help or let my friend die?"

I swear that is really what I said and I didn't take a breath throughout the whole speech. I remember a lot of things I've said over the years, but usually I don't get it verbatim. I can get about a 90 percent approximation. That soliloquy was exactly, to the letter, what I said to the poor bastard who picked up the phone. I must have sounded like I was hanging from the edge of a cliff by my fingernails, because that guy's next words were, "Bring him in. We'll work something out."

And I did. And they did. And the next day, Gideon was in rehab, where he stayed for the next several months.

•   •   •

Like every single band ever covered on *Behind the Music,* our band broke up because Gideon went to rehab and we didn't have the heart or energy to find a replacement. Ira had already defected to play for Ritalin Cowboys full-time, so C.C. and I were back to our original duo. If we had been a little more daring we could have tried a White Stripes setup, but we stuck to our original roles of me writing and singing and him playing guitar.

C.C. and I never played out again but kept playing together in our apartments, and writing and recording whenever we had the time. We had fun, but without the toxic yet incendiary energy Gideon brought into the room, our fantasies of rock stardom were starting to fade. It didn't matter. C.C. and I had both proven to ourselves that we could do and be whatever we wanted and we weren't stuck in our roles as lawyers, good boy and girl, or whatever other labels we had assigned to ourselves long ago. I wouldn't dare to say what the upshot of the whole band experience was for C.C., but as for me, it gave birth to a more powerful creative outlet than Throws Like a Girl had been.

Writing all those lyrics gave me more confidence about my writing abilities and got me thinking about other writing I might do. Maybe I'd try writing magazine articles, possibly even a book. I spent my days selling and promoting other people's written work; why not try producing something of my own? The old chestnut that everyone has one book in him or her rang in my ears and rang true. Everyone goes through a transformative or, at the very least, unusual moment in their lives that they should share if they can find the words. I say "should" because any opportunity to connect with other people and let them know they're not alone in their experiences (and reassure yourself that you aren't either) seems like a fine idea to me. After everything I did during my stint as a Very Bad Girl I knew that I finally had a story to tell that I thought other people might learn from or relate to. And I owed a debt of gratitude to C.C., Gideon, and Ira, who, in the studio and onstage, had helped me to find the voice with which to tell it.

• • •

While Gideon was going through the rigors of therapy, withdrawal, gaining weight, all the usual rehab stuff, I had my own crap to wade through. It started with my job. Finally, the layoffs got to me. Which was so inevitable and obviously coming that I barely reacted when it happened. I had some money saved up and would get unemployment insurance, so I'd be okay. I also had, if it was needed, my parents' help. I didn't want to have to take their money. I felt that at thirty-two it was wildly inappropriate, but eventually it became necessary and they were lovely about it. Their assistance paid my rent at the loft, where I still stayed on and off when Andrew wasn't there and I wasn't at Gideon's place watching him disintegrate. Without my parents, the second D, destitution, would have been knocking at my door. So they saved my skin and life went on.

I spent a lot of time with Gideon, but he was increasingly becoming a source of the third D, depression. He had so much to handle that dealing with him was so exhausting I had no time or energy left for myself. I gave Gideon the consolation prize of hanging out with Oscar when rehab wasn't in session (his program was outpatient, half the day, every day) and it seemed like that was enough for him. He couldn't handle having a girlfriend anyway. He was no use to me and I wasn't much use to him. The program had to be his support system, not me. So we stayed together but our sex life, which was really the glue that held us together whether I had wanted to admit it or not, dried up. We still had sex but it was more about clinging to each other for comfort than passion and desire. We also spent a lot of time watching movies on TV. Or we'd go to a movie theater if we were feeling really adventurous. If proof of my love for Gideon ever needed to be provided, I could always say that I sat through what seemed like six hours of *Apocalypse Now Redux*. It was, without exception, one of the most excruciatingly boring experiences of my life.

I looked for a new job and joined the Al-Anon support group the hospital provided for the family members and significant others of the patients in rehab. I joined because I was asked to. I thought I'd go with the flow and see what happened. I hated it the minute I got there. I hated the people, who were all whining about their addicts. I hated the therapist, who had an inscrutable quality that I found deeply unnerving. I hated that every-one in the room seemed to be jockeying to be the one with the most problems. And most of all I hated being there because I didn't belong there. I wasn't like these people and didn't share their problems. They were all codependent basket cases. I was a strong person who had almost single-handedly saved her boyfriend's life.

The thing is, everyone who joins a support group like Al-Anon thinks they don't belong there. It's almost the exact same thing as what happens to people who go to rehab. You think you're special and different, everyone else is a lunatic, and you've got a handle on what your problems are. All you need is a good rest and you'll be back in shape. You think this for a few weeks and then you come to the horrifying conclusion that you were wrong. You are a lunatic. You are a codependent nutcase, and at the moment you really need these people, whom you hate and hope to never see again in your life, to bust you on your bullshit and rationalizing. You need them because no one knows what it feels like to be swept up in an addict's destructive drama like someone who is liv-ing in the same ring of hell. So you finally give in and listen to what they're talking about. And then you do the unthinkable and share your own feelings and general mishegas. And then you're part of the group. And then you hate the other members a little less, but you never really like them too much because the point of the group is not to stay there forever. You should want to get your head together and go.

That's what happened to me. My support group of friends all came out of the woodwork, even those who, unlike Brynne and Alex and Edward, had taken a powder during the worst parts of what I had put myself through. They were ready to help me now that my head was finally emerging from my ass, I was trying to pull myself together, and I was beginning to resemble myself again. My life as Squeaky Fromme to Gideon's Manson was drawing to a close and my pals could sense a shift in the atmosphere. I had a family who, in their own strange way, loved me to bits. I had a career to resurrect. I didn't have the time to hang out in self-pity city. The Al-Anon group had managed to show me that I didn't need Gideon or any other man for anything, everything I did was a choice for which I had to claim responsibility, and I couldn't control everything. I got the message, "graduated" out of the group, and have tried to remember those three simple lessons every day of my life every day since I left. Those lessons never get old and they never go out of style. I recommend them highly as a lifestyle choice. While Sex, Drugs, and Rock 'n' Roll was an excellent short-term lifestyle choice, Independence, Responsibility, and Letting Go works far better in the long run. Which is not to say that I regret a second of what I did—I don't, because of what I learned from it—but making short-term fun and glamour into a long-term affair is simply too much work. It's exhausting, which makes you cranky and leaves you with bags under your eyes, bad skin, and questionable fashion choices. And don't even get me started on what it does to your hair.

12

THE TWELFTH STEP

Straightening out my life became my full-time job. Andrew and I worked hard to figure out how to separate amicably, which we did successfully, much to the disbelief of almost everyone who knew us. Most people thought that Andrew should have kicked my ass. They might have been right, but that wasn't Andrew's style. So while we seemed truly bizarre to a lot of the people around us, our need to find a way to keep calm and carry on was important to us. That was the Letting Go portion of the program.

I had to find a new place to live because our lease at the loft was up and there was no way that we were going to continue living together. So Andrew stayed in Williamsburg and I went, like a homing pigeon, back to the Upper East Side. I found a cute little apartment and some of my oldest girlfriends helped me to move in. I will never forget the sight of my very oldest friend, Nina, putting plates away in my new cupboards. It wasn't a big deal, it was just stacking plates, but having her there in that period of terrifying transition was the best example of friendship I can ever come up with. She wasn't doing anything special, but she was there. Having friends like Nina around as much as possible to keep me company in my apartment for the first few weeks was crucial. I had never lived alone and the thought of it scared the pants off me. Her presence and that of my other friends helped to take the edge off. But the first night I didn't have something to do and had to hang out in the apartment alone without a husband or a friend or Gideon (who spent most of his time holed up at his place staying away from the rigors of the world), I freaked out. Then after a few weeks I got used to it. Then I liked it. Bingo, the Independence portion of the program sprang to life.

And, finally, Responsibility came calling. I got my act together and spent most of my time looking for a job. Any job as long as it was at least tangentially connected to publishing. After a relatively short search I found a job heading up Infinity Press's new book packaging program. Without doing much research about the company or really caring about anything beyond the salary, I took it. It was a big pay cut, but it was a job and I had to do what I had to do. Word to the wise: sometimes it's not a bad idea to wait. I'll always be grateful that I got that job because it came through when I needed it most. But really, believe me, sometimes it's better to wait.

I hated everything about the job and everything about Infinity Press. I despised the duplicity of their bait-and-switch hiring practice, which brought me in as the head of a department and then put me to work selling printing services. I hated that I had fallen for their ploy and was less than overjoyed that within the first few months of my employment I had been sexually harassed by one of the company owners' brothers (but what's a little ass grabbing among friends?). I was horrified by the environment these guys had created.

Things got even stranger when I found out shortly after joining the company that the brothers who owned it were all Hare Krishna and ran the company using fear tactics in a decidedly cultish manner. All three of the brothers were oddly minuscule to the point of possibly being legitimately "little people," they had notoriously double-barreled sex drives, and they sported year-round George Hamilton tans. They also seemed to hate each other and backstabbed one another to the staff on a daily basis.

It was the closest I could get to being in a cult without actually joining one. It was clear that the brothers kept the employees on their toes by giving them contradictory instructions, encouraging company-wide negative gossip, and requiring that employees align themselves with one brother or another to ensure the security of their employment. Working for those tiny little control freaks was like being on the receiving end of mind control in Munchkinland. The mini moguls caused heartbreak and paranoia everywhere they went, but they could never be accused of being boring.

While I detested these guys, I couldn't hate them completely. They supplied me with the one thing I needed most at that juncture in my life: the means to support myself. Without them and their perfectly timed job offer, I would have had to seriously consider moving into my parents' apartment. Which my parents would have enjoyed even less than I would, and I would have had to face the total defeat of living my worst nightmare: over thirty, broke, living with my parents, divorced, and romantically involved with a recovering drug addict. Not exactly the best résumé and not a situation for my parents to brag about at one of the endless series of weddings of the children of their friends that they seemed to attend on a weekly basis. I could just hear it now, the innocent question and classic Dorfman response:

"So, how's Jessica doing?"

"Terrific when she doesn't have her head in the oven. Which she should."

Working at Infinity was an intense process and I was watched over like I hadn't been for years. The brothers were suspicious little buggers and checked in on me on a regular basis. There was no time for fucking around, so the level of attention that Gideon was used to receiving from me during the day was reduced by at least 75 percent. That did not go over well. The only thing that made Gideon happy about the arrangement was that I couldn't bring Oscar to the office, so I left him with Gideon most days. Oscar was the perfect companion for Gideon while he was in recovery; he basically worked as a therapy dog. Oscar would play with Gideon, take his mind off the misery of getting off drugs, snuggle with him when it was time for a nap, and watch TV with him for hours on end. In Oscar, Gideon had found the perfect mate. My little dog didn't talk back, had no expectations, and was up for whatever Gideon wanted to do. Oscar was actually a much better life partner for Gideon than I could ever be.

I had been with Infinity for a few months when

Gideon's struggle with recovery and my strain from dealing with him and my job came to a head. By the time
Fridays rolled around I was ready to collapse and, if I was
lucky, maybe even have some peace, quiet, and perhaps a
little pampering.

One particular Friday a few months into my stint at Infinity, I went to Gideon's apartment before I went home
so I could pick Oscar up and firm up whatever evening
plans Gideon and I had. I let myself into the underground
lair, which had become even more depressing than usual
because in his postdrug depression, Gideon had let his
fastidious habits go by the wayside and the place looked
like a trashed dorm room. I picked my way through the
crap on the floor and sat next to Gideon on what had
once been the love couch but was now more of a sofa of
slack.

Gideon was filing his nails with a nail file that looked
like something he must have inherited from his mother.
It was one of those old-fashioned metal nail files from
the seventies or earlier that had a pink plastic handle with
gold writing on it, possibly "Revlon," and the file came to
a point at the end. Gideon always kept his nails short and
well groomed, for playing guitar and for the ladies, but I
hadn't seen him use this particularly campy implement
before. If I had, I had blocked it out because it was just
such a ridiculous item. As he slowly and meticulously
gave himself a manicure, Gideon looked amazingly like
Joan Crawford, or at least Joan Collins during her Alexis
Carrington era. The whole scene of him sitting in the
middle of all that shit, not saying a word to me, keeping his eyes glued to the TV, and filing his nails was high

camp. It was also creepy in a *What Ever Happened to Baby Jane?* kind of way. I sighed deeply as I surveyed the room and asked Gideon what he wanted to do that night. No answer. I tried again.

"Gideon, what do you want to do tonight?"

No answer. He kept filing those nails and staring at the television set. My patience had already been worn thin by a week of cold calls and no sales at Infinity. I wasn't in the mood for theatrics. I stood up and repeated the question louder this time, trying to snap him out of whatever rehab-induced sulk he was in.

"Hey! Did you hear me? Do you want to go out tonight? What do you want to do?"

"What did you ask me?" He slowly turned his head in my direction with a slightly manic grin on his face. He looked like Chucky of horror movie fame.

"I said: What. Do. You. Want. To. *Do!*" I was admittedly a bit shrill at this point. The Chucky thing had weirded me out.

Gideon kept smiling at me steadily, turned the tip of the pointy nail file in my direction, and with a steady, menacing voice replied, "I want to stab you with this."

I couldn't believe my eyes, ears, or any other organ that might have been functioning at that moment. Gideon had been a dick on more occasions than I could count, but a violent dick he was not. My adventure with Gideon had been largely about discovering what my personal limits and boundaries were. This special moment was no exception to the rule of life with Gideon. This was a boundary test, not only for me but for him too.

And he failed it. From the moment the words left his lips, I knew that an inviolable boundary for me was not only violence but also the mere threat of it. I didn't care if he was joking. It didn't occur to me to stop to ask if it was a joke. He said what he said, it was a threat to hurt me, and in a flash everything I had known for the last two and a half years changed.

I stood exactly where I was, stock still, barely breathing. Gideon had a half-expectant smile on his face, waiting to see if he could get me mad enough to have a fight with him. He was so contrary, lost, and angry during his recovery, it seemed to me that a fight about anything at all was a welcome release to him. I didn't react, which confused him a little. The expectant cocky smile stayed on his face. I don't know what I looked like, but I will never forget what I felt like. I had never felt anything like it before, nor have I felt it again so strongly since.

I never broke his gaze, and as I stared at him I felt an incredible sense of calm come over me. It was as though I had taken the biggest, most beautiful Klonopin in the world. I was instantly calm, composed, and fully in control of all my faculties. I was emotionally impenetrable. I felt a warmth start at the top of my head and in the easiest, gentlest way imaginable work its way down my body, washing over my face, then my neck, my chest, all the way down to my feet. All the concern I had ever had about keeping Gideon happy so he would stay connected to me melted away as that warmth engulfed me. What Gideon thought and what he felt was no longer of the least consequence to me. I was, in that instant, set free

not only of Gideon, his needs and the emotional stranglehold he had on me, but also of my own inability to let
both him and what he had represented to me go. There
weren't any ties left between us. He cut them with that
fey nail file when he threatened me, and he didn't even
know what he had done until I started moving.

The physical and emotional experience I had just
sustained stayed with me as I went into his kitchen to
find a shopping bag large enough to hold any clothing,
books, and dog paraphernalia that were in the apartment. I walked around his place and methodically filled
that bag with anything that could be carried out of there.
It wasn't until I was almost finished that it dawned on
Gideon what was happening. He leapt off the couch and
started screaming at me that I was crazy and that I was
an asshole if I was trying to leave him. I didn't answer
him. I just kept picking up all of my stuff and putting it
in the bag. Gideon got progressively crazier and crazier
as his panic mounted. He knew what he had done and
didn't have the ability to take it back. It didn't matter anymore what his motivation or lack of it might have been.
I could barely hear him as he railed against me, following
me around his place, trailing me a little too closely but
never touching me. My final task was to rescue Oscar,
who had been cowering in a corner overwhelmed by
the noise and fury; put his leash on; and get him out the
door along with my jacket, briefcase, and shopping bag
of belongings.

Gideon didn't stop shouting invectives at me even when
we were on the street. I was a jerk, an asshole, a bitch, a
fucker, a liar, and a few other things I can't and don't care

to remember. Then his anger subsided and the terror set
in. He knew I wasn't kidding. This was it. This was how
the story ended. Gideon's fear made him weepy and he
begged me over and over not to leave. As I walked down
the street toward the avenue to find a cab to take me
home, Gideon called after me. He cried out that he didn't
understand, he loved me, he was only kidding, we were
a family, why wasn't I stopping, and didn't I love him?
My heart was breaking as I listened to Gideon vacillate
between rage and sorrow, but because I was still in the
state of numb, warm enlightenment I had achieved only
fifteen minutes or so before, I was only dimly aware of
the ache in my chest as I kept walking in search of a cab.

Mercifully, a cabbie pulled over almost immediately
and I threw everything into the backseat except for
Oscar. Gideon had stopped screaming, but there wasn't
any doubt in my mind that he was still standing in the
street. I refused to allow myself to look back while I was
getting the taxi and settling in with the dog in my lap,
but once I was in and the door was closed I couldn't help
myself. I turned to my left and looked out the window to
see the man who would always be one of the great loves
of my life, and certainly the biggest catalyst for change I
would ever know, standing midway down his block, staring in disbelief as the car pulled away.

At just that moment Oscar, who had been sitting in my
lap, stood on his hind legs, put his paws on the window,
and whined as he watched Gideon fade into the distance.
I couldn't blame him for crying. I was too. I settled Oscar
back down into my lap and muttered, "Traitor," into his
ear as he snuggled down between my knees. The driver

picked up speed while dusk fell and we made our way back home. I leaned my head against the window and watched the lights go on in the apartments that lined the avenue as their residents arrived home. Knowing what I now knew, I looked for a figure in every window I passed and wished out loud to each one I found, "Good luck."

Epilogue

The best stories are the ones that come full circle. The ones where the protagonist goes out into the world on some kind of mission and encounters all the happiness and all the horrors that it has to offer, but returns home with more knowledge, compassion, or whatever they lacked in the first place.

I never thought about this period of my life being a story like that. In fact, it took me a long time to even see it as a story with any kind of beginning, middle, and end at all. For me, it was a series of anecdotes only, because that way I could keep the full emotional impact of what had happened at bay. By reducing what I had done and what happened to me to bite-sized pieces, I could keep the good, ignore the bad, and get some good cocktail party chat out of the whole mess.

But enough time went by and I finally saw that, of course, this was a story with a beginning, middle, and end. It started with an unhappy person who was living the wrong life, then became a story about that unhappy person trying to figure out what was wrong by challenging herself to be everything she thought she never could or would be, and then ended with the unhappy person becoming a much happier person because she was on the road to figuring out what the right life was for her.

While that's a good kind of story, as I've already made clear, it's not the very best. It doesn't come full circle. But it turned out that I was lucky enough to have the best kind of story, one that came all the way back around again to where it started.

Here's the thing: while Gideon was the catalyst who got me riled up enough to start trying new things, and he was and will always be one of my great loves, he's not the most important person in this story other than me.

I started my adulthood with Andrew by falling in love with him when I was eighteen. He was the first true love of my life, and no one and nothing can ever rob him of that title, whether he likes it or not. I grew up with Andrew, and while I was truly with him I learned more about myself, and how to be in a relationship, than it's possible to express without gushing and sounding like I'm still high as a kite. But then things changed, as they do, and we stopped learning from each other. A fault line opened up between us and before we knew it, the gap was big enough for someone else to step in. Which is what Gideon did, with a healthy push from me.

But then something surprising, at least to me, happened. Even as things were going south with Andrew and then got even worse with Gideon, Andrew was never cruel or vindictive. He was restrained and tried harder than I've ever seen anyone try to be kind. Andrew had displayed these qualities throughout our entire ordeal and I had never fully understood where he was coming from. Even though he had struggled with his own heartbreak and confusion, he had never stopped being the caring person he was and is. Andrew showed me that the cynical old saying "Nice is a dime a dozen" couldn't be further from the truth.

Once things came to their messy conclusion, Andrew tapped into his native goodness and had the presence of mind and maturity not to toss out our fourteen years together, but instead he waited to see what we could preserve and how. The ball was completely in his court. If he had vowed never to speak to me again, it would have been reasonable and I would have understood and accepted it. But that's not what he did.

I don't remember if it was his idea or not, but we decided to go to couples therapy to work out how we could get past all that we'd been through, stay friends, and remain in each other's lives. When we told the therapist what our goal was, she laughed us out of her office, saying that if we could articulate that goal, we didn't need her. We saw her a few times anyway, and Andrew got to yell at me a bit, so that was good, for both of us. He needed to vent after what I had put him through and I needed to hear exactly what I had done to him. I heard all about the shame, anger, hurt, and sadness that he had sustained while I was out finding myself, which instantly heightened my understanding of my impact on other people. And Andrew got to see me shoulder that burden. But at the end of the day, that therapist was right. We didn't need her. Because we had already decided we weren't going to throw something out if there was still some good in it.

The point of all of this is that Andrew's decisions and his compassion and wisdom blew me away at the time and still do today. His grace and intelligence showed me that while I had certainly learned a lot about who I really had been all along and who I was in the present partly from being with Gideon, there were other qualities that I knew I had to find a way to incorporate into my future. And they were the qualities that Andrew had displayed throughout and after our ordeal.

This story is one that comes back around to become a full circle all because of Andrew. His decision not to throw out the baby with the bathwater sealed the deal. We started our lives out together having a blast and learning from each other, and even after we had catastrophically split and were no longer a couple, he made the decision to allow us to create a new relationship in which we could start to learn from and enjoy each other again. It's definitely been insanely hard to keep it together at certain points since then, but the mission has never changed. And even now, if I need to talk to someone who understands me better than I do myself, I'll call Andrew. To my infinite joy, he does the same.

So, Andrew, and you know who you are, this is for you. Thank you for what you did, what you continue to do, and what I know you'll do in the future. I'm lucky to still have you around, and as you know, the only way to properly celebrate the way in which we've created a shared life story as well as our individual stories is to demand of anyone who will listen, at top volume:

"We want the finest wines available to humanity! We want them here, and we want them now!"

Acknowledgments

First and foremost I'd like to thank Dan Conaway, the best agent and friend anyone could have, for relentlessly challenging me creatively and getting this book to Crown Publishers. Lieutenant Dan, you are a true rock star. And a shoutout to the long-suffering Stephen Barr, you know what you did. Thanks also go to the fantastic Julia Pastore for shaping this book so expertly and helping me to pluck the story I needed to tell from what was originally an emotional tangle. Annie Chagnot, thank you so much for your help and support too. And of course, special thanks go to Molly Stern and Christine Pride. Major gratitude as well to every person at Crown Publishers who had something to do with getting this book out into the world. They deserve thanks, praise, and probably a Valium. Deb Shapiro, you are a publicity ninja and all-around smarty-pants.

A very special and weepy thanks to all of the people who were part of my life during the time period represented in this book. Each and every one of you made a big difference in my becoming who I am today. Whether or not that's a good thing may be up for discussion, but as far as I'm concerned, it's a very good thing.

A major debt of thanks goes to my parents (who decided not to move to another state and change their names), my brother, John, and the innumerable friends who read the many iterations of this book and have helped me along the way. They are, in no particular order, Terry Deal, Kim Fields, CJ Gedeon, Nikki LaRosa, Gerard Lynn, Nina Peek, Amanda Monaco, Helen Clarke, Debbie Lublin, Bronwen Epstein, Elizabeth Ashworth, Jim Hubbell, Bascha Satin, Sasha Cookson Wilson, Nathaniel Marunas, Suzanne Crane, Anne Cole, Kerby Neill, Laurie Dolphin, Alejandra Pero, Cathrine Westergaard, the genius who served me that life-changing Klonopin lunch, and, of course, Gideon (you know who you are).

Finally, thanks to my crack team of psychiatrists and last but not least, General Tso, without whose outstanding chicken writing this book would not have been possible.

About the Author

A die-hard native New Yorker, graduate of the Nightingale-Bamford School (she still has the white gloves to prove it), Kenyon College, and Cardozo School of Law, Jessica Dorfman Jones started her life in publishing in the publicity department of Simon & Schuster. She continued on as a literary agent (responsible for bringing *Legally Blonde* into the world) and a book packager, among other jobs. She is the author of *The Art of Cheating: A Nasty Little Book for Tricky Little Schemers and Their Hapless Victims,* which she is adapting for television. Jessica is currently at work on a novel, as well as a musical titled *Friends Like These* about the triumphs and trials of female friendships. She is also the cofounder of Glass Elevator Media, a creative development company based in LA and New York. Jessica lives and works in New York City.

JessicaDorfmanJones.com